Harmonizing Sentiments

Masterworks in the Western Tradition

Nicholas Capaldi
General Editor

Stuart D. Warner
Associate Editor

Vol. 4

PETER LANG
New York • Washington, D.C./Baltimore • Boston • Bern
Frankfurt am Main • Berlin • Brussels • Vienna • Oxford

Hans L. Eicholz

Harmonizing Sentiments

The Declaration of Independence and the Jeffersonian Idea of Self-Government

PETER LANG
New York • Washington, D.C./Baltimore • Boston • Bern
Frankfurt am Main • Berlin • Brussels • Vienna • Oxford

Library of Congress Cataloging-in-Publication Data

Eicholz, Hans L. (Hans Louis).
Harmonizing sentiments: the Declaration of Independence
and the Jeffersonian idea of self-government / Hans L. Eicholz.
p. cm. — (Masterworks in the Western tradition; vol. 4)
1. United States. Declaration of Independence. 2. United States—Politics and
government—1775-1783. 3. Jefferson, Thomas, 1743-1826. I. Title. II. Series.
E221.E48   973.3'13–dc21   97-039404
ISBN 0-8204-3961-4
ISSN 1086-539X

Die Deutsche Bibliothek-CIP-Einheitsaufnahme

Eicholz, Hans L.:
Harmonizing sentiments: the declaration of independence
and the Jeffersonian idea of self-government / Hans L. Eicholz.
–New York; Washington, D.C./Baltimore; Boston; Bern;
Frankfurt am Main; Berlin; Brussels; Vienna; Oxford: Lang.
(Masterworks in the Western tradition; Vol. 4)
ISBN 0-8204-3961-4

Painting of Thomas Jefferson courtesy of Independence National Historical Park.
Reproduced from the *Dictionary of American Portraits*, published by Dover Publications,
Inc., in 1967.

Cover design by Joni Holst

The paper in this book meets the guidelines for permanence and durability
of the Committee on Production Guidelines for Book Longevity
of the Council of Library Resources.

Printed in the United States of America

For my son, Tristan Alexander Eicholz

Acknowledgments

The idea for this book grew out of two concerns. The first was a basic dissatisfaction with the growing consensus among historians that the American revolutionaries and the entire founding generation were bereft of a coherent political tradition, but spoke numerous conflicting political tongues, with very different meanings attached to even such commonly used words as "liberty." The second has been an ongoing concern with the way Americans presently think about the nature of self-government. Today self-government is typically taken to mean the collective expression of the majority will in government, and there is little recognition that it once meant primarily to control oneself. "Government of the self" was the original basis for republican government, reflecting the view that civil society was much more than politics. Society was made up of men and women who gave order to their lives by entering into associations on a voluntary basis, quite apart from government, for all of the various reasons of fellowship, philanthropy, faith, and commerce. It was the flourishing of this order that a limited government was meant to protect, but it was never conceived of as the source of that order, except perhaps among a few Tory loyalists. Now it appears that we often use "government" and "society" interchangeably.

To gain a better sense of the earlier definition, it seemed necessary to go back to the original statement announcing and giving the reasons for America's independence from Great Britain: the Declaration of Independence. It also seemed like an excellent place from which to address the issue of the coherence of early American political thought. The work is thus directed to a broad audience of students and the interested reader, covering the major interpretive schools on the subject, from history to political theory. The hope is that this work will encourage continued interest in and exploration of the meaning of American self-government and society, so as to further our civil discourse about who we are as a people.

Over the course of writing this work I have incurred a number of intellectual debts. For suggested readings, comments on various rough drafts of some of the early chapters, and moral support, I want to thank John Alvis and my colleagues in history, William C. Dennis and George M. Curtis. Michael Zuckert was generous with his time and provided exceptionally helpful comments on a late draft of the manuscript. My friend Richard B. Vernier was of considerable influence in shaping my understanding of early Whig thinking on civil society and its role in America, and I am especially grateful for his extensive comments on the third chapter. James E. Bond was very helpful both in conversations about the relationship of natural rights to the Constitution and in his close reading of the fourth chapter and the conclusion. For his assistance in ferreting out the history of the idea of Parliamentary supremacy, I am thankful for the breadth of knowledge and the library of Emilio Pacheco. On the sources of early Whig thought, especially in regard to common law and the ancient Saxon constitution, James McClellan was generous with his sources and time. Steven D. Ealy helped me to understand the Straussian perspective, especially that of Harry V. Jaffa, and provided helpful comments on the bibliographic essay. I am also grateful to Eugene Miller who first suggested that I consult Jaffa's work and to Karl Walling, who introduced me to the essays of Martin Diamond. Jean M. Yarbrough was very kind to let me read an early draft of a chapter of hers on the meaning of Jefferson's pursuit of happiness. I also benefited from more informal discussions with Randy Simmons on the history of power and the meaning of government; Douglas Rassmussen on the history and implications of natural law philosophy; Tom Palmer on Thomas Paine's notion of social order; M. Stanton Evans on the medieval origins of constitutional thought; Leonard Liggio on Destutt de Tracy and the influence of French liberalism; Barry Shain on Christianity and politics in early America; Susan Collins on the ancient meaning of autonomy; and Nicholas Capaldi on the early conceptualization of this project. Finally, Joyce Appleby provided important references to sources at the very outset of the project and helpful comments on the final drafts, but my debt is considerably greater. Relying, as I do, on her insights into the centrality of economic thought to early liberal ideas, my thinking on this topic reflects the enduring influence of her mentoring in my graduate years. In addition to the encouragement of all those just mentioned, their disagreements also helped to clarify my thinking and any errors that remain are due entirely to my own stubbornness. In locating materials, Lorraine Whitney of the Liberty Fund Library was of tremendous assistance, as were Susan Thomlinson and Carrie Rosar before her. Dan Kirklin and Patty Ordower were very helpful to me with their advice on how to prepare the manuscript. Also my assistant, Nila Spears, must be thanked for her patience and diligence during those times when my focus on this project threatened to pull me away from the pressing duties of a Liberty Fund Fellow. And to my family, for their understanding and patience during what was a difficult and trying two years, thank you is not sufficient.

Contents

Engaging the History of the Declaration

During the first four decades of the American republic, the irascible William Findley was the leading state politician of the western Pennsylvania backcountry. He had seen action as a captain in the American army during the Revolution, was an outspoken Antifederalist during the state's ratifying convention, and was a persistent critic of both state and national public finances. Many a high-born Philadelphian of the likes of Robert Morris and James Wilson, crossed swords with William Findley, only to come away with a healthy respect for his tenacity and shrewd political sense. It came as little surprise that Findley would write the definitive critique of the first administration's handling of the western counties' resistance to the federal excise tax on whiskey in the early 1790s. In that work Findley felt compelled to remind his readers that America was not great because of those in power or because of its "privileged orders," but derived its "dignity and importance, through the natural and honourable channels of prudence and industry."[1] These were not political qualities, but social values of individual responsibility and integrity. Government in America was not their source. They sprang from the people through their own private and civil associations. But when government exercised power badly, it threatened to break up those "natural and honourable channels." State and society were not the same. It was not so long ago that this distinction was still part of American understanding.

In the earliest dictionaries of American English, the definition of self-government was not political, but reflected the same personal quality expressed by Findley—it was the "government of one's self." This remained true as late as 1959 when the Merriam-Webster dictionary defined self-government as "Self-control; self-command," and self-control meant simply, "control of one's self." The second definition followed, and is the one usually expressed today as majority rule. What was unusual for a dictionary definition was that this second definition was made dependent on the first: "Hence, government by the joint action of the mass of people constituting a civil body; also, the state of being so governed; specifically, democratic government." By the inclusion of "Hence," the dictionary reflected the view that you could not have democracy or the rule of law without individuals capable of governing themselves. The present edition of the dictionary has dropped that beginning, and today, we appear to think primarily of the collective, governmental meaning of self-government.[2] Indeed, many current English dictionaries simply list majority rule as the only definition of the term. To recapture a sense of the older notion, we need to go back to a time when Americans still maintained a clear conception of themselves as a people composed of individuals capable of self-government.[3] The American Revolution was the dramatic culmination of just such a moment.

I. The Objective of the Present Work

The Declaration of Independence holds "that mankind are more disposed to suffer while evils are sufferable, than to right themselves by abolishing the forms to which they are accustomed." But when is the point surpassed where a people react to the frustrations of the day and take a chance on a new political order? Resisting the familiar, they might improve their lives or—just as likely—bring on something far worse. By what reasoning do they summon the courage to confront that uncertainty? This was the political and social dilemma facing the British colonists in North America in 1776. The Declaration was the synthesis of reasons and principles by which the colonists, united in a confederation of states, fortified themselves to plunge into the unknown condition of independence.

This work attempts to explain the basis for that decision by relating it to the essential themes running through Anglo-American political thought. The intention is not to be original, but rather to introduce the reader to the primary reasons underlying America's resolve to declare for independence. Different schools of interpretation are introduced to illustrate the wide disparity of views among scholars, but the work is not meant to be an exercise in historiography. Rather it seeks to show that the leading contributions on the nature of the American Revolution in general, and the Declaration of Independence in particular, are actually component parts of a coherent liberal tradition that speaks directly to the meaning of self-government. For the better part of this century, scholars have variously characterized American revolutionaries as Lockean individualists,

Christian communitarians, civic republicans, or radical democrats to the point where many now simply assert that they were all these things and America has no coherent political identity.[4] While not wishing to dismiss the observation that Americans approached the Revolution from many points of view, the notion that these characterizations represent incompatible strains of thought, without a common connecting tie, is unwarranted. Jefferson explained once very emphatically that the Declaration was "Not to find out new principles, or new arguments, never before thought of," but rather to present "the harmonizing sentiments of the day, whether expressed in conversation, in letters, printed essays, or in the elementary books of public right, as Aristotle, Cicero, Locke, Sidney, &c."[5] This work takes that contention seriously.

II. The Historical Conversation

To begin any inquiry into the meaning of the Declaration, it is essential to explain the context that made the move to independence necessary. This is not an easy task, because the history of that endeavor has always been fraught with controversy. The reasons behind the drive for American independence form an essential part of the political identity of the United States, and the Declaration is a primary document in the continuing debate about who we are as a nation. The members of each generation have striven to discover for themselves the truth about the past. In the process, they necessarily engage previous historical interpretations in a conversation about the ideals to be expressed in our civil discourse. The continuous reinterpretation of events can give to history the appearance of so much subjective babble, which is frustrating for those who seek the definitive work. The lesson to be had, however, is not pessimism about history, or abandonment of scholarship, but the real importance of engaging the ongoing discussion about the meaning of America. This is the spirit in which the current work is offered. It is in the style of a comment raised in conversation, and should be viewed, not as a comprehensive examination of the history of the Declaration, but as an introduction to the dialogue about its origins, meaning, and place in American historical understanding. It attempts to draw the student and interested reader into the discourse about America's founding documents by pulling together the major schools of interpretation in a way that emphasizes their points of congruence with regard to ideas of self-government and social order, while retaining a sense of their differences. The primary documents have, where possible, been taken from readily available collections to allow the reader easy access to the original materials. The hope is to draw the reader into what should always be a lively and interesting discussion of the meaning of the United States and its institutions.

III. The Structure of the Argument

The approach of this work is to situate the Declaration in the argument between loyalist and patriot Americans. Among the most important aspects of this debate were the very different notions of social order held by those Americans who supported independence and those who contended against it. Often this division is interpreted as a split within a broader English Whig tradition, which is narrowly construed to mean the defenders of more popular representative government. In this case, one branch of the Whigs favored local colonial assemblies, while the loyalists are seen to have upheld the authority of Parliament.[6] This study breaks from that view by looking deeper into the distinct notions of social order that gave meaning to the different camps' ideas of self-government and social order. The loyalists were Whigs by the standards of late eighteenth-century England, but that had come to mean that they supported rule by Parliament, whereas the patriots were in actuality Old Whigs who were opposed to the abuse of power and in favor of limited government. Since the Glorious Revolution in England (1688–89), the rise of Parliament witnessed a decline in the application of the original Whig critique of power, and its replacement by the notion of Parliamentary supremacy. Parliament, rather than the king, now occupied the principal place of power, and the social order was increasingly seen to be the consequence of Parliament's law. Therefore it can be said that "new" Whigs set their support for Parliament on a Tory foundation, substituting legislative supremacy for the divine right of kings. However, the Old Whigs, both in England and America, continued to hold that social order stemmed not from the government, but from the various institutions of society that had developed spontaneously in law, custom, and the market. They made a strong distinction between state and society that is largely lost today. This work will attempt to recapture a sense of that distinction and show how it rests at the core of both the Declaration and the original understanding of self-government.

By looking at the different conceptions of social order held by early English Tories and Whigs and their later loyalist and patriot counterparts in America, this study underscores the centrality of economic theory to early Whig thought. It was precisely because Whigs believed that large segments of human life were not dependent on political governance, but formed a parapolitical dimension of human association, that they came to endorse the idea of limited and balanced government. The notion of rational self-interest operating through the economy was later supplemented by the Scots to include a "moral sense" that further vindicated the liberal arguments for a minimal state. It was this conception that informed the Whig idea of civil society and self-government in the eighteenth century, and it was the flourishing of such a society, predominantly self-regulating and composed of non-governmental associations and institutions, that gave meaning to the Whig ideal of "happiness." The Tory perspective, on the other hand, evinced a profound mistrust of such a limited government. The Tories espoused the importance of an ultimate sovereign and supreme power at the head of a historically evolved governmental hierarchy in maintaining social order and stability. American loyalists adopted this Tory stance once the Revolution was underway, giving themselves over to long pronouncements against chaos and anarchy. Contrasting these two starkly different positions makes manifest the reasons for the confidence that resonates throughout the Declaration, and illuminates why American Whigs were so assured that they could go it alone without the imperial political structure so much revered by their loyalist adversaries.

Situating the story of the Declaration in this manner also allows for a general treatment of the major arguments about the meaning of the American Revolution and the Declaration by looking at the basic questions with which any student of the period should be well acquainted. The work thus serves as an introduction from which the interested reader can then move on to more specific treatments. The first chapter lays out a general outline of the history of the Revolution, introducing the major participants and answering in broad fashion the general question, Why the Revolution? It is here that the Whig and Tory, or patriot and loyalist, distinction is first made, and the reader introduced to some of the revolutionary literature written just prior to independence. The chapter ends on the eve of the Declaration. The second chapter then moves directly to the drafting of the document, its adoption by Congress, and the loyalist response.

This approach is unorthodox by the standards of previous studies, but valuable precisely because it begins, not with Jefferson's preferred version of the Declaration, but with the final congressionally approved draft of the document that most people, then and now, read. After briefly recounting the story of the Declaration's composition (a process that has been exhaustively studied elsewhere) the document is treated as the public, political expression it was intended to be.[7] The loyalist reaction allows for a serious appraisal of the various charges levied against the King of England, and sets in stark relief the different ways in which loyalists and patriots interpreted and used the constitutional history of the empire. For this endeavor, Thomas Hutchinson's *Strictures upon the Declaration of the Congress at Philadelphia* provides the window through which the loyalist position is evaluated, and answers the question, What were the patriots arguing for and against?

The third chapter addresses in detail the various strands of Whig political and social thought, and their influences on American Whigs in general and on Thomas Jefferson in particular. By keeping Jefferson's contribution as a mouthpiece of the American Whig tradition clearly in view, the book tries to avoid the pitfalls that come from his elevation to prophet. Jefferson's flair for just the right phrase, and his broad acquaintance with the ideas of the Revolution, made him the ideal choice for drafting the Declaration. Yet it was not *his* composition, so much as it was an expression of the American mind at the time, as he himself was keen to point out. Consequently, this chapter puts forward an explanation of how the Whig understanding of common law, of the ancient Saxon constitution, of the Christian religion, and of civic republican political institutions, melded with more current developments in natural law and political economy to form a coherent political tradition upon which Americans like Jefferson could draw. To illustrate this point, particular attention is focused on why Jefferson chose the phrase, "Life, Liberty, and the Pursuit of Happiness," rather than the traditional Lockean "Life, Liberty, and Estates." That understanding is then used to clarify the meaning of the Declaration's opening paragraphs. The main thrust of this chapter is to address the question, What is the meaning of the Declaration?

The fourth chapter develops around the enduring question, Was the Constitution of the United States a rejection or fulfillment of the meaning of the Declaration? It is here that the Whig understanding of the nature of power and the institutional mechanisms necessary for the protection of liberty are explored. The Declaration is not seen to be necessarily in conflict with the Constitution, but certain readings of the latter document might be. The Jeffersonian constitutional approach of strict construction, robust federalism, and a bill of rights is taken to be more in line with the spirit of 1776, and more in keeping with the original argument offered by Federalists at the time of ratification that theirs was a government of delegated powers only. It is during this stage that Jefferson's authorship of the Declaration became the focal point for the development of a distinctive political movement that eventually drove the Federalists from the field in what Jefferson called the "Revolution of 1800." Combining a strong sense of the powerful potentialities of a civil society of free individuals with a jealous regard for limiting political power, Americans molded Whig thought into a uniquely American form that can properly be called the Jeffersonian political tradition. That tradition was much more than just Jefferson, who became a symbol, along with the Declaration, of a movement that upheld, not just the Whig theory, but the American fact, of self-government.

The concluding chapter ends with a brief overview of the subject and observations about the course of development of our present understandings of the Declaration, government, and society. It intimates that certain gains for our current reading of the Constitution might be had from a more studied appreciation of the original Whig conception of social order that is embedded in the Declaration. While it is not itself part of the Constitution in any legal sense, the Declaration does provide a window through which to understand the original character of the later document and the purpose behind America's political institutions. As an expression of a particular moment in Whig thought, the Declaration stands alone in its powerful integration of the different strands of the Whig tradition. While it was part of a long chain of written documents in English and American history, no other document did exactly what it did, and to that extent it was an original American contribution to western political thought.

IV. The Declaration of Independence in Perspective

The composition of the Declaration was the culmination of a synthesis of uniquely modern principles and profoundly ancient practices. The colonists were inheritors of a long tradition of parchment proclamations of rights, grievances, laws, and customs dating back at least as far as the beginning of the twelfth century to the coronation charter imposed by the English barons on King Henry I. This could be extended even further back when one considers that the practice of written law and legal codes is a fundamental part of the evolution of western law.[8] From this perspective, the Declaration is simply another document in a long series by which people have attempted to appeal over the heads of tyrants to some notion of a higher authority. In the English Declaration of Rights in 1689, which set forth the wrongs of King James II and placed limits on the actions of future kings, the appeal was to the age-old practices of Parliament and tradition. The King was limited to acting in accord with procedures established over "time immemorial." In the Declaration of Independence the appeal was made to the authority of the "laws of Nature and Nature's God," and the opinion of the world. It was here that the American document was distinctly modern. Like its predecessors, the Declaration of Independence set forth the limits of power and called to judgment the King's perceived violations of justice.[9] Like the English Declaration of Rights, which provided one of many models for the author of our document, the Declaration of Independence was a legal brief presented to a court of higher authority.[10] Its purpose was to set forth the reasons and principles upon which opposition to power was being conducted. It presented a historical case, and that case was itself rooted in an interpretation of the colonies' proper relation to the mother country. But it was also profoundly modern in the way it judged the abuses of power. King and Parliament were not limited only by traditional practices. Rights were not merely the historical privileges of the barons, but were founded in nature and held by all individuals, inalienably. For government to violate these rights was to violate a universal sense of justice that was powerfully laden with implications about the nature of human society and liberty. If the charges against the King of England in the Declaration of Independence are to be believed, the unfolding of imperial policy after 1760 constituted an affront to the moral life of a free people.

Historians now recognize that British imperial designs towards America began to change well before the French and Indian War, but the American perception of that change did not reach crisis proportions until the Stamp Act of 1765. It is with this act that the first historians of the Revolution generally start their narratives, and is a good place to initiate an examination of the specific claims leveled against the British Empire in the Declaration, weighing them against the counterarguments of the loyalists.[11] From here, we can move to an evaluation of subsequent historical interpretations that attempt to further elucidate the underlying causes of American resistance, and take a closer look into the sources influencing Jefferson's authorship. What becomes apparent is the fundamental importance to the American colonists of the need to limit the use of political power in society. This translated into a strong attachment to certain Whig principles of order and liberty that were assumed implicitly in the early debates between patriots and loyalists. The conversation thus comes full circle to convey the primary importance of the first arguments against parliamentary power for understanding the political tradition inaugurated by the Declaration. That tradition shaped the constitutional era that followed and provides the measure by which we can gauge our own fidelity to the concept of self-government that comprises the essence of the Declaration.

Chapter 1

"A History of Repeated Injuries": The Designs of Empire

The Declaration of Independence puts forward, in its final congression-ally approved form, a list of some nineteen violations of American rights, including nine subcategories in the thirteenth charge. The list draws from the experiences of all thirteen colonies over an extended period of time. The charges against the crown ranged from the most general neglect on the part of the King in approving laws passed by colonial legislatures, to the very specific charges of raising foreign troops and inciting American Indian tribes against the colonists. These charges, when published, were attacked by loyalist writers as vague and unsubstantiated or simply dis-missed as false. To properly assess the Declaration and the counterclaims of detractors, it is necessary to retrace the source of American discontent within the empire. The political perception of the American people was shaped by the course of British attempts to raise revenue from them, and it was in the unfolding of events after 1750 that Americans detected the designs of empire. That perception prompted the colonists' efforts to understand the nature of power and its relation to liberty and society, and sparked a remarkable debate among Americans between those who wanted to preserve imperial authority and those who sought to check its exten-sion and consolidation in the colonies. Over the course of these debates, we increasingly see American resisters to British authority incorporating historical, customary, and constitutional arguments with assertions of natural law and natural rights. Their opponents, on the other hand, ap-pear to rely almost exclusively on historical precedent and the necessity of maintaining the existing imperial hierarchy for the preservation of society.

I. The Origins of Imperial Reform

Often historians explain the Revolution as a response to the British Parliament's attempt to find tax revenue to pay for the Seven Years War, or as it was called in America, the French and Indian War, in which the French were roundly defeated in North America by 1760. This argument was originally raised by loyalists and Parliamentarians who contended that the colonists were ungrateful for the defense of their settlements by England, and were unwilling to pay their fair share of the expenses. Revolutionary writers felt duty-bound to refute this charge and asserted that the colonists had willingly shed sufficient quantities of their own blood and treasure on behalf of the King. As a result of this controversy, historians often assumed the accuracy of the claim that the debt from the war led to a change in imperial policy, which in turn led to the war for independence.[1]

More recently this interpretation has been revised, and the new perspective actually comports better with the understanding of the Revolutionaries. Rather than seeking revenue to pay the debts of war, Parliament was attempting to streamline and strengthen its control over the empire. This move predated the French and Indian War by nearly a decade, extending back to the policies of Henry Pelham's administration under George II, beginning with the substantial electoral victories of Pelham's party in Parliament in 1747.[2] The following year, the Treaty of Aix-la-Chapelle brought a temporary close to hostilities that had been raging since 1739 between France and England. Now, for the first time since the establishment of the colonies, there were no significant internal political divisions in England to distract the attention of Parliament, and no wars outside to channel off imperial energies. The colonists were not far off when they claimed to have detected a design "pursuing invariably the same object."

Since about 1720, the activities of the Board of Trade and the enforcement of the Navigation Acts had been intermittent and minimal. The colonists had been, for all intents and purposes, left to fend for themselves. Edmund Burke called this period a time of "wise and salutary neglect," but it was not what Pelham and the ministry wanted. The hope of imperial administrators was to reinvigorate central controls over North America to prepare for future international conflicts, and it was a significant source of anxiety that the colonists were becoming increasingly populous and prosperous. As one historian has pointed out, many in England believed that if the American colonies were not quickly reined in politically, they would soon be ungovernable by the mother country.[3]

After 1748, the Board of Trade under the leadership of Lord Halifax began a more vigorous supervision of its colonial responsibilities, including the strengthening of Nova Scotia by the promotion of further settlement through a parliamentary subsidy for colonists willing to settle in the territory. The Board also instructed the royal governors of the colonies to assent to no laws which contradicted imperial policies and the laws of Parliament. The problems of managing the colonies were staggering, and the newly invigorated Board of Trade came up against the realities of colonial obstinacy and an increasing volume of complaints from royal governors. Despite these obstacles, the Board was still able to get certain measures through Parliament with the support of the Pelham Administration. Most important of these was Parliament's prohibition in 1751 of the use of paper money as legal tender in the New England colonies. A year later this was followed by additional grants of power to the Board of Trade. Henceforth, the Board would have sole power to appoint royal governors, attorneys general, secretaries, and councilors, and these would all answer directly to the Board. Before the effectiveness of these new powers could be properly assessed, the empire was plunged into yet another conflict with France in 1756. Once more in need of colonial support to prosecute imperial aims in North America, the Board of Trade relaxed its power and the colonists were spared the full brunt of England's determination to regulate them until the French defeat of 1760. Now the British Empire would attack colonial administrative problems with renewed vigor, and with the presence of the victorious imperial army in the colonies and the royal navy along the coast, conditions seemed especially well suited to the task. The moment was at hand, or so it appeared, for England to make good on its administrative designs.[4]

II. The Application of Imperial Policy

In 1763, the King and Parliament were ready to resume strengthening the central administration of the colonies. A number of policy decisions and parliamentary acts were annoyances, but did not offer clear grounds for a unified colonial protest. The prohibition on paper money, for instance, was extended to include all the colonies. The usefulness of paper currency had declined with the war's end, but the ban continued to be a point of irritation with the colonists. Another act sought to alleviate tensions with the Indian tribes by restricting western settlement to the pre-war British Appalachian border, but this irritated mainly western interests, and was generally ignored besides. More aggravating was enforcement of the White Pines Act. That law had been designed to protect wood supplies for imperial war ships by prohibiting colonists from cutting white pine trees that were not on privately owned land within a recognized township. It had been invoked only intermittently over the years, but in 1763 the Surveyor for the Crown began taking the new policy more seriously. He confiscated large colonial stores of white pine logs on the mere presumption that they had been illegally felled and got his decisions affirmed by the admiralty court in Boston. Other acts angered the colonists more for their assertion of authority than their actual application. The Quartering Act of 1764 required unoccupied buildings to be given over for use by the Royal Army in the event that no alehouse or barracks was available and to furnish funds voluntarily for the support of the troops, but this was never invoked until revolutionary hostilities erupted.[5] As disagreeable as these acts were, it was the stricter enforcement of trade regulations, and in particular the collection of revenue from those regulations, that evoked the most grumbling.

For George Grenville, the newly elected prime minister, the critical issue facing Parliament and its administration of the empire in 1760 was one of fiscal responsibility. The Bute ministry, which preceded Grenville's, had made commitments to maintaining a larger military presence in the colonies. This was in part a response to the 20,000 French troops still in the Caribbean West Indies, and the ongoing tensions with native tribes on the frontier. In a larger sense, however, it was simply a logical step in the expansion of imperial power and a response to the fear that the colonies were becoming too self-reliant. Defense and fiscal responsibility formed a convenient pretext, however, and it was assumed that this burden would be borne by the colonists themselves. Upon review of the existing sources of colonial tax revenue, Grenville realized that imperial designs in America would require additional levies. Who better to pay them than the colonists themselves?[6]

Grenville well understood that any effort to increase the meager taxes already in place would meet with discontent, but he thought that after some show of protest, the Americans would settle down and accept the new laws, furthering Britain's long-term goals. The first difficult lesson would be the enforcement of strict compliance. The Molasses Act of 1733 had been established to prohibit trade between the French West Indies and the American colonies. The duty was a hefty 100 percent tax on molasses imported from the French islands, but it was routinely evaded. Customs officers were given a small consideration to look the other way. Smuggling was rampant, and as one contemporary observer noted, Parliament was for years content to ignore the trade because it produced the income with which the colonists bought manufactured goods from England. Consequently, revenue was a mere £700 per year when Grenville checked the books, hardly enough to support imperial objectives in the New World. His proposal was the first of a number of makeshift reforms designed to correct the imbalance of accounts. The Sugar Act of 1764 actually reduced the duty on molasses by half. The law recognized the importance of the sugar trade, but the reduction in the duty was combined with provisions for ensuring its vigorous enforcement by customs officials and the British navy.[7] No longer would smuggling be conveniently overlooked. The response to this act in America heralded arguments that would be raised later against taxation by a Parliament in which the colonials were not represented. James Otis' *Rights of the British Colonies Asserted and Proved* covered ground that anticipated the course of later arguments.

An outspoken critic of the royal government of the Massachusetts Bay colony, a graduate of Harvard, and a leading colonial attorney, Otis presented a formidable character to royal officials, but his course of argument must have appeared odd and antiquated, revealing the distinctive lines along which American thought had diverged from the British political mainstream. Citing Edward Coke, the great jurist of the seventeenth century and a great thorn in the side of the Stuart monarchs, Otis asserted that legislative acts that went contrary to natural law and the ancient constitution were null, and void of any force. He based his argument both on precedent and on the language of natural rights and natural law that were put forward in an earlier age when Parliament was trying to protect itself from the power of the King; but to English officials of the late eighteenth century, Parliament was now supreme, and talk of natural rights and the ancient constitution seemed out of date. Not so in America, and Otis' position was a forewarning of things to come. The Sugar Act, however, did not elicit a unified colonial response. It was unclear to many how much of the law was a novel attempt to raise revenue and how much of it was consistent with earlier mercantile trade regulations, but as Otis warned, it did portend the coming of more ominous interventions.[8]

The measure that finally galvanized colonial opposition was the Stamp Act. This law touched a wide range of individuals throughout the colonies, and was clearly a form of direct taxation, as opposed to regulation. Unlike the Sugar Act that was still, in practice, the same sort of nominal intervention as the Molasses Act of 1733, the Stamp Act was an entirely new form of legislation, explicitly designed to collect revenue.

III. The Stamp Act

The plan for the Stamp Act was known in the colonies long before the bill was actually passed. In addition to following the proceedings of Parliament, colonial officials were invited to a meeting with Grenville on May 17, 1764 and informed of his determination to impose stamp taxes. He even suggested that they might propose an alternative plan so long as it was not the old system of voluntary requisitions, but that was the only alternative the colonists could agree upon. Consequently, a circular letter was sent to the colonial governors in August of that year requesting details of all of the various instruments at their disposal for collecting revenues so as to assist in the planning of the Stamp Act. Colonial protest thus began as early as 1764, and through both the press and official communications, Parliament was well informed of American criticism of the proposed law's legitimacy. With these arguments before them, Parliamentarians in England made sure that the Stamp Act contained strong language concerning the ultimate sovereignty of Parliament in the empire, thereby attempting to settle any question of proper authority and jurisdiction. When the Stamp Act received royal approval in March of 1765, it laid out in no uncertain terms Parliament's claim to a right to tax the colonies. The contemporaneous historian of the Revolution, David Ramsay of Virginia, found the preamble alarming for its assertion of the right of the House of Commons to "give" colonial property to the King, and observed that "the novel claim of taxing them without their consent, was universally reprobated, as contrary to their natural, chartered, and constitutional rights. In opposition to it, they not only alledged the general principles of liberty, but ancient usage." Unlike earlier measures, the Stamp Act directly affected the two groups in colonial society most capable of organizing resistance: attorneys and merchants. Moreover, the novelty and objective of the law were beyond doubt. It was clearly a direct tax levied on the colonies by Parliament for no other purpose than to raise a revenue. The act required that stamps purchased from a government agent be affixed to all legal documents, newspapers, shipping clearances, and a host of other items such as playing cards, dice, pamphlets, and liquor licenses. Additionally, adjudication of the laws created by both the Stamp Act and the Sugar Act was taken out of the hands of local courts and local juries and placed firmly in the Courts of Admiralty, where a royal judge would determine both the application of the law and the facts of particular cases without the use of a jury. Legislation could not have been more effectively designed to anger nearly everyone in America, but this was not apparent to Parliament at the time of passage. Stamp taxes were not a novel practice in England, nor were the costs of the proposed stamps particularly high. Indeed, they were much lower than in England. Defenders of Parliament pointed out that Americans could easily afford to pay the small sums required, but as colonial writers contested, it was a matter of precedent and principle, rather than expense.[9]

One of the most concise examples of this debate is captured in Richard Bland's 1766 pamphlet, *An Inquiry into the Rights of the British Colonies*. This work was highly esteemed by Jefferson, and had a considerable influence on his own *Summary View of the Rights of British America* of 1774, which in turn influenced the composition of the Declaration. As historians have pointed out time and again, those who argued against Parliament's right to tax the colonists did so on the grounds that Americans possessed the same rights as Englishmen, and among these was the right not to be taxed without the consent of their own legislatures. Bland's work is useful for its elucidation of the intellectual roots of colonial opposition to Parliament and its clarification of the colonial understanding of proper legal practice, legislative representation, and English liberties. The target of his pamphlet was an essay written late in the previous year by none other than the author of the Stamp Act himself, Secretary of the Treasury and confidant of Grenville, Thomas Whately. Whately vigorously defended Parliament's authority over the colonies, and justified the efforts of the British ministry to "cement and perfect the necessary connection between the Colonies and the Mother Kingdom." For Bland this was confirmation that Parliament was endeavoring to "fix shackles upon the American colonies." The first point he attacked was the notion that Americans did not need to be directly represented in Parliament to be subject to taxation.[10]

Whately asserted that few subjects in England were themselves directly represented in Parliament, but all were *virtually* represented. Numerous populous areas of Britain had no representative to that august body, but they were still subject to its authority. Parliament supposedly presented the voice of all the commons, wherever they resided, including the colonies. For Bland, this was not a justification of Parliament's right to tax, but an example of the flaws in the English constitutional order—flaws that should not be transferred to the colonies. Yet the issue was even more complicated than that because, it was generally argued, individuals could implicitly consent, by their obedience, to the actions of government. Could it be said that the colonists had ever voluntarily consented to direct taxation? Two principles, ancient and modern, were brought to the fore by Bland to answer this question. One was the invocation of custom and the development of English law from ancient times. The other was the natural right of all men to quit one society and form new associations of their own choosing. Both approaches illustrate the unique blend of philosophical and historical arguments that formed American thinking.[11]

Bland described at length the origins of English liberties from ancient Saxon times to illustrate that the right of representation in Parliament was originally a general right extended to all freeholders, or property owners of whatever extent. Virtual representation was unheard of until such time as a forty shilling minimum for the right of voting was instituted centuries later. But this was not really a negation of the natural right of consent in the formation of the laws so much as it was an abdication of exercising that right by those who acquiesced to the decision. By simply remaining in England, for whatever reason, those freeholders possessing property of less than forty shillings were consenting to abide by the law. This was a grave defect in the English legal system, by Bland's reckoning, but one that was corrected throughout most of the American colonies. All men everywhere, according to Bland, retained the right to leave one society and form another. This was founded in their natural right to pursue happiness. When a particular society was no longer conducive to that pursuit, it was time to leave and enter upon another social order. When the colonists departed England, they entered voluntarily into a contract with the king to establish colonies under his protection in the New World. Referring specifically to Virginia, Bland noted that the colony had never willingly submitted to the authority of Parliament, but only to the king, and that the monarchy had recognized this relationship by appealing in the past to the general assembly of the state for requisitions of revenue. To submit now to the authority of Parliament in the matter of the Stamp Act would establish the terrible precedent, contrary to natural right, that the Americans were the subjects of subjects, reducing their government to "even below the Corporation of a petty Borough in England."[12]

IV. The Different Ways Americans Respond

Bland only begrudgingly admitted that if Parliament had any authority over the colonies, it was the result of a painful acquiescence to superior strength after the restoration of the monarchy with the ascension of Charles II, and not a matter of right. Thomas Whately, on the other hand, asserted that these submissions to the regulation of American commodities for export and import conceded the historical legitimacy of the stamp taxes. Where Bland asserted that Parliament's taxation of the colonies constituted an "unnatural Difference between Men under the same Allegiance, born equally free, and entitled to the same civil Rights," Whately argued from history and precedent to defend the extension of imperial power in line with the exigencies of international politics. Both used history, but Bland also invoked the natural right of consent for the old ways of colonial–imperial relations. England was limited to regulating the trade of the colonies, Bland averred (conceding that point reluctantly), while leaving everything else—especially the raising of revenue—to local colonial assemblies.[13]

This was a common line of argument among Americans, but there were some subtle distinctions even here that were important enough to separate future loyalists from revolutionaries in the controversies ahead. Daniel Dulaney of Annapolis was willing to accept the legitimacy of Parliament's regulation of colonial trade, though not its power to raise revenue by the imposition of internal taxes. Regulating trade, he argued, was necessary to defend the empire and was consistent with the accepted practices of the past. Thus, when revenue was derived incidentally from the regulation of colonial commerce, that was admissible. Legislation intended to take the property of the colonists was not. Like Whately's, Dulaney's argument was entirely historical rather than philosophical, but his account emphasized the past intentions of Parliament's laws, arriving at a distinction between commercial regulation and taxation not unlike Bland's argument. Where Dulaney differed markedly in his analysis was the degree to which he ascribed social stability and order to the fortuitous development of English and American history, rather than to the advancement of man's conceptions of natural rights and reason. Like others who were ultimately unable to support independence, despite having been initially opposed to Parliament's taxation of the colonies, Dulaney warned of chaos should the empire be dissolved. For him, Parliament's right to regulate American commerce was founded in the basic historical relationship of a superior power to an inferior one, where the latter accepted a lower rank for the sake of enjoying certain privileges and protections. "The subordination of the colonies," Dulaney asserted, "and the authority of Parliament to preserve it, have been fully acknowledged. Not only the welfare, but perhaps the existence of the mother country as an independent kingdom, may rest upon her trade and navigation, and these so far upon her intercourse with the colonies, that if this should be neglected, there would soon be an end to that commerce whence her greatest power is derived." This conception marked a common fear among loyalists of the potential for disorder should the familiar hierarchical structure of the empire be undermined. The basic arguments dividing colonials over the issue of Parliament's authority consisted of a number of subtleties regarding theory, history, and prevailing circumstances. These distinctions went to the heart of what late eighteenth-century Englishmen considered the basis of law and justice.[14]

V. The History of Parliament and the Whig Tradition

If one consults the leading texts of English law created during the period of growing tensions between England and the colonies, two converging understandings of constitutional jurisprudence are apparent. The first is a conception of fundamental law that holds all precedents to possess potential legal merit. From this view, English history constituted a powerful basis for asserting a legal claim or right if it could be shown that such a claim was consistently recognized or permitted by the government and the people so that its performance came to be expected by the subject or citizen. Englishmen of this era were deeply impressed with the importance of past practices, and the greatest jurists were of necessity great historians. Consequently, small transgressions of what were thought to be sacred rights were attacked with great tenacity, to avoid the establishment of an evil precedent. William Blackstone, citing the great chief justice Edward Coke, who made it his work to thwart the desires of James I for an independent source of tax revenue, cautioned against legislative innovations as the source of "almost all the niceties, intricacies and delays" in the common law itself. Americans shared in this view as profoundly as their English counterparts did, but England's history and the history of the colonies had, by this time, diverged radically.[15]

The fight between Parliament and the King over who would decide matters of law determined the whole course of English politics in the seventeenth century. Parliament was particularly determined to force the monarch to accept its jurisdiction over taxation. In this constitutional power struggle, Whig writers, in defense of Parliament, put forth the argument that taxation demanded the consent of the governed. The essays of Trenchard and Gordon (writing as Cato) were an early eighteenth-century continuation of this train of thought which dated back to Coke, Milton, Locke, and Sidney. It was from these sources that Americans imbibed a considerable portion of their legal and political theory. Intimately connected to the right of consent was the development of ideas of natural law and natural rights as ultimate sources of moral authority to which the Whigs in Parliament could appeal in their disputes with the King. With Parliament's victory in the struggle over the power of taxation, however, these earlier ideas were increasingly displaced in England by a greater concern for maintaining Parliament's preeminence in the empire. Ideas about natural rights and the constitutional limits of power were superfluous to this end. The result of the struggle between Parliament and the King was to put Englishmen on their guard against any threat to undermine Parliament's position of authority—little thought was given to containing the power of Parliament itself. Thus William Blackstone, who wrote about legislation as the source of corruption in the common law, could write with equal conviction in the same book that every state required an ultimate sovereign power; in Britain that was Parliament. Against John Locke's assertion of the authority of the people to remove the legislature at its pleasure, he contended, "So long therefore as the English constitution lasts, we may venture to affirm, that the power of parliament is absolute and without control." To allow for the nullification of parliamentary laws would invite chaos. "[S]o desperate an event," he continued, would "render all legal provisions ineffectual." Consequently, when Bland argued that Americans had voluntarily consented to their governance in a compact between themselves and the King, a warning knell was struck throughout England. The King, by this theory, might yet claim a source of revenue independently of Parliament, and there was little comfort in the idea that this other jurisdiction was to be based upon the consent of so many little colonial assemblies. By the middle of the eighteenth century, neither the King nor Parliament was willing to consider anything so disturbing after the turmoil of the previous century. Indeed, even lawyers in Britain who were troubled by the unconstitutionality of taxation without the consent of the colonists, nonetheless frequently argued that Parliament possessed the absolute legal authority to do what it pleased.[16]

Americans who resisted imperial taxes, on the other hand, continued to espouse the older positions of those who had struggled to limit the power of the monarch on the basis of consent and its foundation in natural law. They could not fathom the idea that anything but their own assemblies was consistent with that notion. Parliament was not their elective body. The very idea of virtual representation as presented by Whately was anathema and tantamount to asserting that colonials were the inferiors of their British cousins. "Strange doctrine," wrote Silas Downer of Providence in 1768, "that we should be the subjects of subjects, and liable to be controlled at their will! It is enough to break every measure of patience, that fellow subjects should assume such power over us." And as the American dissidents soon made very clear, most American revolutionaries did not share Blackstone's fear of social or legal chaos resulting from the nullification of what they saw as an unjust assertion of power and the toppling of a corrupt hierarchy. For them, such opposition was the very foundation of law, properly understood. It was the abuse of power itself, not the resistance to it, that undermined social order. Law originated from society, not from the wielders of power, and everyone, high and low, was subject to the dominion of law. "To suppose otherwise," wrote John Tucker of Boston, "and that without a delegated power and constitutional right, Rulers may make laws, and appoint officers for their execution, and force them to effect, i.e. according to their own arbitrary will and pleasure, is to defeat the great design of civil government, and utterly to abolish it."[17]

Opposition to the Stamp Act was played out not only in the public papers, but in the first united effort of protest in a convention known as the Stamp Act Congress in 1765. In June of that year, Massachusetts sent a circular letter to the other colonial governments requesting the formation of an intercolonial committee to meet in New York the following October, to compose a petition presenting a "humble representation of their [the colonies'] condition to his majesty and to the parliament, and to implore relief." Nine colonies answered the call, but North Carolina, Virginia, and Georgia were prevented by their royal governors from attending. New Hampshire did not send representatives, but did ratify the convention's "Resolutions," published on October 19. That document presented an argument based on precedent and received English liberties, which asserted that the Stamp Act was a dangerous innovation abridging the sacred right of subjects not to be taxed without their consent. It made no mention of the more radical argument from the law of nature, but sought a conciliatory tone that emphasized a return to past practices. It concluded with further observations that the proposed taxes would impose an unacceptable burden on the colonial economy that would redound to the misfortune of Britain herself.[18]

Historians have differed over the essential character of colonial opposition to Parliament's attempt to impose taxes on the colonies. Some have argued, as was believed in England and by some colonials, that the Americans were opposed only to internal, and not external taxes. In its official protest to the King, however, no such distinction was made by the Stamp Act Congress. It seems far more likely that Richard Bland's original opposition to taxation by Parliament in general, and his grudging acceptance of the regulation of trade, was more illustrative of the opposition to the Stamp Act and of colonial dissent overall. Nonetheless, it was the supposed difference between internal and external taxes that was being expediently sold to the British by some Americans in England, to obtain the short-term objective of repealing the onerous stamp duties. Benjamin Franklin said as much in his presentation to Parliament in 1766 while that body was considering repeal of the law. In replying to the question of what difference there was to the colonists between an external and an internal tax, Franklin sought to avoid controversy by not raising the colonists' general objection to Parliament's authority to tax the colonies, which bordered on denying all legislative power over America. Instead, he answered that "the sea is yours; you maintain, by your fleets, the safety of navigation in it, and keep it clear of pirates; you may have therefore a natural and equitable right to some toll or duty on merchandize carried through that part of your dominions."[19] As it turned out, this was a dangerous misstep that placed the short-term benefit of rescission of the Stamp Act against the long-term machinations of imperial power.

VI. The Townshend Acts

With Franklin's testimony before the House of Commons regarding the distinction between internal versus external taxation, Parliament entered upon a new phase in its design to secure control over the empire. The colonists had essentially nullified the execution of the Stamp Act by compelling most of the appointed distributors of the stamps to resign even before assuming their offices. This, combined with the voluntary compacts among merchants to cease importation or exportation of goods with England, placed pressures on Parliament to reevaluate its course. More importantly still, the Grenville ministry had lost favor with the King, and Grenville was dismissed in July of 1765.[20] The new prime minister, Lord Rockingham, was no enemy of the colonists and favored, on Franklin's assurances, repeal of the Stamp Act, which was accomplished March 18, 1766. Just to make certain that no precedent would be established conceding legal legitimacy to the American position, Parliament also issued the Declaratory Act, asserting its right to make laws binding upon the colonists "in all cases whatsoever." It also passed another resolution, even more ominous in many respects, that called for alleged traitors to be brought to England for trial. This was based on a very old, and disputed law of Henry VIII, and most lawyers in the colonies, for the time being, simply dismissed the resolution as so much unconstitutional venting of steam having little real significance. Thus, for a short time, colonial relations seemed to ease, but the Rockingham ministry quickly ran afoul of the King as well, and was replaced by the administration of William Pitt, Lord Chatham, in July of 1766. From the start, the ailing Pitt chose to leave colonial policy in the hands of his Exchequer, Lord Townshend, who was more than willing to offer his own independent solutions to the problem of colonial taxation. Taking Franklin at his word, Townshend introduced a whole new set of duties to be levied purely on goods sent into the colonies from England. This would help defray expected short-falls from a major land tax reduction within England just passed by Parliament, while seeming to sidestep the stated objections of the Americans to the Stamp Act.[21]

Like the tax on sugar with which the Americans had been reluctantly complying, the Townshend duties on lead, glass, paper, paint dyes, and tea imported into the colonies from Britain were small sums that were to be vigorously enforced. Even more irritating, however, was the provision directing the revenues to pay the salaries of royal officials and governors, making these independent of the colonial assemblies. Colonial legislatures were known to periodically withhold the salaries of royal governors until they complied with the assemblymen's wishes, but the Townshend duties were designed to ensure that royal appointees would be dependent for their pay on the will of Parliament instead. Additionally, other acts were passed to enforce compliance with these new laws. They included the establishment in Boston of a Board of Customs that assumed authority from the distant Board of Trade in London for enforcement of British policies. Another act suspended New York's assembly from conducting any business until it had complied with the Quartering Act (discussed earlier) by raising a certain amount of revenue for the support of imperial troops.[22] No sooner had these acts been passed than the American opposition to them formed, and no more vigorous denunciation was to be found than John Dickinson's *Letters from a Farmer.*

Born of a distinguished colonial family and educated in the law at London's Middle Temple, Dickinson established a thriving legal practice in Philadelphia in 1757. As a member of the colonial elite, he had much to lose by opposing British rule. His love of English history and legal institutions, on the other hand, had nurtured a profound distrust of unrestrained power, whether by a king or a parliament, and inspired him to bring his considerable learning to bear upon the subject of colonial versus imperial jurisdictions. Though he did not hesitate to cite Locke in support of his arguments, Dickinson rested his case more emphatically on the grounds of historical precedent. He also rejected Franklin's earlier testimony to Parliament about the distinction between internal and external

taxation. Dickinson's letters reveal just how deeply situated was the distrust of centralized power running through colonial protests, as well as
the highly developed sense among Americans that the constitution of the
empire was fundamentally federal in character. Historical practices had
defined, in good English constitutional fashion, the proper spheres of the
various agencies within the empire, and these comprised for Americans
an absolutely essential constraint upon the use of power that protected
English liberties.[23]

There was, indeed, for Dickinson, a distinction to be made between
internal and external impositions, but *not* internal and external taxation.
The Townshend duties began with the explicit recognition that the acts
constituted measures for raising revenue for Parliament, but even if they
were not so explicit, they would still be innovations of a sort dangerous to
the constitutional order of the empire. Like previous writers, Dickinson
firmly grounded the power to tax on the right of consent as revealed in
British historical experience. That sacred right, according to Dickinson,
prohibited Parliament from levying taxes upon Americans, but historically the colonists had recognized Parliament's right to regulate the trade
of the empire as part of their natural obligation to ensure the well-being of
the whole system of trade. This meant that Parliament could, and did,
prohibit the exportation or manufacture of certain items not deemed essential to the well-being of the colonies, but possibly detrimental to the
empire in general. Thus Dickinson wrote that "External impositions, for
the regulation of our trade, do not 'grant to his Majesty *the property of
the colonies.*' They only *prevent the colonies acquiring property*, in
things not necessary, in a manner judged to be injurious to the welfare of
the whole empire." If the object was to raise revenue, however, that same
power to regulate trade could and would be used to compel the payment
of taxes on designated items: "If you ONCE admit, that Great Britain may
lay duties upon her exportations to us, *for the purpose of levying money
on us only*, she then will have nothing to do, but to lay those duties on
the articles which she prohibits us to manufacture—and the tragedy of
American liberty is finished."[24]

In essence, the very claim that Parliament could control the disposition
of colonial property was the point against which the Americans were
contending. This was the substantive issue in regard to the Townshend
duties, not the distinction between different types of taxes. Citing the
resolves of the Stamp Act Congress, which he referred to as an American
Bill of Rights, Dickinson noted that "NO TAXES ever have been, or can
be constitutionally imposed on [the colonies], but by their respective

legislatures." His conception of external versus internal impositions reveals the federal nature of the American perception of the empire, where the different jurisdictions of colonial legislatures, Parliament, and the King formed limits on power. Yet, as he was quick to point out, "All artful rulers, who strive to extend their power beyond its just limits endeavor to give to their attempts as much semblance of legality as possible." Thus the Townshend duties appeared to be mere regulations of trade, while actually doing little to alter the flow of goods. They were imposed not to discourage commerce, but to gain revenue from its practice. All regulations preceding these duties and the late Stamp Act, he observed, were "calculated to regulate trade . . . or promote a mutually beneficial intercourse between the several constituent parts of the empire; and though many of those imposed duties on trade, yet those duties were always imposed *with design* to restrain the commerce of one part, that was injurious to another and thus to promote the general welfare." Any revenue from the previous regulations was merely incidental. Townshend's plan was something quite different from mere regulation, and not substantively different from the hated Stamp Act. Like that act, the Townshend acts were a direct challenge to the core principles of Americans, argued Dickinson: ". . .that we cannot be happy without being free—that we cannot be free without being secure in our property—that we cannot be secure in our property, if, without our consent, others may, as by right, take it away—that taxes imposed on us by parliament, do thus take it away—that duties laid for the sole purpose of raising money are taxes—that attempts to lay such duties should be instantly and firmly opposed . . ."[25]

Opposition to the Townshend acts escalated as royal port officials and the newly seated Board of Customs in Boston began to vigorously enforce the new duties. Joseph Harrison, the collector of the Port of Boston, stood to receive, according to the new laws, a portion of all the proceeds from the seizure of smuggled goods—goods upon which the proper taxes had not been paid. That provision essentially closed off any chance of bribing port authorities to look the other way. On June 10, 1768, Harrison decided to make an example of John Hancock by seizing his sloop, the *Liberty*. The vessel was impounded for landing Madeira wine without payment of the proper duties, and for obstructing enforcement of the laws by detaining a customs officer in the ship's cabins below deck. As Harrison, his son, and another official were departing the docks where the *Liberty* had been detained, they were set upon by an angry mob of protesters. Though they escaped unharmed, such instances of open hostility eventually led the ministry in England to alert General Thomas Gage, commander in chief of British forces in America, to move troops to Boston to maintain law and order. Gage's soldiers inspired only more heated outpourings of protest, against both the Townshend duties and the keeping of a standing army in peacetime. In the English Whig tradition, the presence of armed troops in times of peace was a signal feature of tyranny. The sending of two regiments of relatively young and inexperienced troops into the agitated environment of Boston was an especially poor decision on the part of the ministry. When faced with the jeers and stones of an angry mob of Bostonians on March 5, 1770, the soldiers panicked and shot into the crowd, killing five. Dubbed the "Boston Massacre," the incident ratcheted up tensions and underscored the inability of the British to govern their dominions. The newly seated governor of the state, native Bostonian Thomas Hutchinson, was compelled to obtain the removal of one regiment to beyond the boundaries of the city, and the other to Fort Castle William on a small island in the harbor, thus restoring a degree of calm to the streets. The attempted use of force was a clear indication of the failings of imperial government in America. Such tensions, combined with the petitions from colonial legislatures, the escalating pamphlet literature against taxation without representation, and the numerous nonimportation agreements in which merchants refused to trade with British suppliers, put pressure on Parliament to repeal the Townshend duties.[26]

In September of 1767 Townshend died, and the following year a new ministry, with little affection for his duties on exports, came to power. While the new ministry under Lord North was no more willing to tolerate colonial disregard for Parliament, as evidenced by Secretary of State Lord Hillsborough's commitment of troops to Boston, there was a general consensus within the ministry that taxing exports to the colonies was bad policy. It contradicted old mercantilist ideas that colonies were to provide an outlet for goods produced in the mother country. By taxing the American importation of such goods, England only undercut her own productivity. Besides, the revenue from the Townshend duties for the previous year was abysmally low. Many were concerned, however, that a repeal of the duties would irreparably damage the authority of Parliament in the eyes of the colonials and fuel their contempt of imperial power. To placate such fears, Parliament chose to retain the duty on tea as a token of its claimed right to tax the colonies. When the repeal of the remainder of the duties in March of 1770 was announced in America, tensions subsided and a general quiet resumed, but this proved merely to be the proverbial calm before the storm. England had no intention of relinquishing her imperial objective of tightening colonial controls and imposing taxes on the colonies.[27]

VII. A Whig Assembly versus a Tory Governor in Massachusetts

For the next three years, tensions remained just under the surface of colonial society. One delicate matter that continued to agitate American politicians was the issue of who would pay the governors' and judges' salaries in late 1772. Thomas Hutchinson, who once acted to ease tensions by removing troops from Boston's streets, now added fuel to the fire when he pressed for executive independence from the fiscal restraints of the Massachusetts legislature. He was proceeding under the authorization of Lord Hillsborough to pay the Massachusetts Superior (i.e. Supreme) Court Judge, Chief Justice Peter Oliver, and the associate justices, their salaries out of the proceeds from the remaining duty on tea. Announcing that he and the judges of the colony would be taking their pay directly from the Crown in the summer of 1772, Hutchinson tried to make quick work of the opposition. What he failed to anticipate (strangely, for a native of Massachusetts) was the degree to which this would inflame the legislature. The controversy went on into 1773 and eventually produced an engaging exchange between Hutchinson and John Adams, who was commissioned to write the response to the governor's address to the Massachusetts legislature.[28]

Thomas Hutchinson was long involved in Massachusetts politics, and was the distinguished head of one of the colony's oldest and most esteemed merchant families. He had been a respected representative from Boston to the state legislature from 1737 to 1749 and a member of the Governor's Council for the following seventeen years. Subsequently he was appointed lieutenant governor, and then governor of the colony, succeeding Governor Bernard in 1769. During his long career, Hutchinson had championed the colony's territorial integrity against competing claims by its neighbors, and had been a force in defending Boston's mercantile interest in hard money against the promoters of inflationary paper currency. He had even been a cautious critic of the Stamp Act, contending against its impolitic circumvention of the colonial assemblies to raise revenue. All of this served to endear Hutchinson to his constituency, until the press of events became too contentious for him to avoid the question of allegiance. His was not a revolutionary temperament. Indeed, as the biographer of Hutchinson has pointed out, he was extremely cautious in all of his endeavors, never risking an importunate sentence where calmer, if less inspiring, prose would suffice. He was distinctly out of place in his last years of political service, pleasing neither the colonists, who thought him a traitor, nor the ministry, who thought him inept. However, his arguments against resistance to Parliament are instructive for what they reveal about the loyalist position.[29]

When it was discovered that Hutchinson had obtained salaries directly from the Crown for himself and the judiciary, Boston's town meeting issued a condemnation of the action as a violation of the constitutional protections against the abuse of power. This was quickly followed by endorsements from other towns which spread like wildfire and took Hutchinson completely by surprise. Hoping to stave off what he feared was a general crisis, he called the legislature into session and lectured the representatives on the essential principles of the English constitutional system. What resulted was a deeply engrossing exchange, in which the lower house responded in writing to Hutchinson, who countered in turn. There had been other exchanges between governors and legislatures, but as Bernard Bailyn has pointed out, "never one so deliberately aimed at probing the most sensitive issues of Anglo-American relations."[30]

The leading voice of Hutchinson's opposition was a rising star among the resistance, John Adams. Adams was the cousin of the already well-known Samuel Adams, who was infamous among the members of the royal administration, and an irascible defender of Massachusetts liberties to his friends. John Adams was not the skillful local politician that his cousin was, but he had a keen intellect and an abundance of legal and historical knowledge gathered by voracious reading, making him a force to be reckoned with in any argument. His family was not as prominent or wealthy as Hutchinson's, but they had been in the colony just as long. Indeed, there might have been a touch of rivalry that animated Adams' feelings towards the governor beyond merely the political. He could hardly restrain his oratory against him. Like Hutchinson, Adams was educated at Harvard, but rather than entering immediately into politics, he developed his law practice and tended to his farm in Braintree. It was a course that denied him the quick rise to prominence that Hutchinson experienced, and which Adams may have privately envied. Moreover, Adams' education focused on constitutional and legal history that encouraged his Whig inclinations, and predisposed him to be anything but tolerant of Hutchinson's conciliatory stance towards imperial reform.

Adams made his first foray into public debate with his attack on the Stamp Act in his newspaper series, *A Dissertation on the Canon and the Feudal Law*, and earned a reputation for fairness by his successful

defense of the troops charged with the Boston Massacre, something only
a known partisan of American liberty could have done. When relations
heated up between America and Britain, John Adams was drawn to politics. He was elected to the state legislature where he found himself composing the response to Governor Hutchinson's address, and charging
him with attempting to set a dangerous constitutional precedent.[31]

The essence of Hutchinson's reply to the charge of constitutional innovation was to assert the authority of past precedent, which ostensibly
demonstrated Parliament's right to legislate for the colonies even with
regard to taxation. While it was true, he reasoned, that both King and
Parliament had exercised that right only sparingly, it was nonetheless invoked at certain times, and had never previously been challenged by the
colonies. The existence of subordinate authorities and corporations in
the empire was a pragmatic recognition that certain measures were best
consigned to local direction, with "Parliament occasionally, though rarely,
interposing, as in its wisdom has been judged necessary." It was, moreover, not to the King alone, which was dangerous in itself, but to the King
as a constitutional and subordinate part of Parliament that the colonists
owed allegiance. The King, Hutchinson observed, must give his assent to
every act of the Parliament, as a requirement of the constitution, so for
Adams to disparage the right of Parliament to legislate for the colonies
was to "alienate the affections of the people from their Sovereign." He
then went on to attack directly those arguments from natural rights that
were circulating among the colonists and raised the terrible specter of
anarchy, observing that such an argument must "be considered as an
objection against a state of government, rather than against any particular form." It was the colonists who were making a constitutional innovation, he cautioned, and it would lead to separation. Surely this was not
what the people wanted? Believing that he had backed his opposition into
a corner from whence they would now be compelled to either recant their
arguments or admit the inadmissible, Hutchinson observed, "it is impossible there should be two independent Legislatures in one and the same
state; for although there may be but one head, the King, yet the two
legislative bodies will make two governments as distinct as the kingdoms
of England and Scotland before the union."[32] What Hutchinson singularly
failed to recognize was that this was precisely the intention of his opponents.

The House of Representatives was not at all uncomfortable with
Hutchinson's conclusion. "Very true," remarked John Adams, writing for
the assembly, "and if they [the two legislative assemblies] interfere not
with each other, what hinders, but that being united in one head and

common Sovereign, they may live happily in that connection, and mutually support and protect each other?" Far from fearing a separation, or the "terrors which your Excellency has pictured to us as the effects of a total independence," Adams went on, "there is more reason to dread the consequences of absolute uncontrolled power, whether of a nation or a monarch, than those of a total independence." Hutchinson was aghast, and could make little response. The opponents of Parliament's authority in the colonies were not averse to independence, nor were they ashamed to admit it.

The issue of the governor's salary remained within the confines of the government, and was not such a pressing issue with the general population. Rather, it formed one of several annoyances that simmered just below the surface until a more widely inflammatory controversy undid the general peace. What the debate between the governor and the House revealed, however, was the continuing divide between the kind of historical arguments favored by those loyal to Parliament, and the more daring historical and philosophical positions of those who aimed to check Parliament's power. Adams met Hutchinson's historical argument with a historical argument of his own, not because the idea of natural rights was unimportant to the colonists, but because he could illustrate and defend the same underlying principle from the Whig's interpretation of the past. At the core of any understanding of natural rights is the absolute necessity of consent to the political order. It was this same voluntary principle that was at the heart of Adams' understanding of the earliest colonial charters. Rather than the relatively recent precedents to which Hutchinson appealed, Adams drew upon *the intentions* of the first colonists and their contractual arrangements with the kings of England (*before* those kings had been subdued by Parliament) to secure those "most essential" rights, without which Americans would be reduced to vassalage. Adams countered Hutchinson's examples by the fact that they were not, as Adams insisted, "voluntarily submitted to." Both the natural rights approach and the historical Whig understanding thus affirmed the same belief in a self-governing social order. The Whig understanding of history, exemplified by Adams, merely pointed to those historical instances that illustrated and affirmed the principle of voluntary consent. For Hutchinson to insist otherwise placed him in the morally untenable position of asserting that all precedent pointed to the intention of making the colonies "the vassals of the Parliament." Certainly that could be a reading of the past, but it was not the history American Whigs embraced. Uncontrolled power was what they feared. Their understanding of both history and natural rights directed attention to what they affirmed. These were sources of authority and order that originated in society, from the people, and not from those in possession of raw power. It was a boldly self-assured faith, much to Hutchinson's chagrin, that the colonists could lead orderly lives independently of Parliament's imperial hierarchy. It remained to be seen whether Parliament would challenge the colonists to act upon that belief.[33]

VIII. The Trouble with Tea and the Intolerable Acts

The intentions of Parliament seemed unmistakably clear to the colonists when in 1773 the focus of Americans was drawn to the one remaining duty, on tea. Had no further alterations to the tea tax been made after 1770, it is conceivable that no revolution would have occurred, but multiple interests in Parliament were arrayed against a hands-off course. Among the reasons given for this were the ongoing desire to strengthen imperial controls throughout the empire and the fears brought on by the growing prosperity of the colonies. Another was the more immediate desire for revenue and the irresistible urge to find sources of taxation beyond the confines of Great Britain to finance those increased controls and imperial aspirations. More immediate in relation to the duty on tea was the declining fortune of one of the great trading companies of the empire—a company in which numerous members of Parliament had invested considerable sums of money—the East India Company.

At the close of 1773, Parliament passed legislation granting the East India Company the privilege of being sole provider of tea to the American colonies, with the revenue from the duty going to pay the company's officers. Fulfillment of the prediction made by Dickinson at the start of the Townshend crisis was at hand. Dickinson had predicted that if ever Parliament assumed the right to raise taxes without the colonists' consent, then the power to restrict colonial trade would complete the destruction of American liberty by compelling Americans to buy only taxed goods. American radicals took this warning to heart, and on December 16, 1773, a group of them, disguised as native tribesmen, boarded the ships that had entered Boston Harbor with the first shipments of tea, and dumped approximately £10,000 worth overboard. The Boston Tea Party, as it came to be called, infuriated Parliament and much of the British populace and produced a general outcry for retaliation. This came in March of 1774 in the form of a series of punitive acts passed to assert control over Massachusetts and exact monetary compensation for the destroyed tea as well as an official apology from the colony's legislature. The first act closed the Port of Boston and allowed no ships to leave or enter until the East India Company was compensated. The second act nullified the Massachusetts charter and made all members of the council appointees of the royal governor, rather than of the legislature. It also restricted the number of town meetings, and increased the power of the royal governor to appoint judges and sheriffs. In a third act, Parliament exempted royal officials from standing trial in the colonies for capital offences, to ensure that they would not face a hostile colonial jury. If an officer of the royal government were charged with such an offence, he had the option of going to England for trial, virtually ensuring that no meaningful action would be taken against him. The final act gave the governor of the colony the power to take over private dwellings for the housing of troops. A fifth act, that was not part of the package directed at Massachusetts, nonetheless angered the colonists by its affirmation of the French tradition of civil law in the former French colony of Quebec. Under the Quebec Act, Quebec would not be required to institute the English jury system. American Whigs interpreted this as a first step towards the abolition of juries throughout the colonies and referred to all of these actions collectively as the Intolerable Acts. Taken together, the acts seemed finely tuned to irritate the colonists on every point which they had contested over the previous decade. As if to purposely exacerbate the situation, the imperial administration installed General Gage as the new governor of the province, replacing Governor Hutchinson. The Whig fear of military authority usurping civilian government was a reality.[34]

By its determined show of strength, the ministry of Lord North sought to isolate Massachusetts from the other colonies, but what in fact occurred was a general outpouring of support from the other colonial assemblies and the rapid formation of impromptu committees of correspondence. These committees maintained communications among the various groups of the resistance and comprised the backbone of what became the revolutionary movement. Soon supplies of food, clothing, and even arms began filtering into Boston and the surrounding area. In May the legislatures of Massachusetts and Virginia, in defiance of their royal governors, declared the fate of one colony to be the fate of all, and announced their intention to send delegates to a general Continental Congress. Other colonies followed suit, and on the first day of September in Philadelphia, the first truly representative intercolonial body, with delegates appointed by the colonial assemblies, met and produced a list of grievances with which to petition the Crown for relief from the oppression of the Intolerable Acts.[35]

IX. Jefferson and the Summary View

Just a month prior to the first sitting of Congress, the colony of Virginia formed a convention to select its delegates to that grand assembly. It was in this state convention that Thomas Jefferson, a young member of Virginia's legislature, the House of Burgesses, hoped to introduce a set of briefs to instruct Virginia's delegates to Congress on the nature and history of the colonial opposition to Parliament. Falling ill en route to the convention, he sent his papers on ahead, apparently not suspecting that his friends would publish them as a complete pamphlet, entitled *A Summary View of the Rights of British America*. As intended, the essay served as the starting point for the discussions that eventually produced Congress's own petition to the King, and as such, was a linear ancestor of the Declaration of Independence which followed two years later.[36]

Under the careful tutelage of George Wythe, a distinguished member of the Virginia bar, Jefferson had imbibed the basic elements of the common law and the legal history of England, and he was admitted to the bar in 1767. Just prior to the completion of his studies in Williamsburg, however, Jefferson had witnessed the first stirrings of protest against British measures. Patrick Henry's daring speech challenging the authority of the Stamp Act filled him with awe, but far more enduring was the influence of his fellow Virginian and distinguished senior member of the House of Burgesses, Richard Bland. Jefferson was impressed by Bland's invocation of the higher law of nature to defend the sacred right of consent to the power of taxation. He was impressed also by the historical argument that proved the colonies to be distinct jurisdictions unto themselves, wholly separate from the legislative prerogatives of Parliament. Yet Jefferson was impatient with what he considered to be Bland's waffling on the essential conclusion demanded by these basic observations. Bland had grudgingly conceded to Parliament the authority to regulate trade. Jefferson sought to deny the legitimacy of all such legislative interference with America and granted to England only that which "it is in our power to give." Unlike Bland, who wrote at the beginning of the conflict between England and her colonies, Jefferson had a decade of additional parliamentary intrusions to call upon to build a more consistent case, and argue that more than bad policy or a few misguided ministers were at the heart of America's woes. He had been in the House of Burgesses only five years when he set out to extrapolate further Bland's original insights. In so doing he formulated an even stronger case against the policies of Parliament as violations of ancient constitutional practice and the law of nature, which was, according to Whig theory, the foundation of the imperial constitution. Thus, contending that Parliament had committed a breach of fundamental law, Jefferson, like a good common law lawyer, had to demonstrate not only the fact of the case, but the criminal intention of Parliament.[37]

In 1766 Bland had accused Thomas Whately of being "guilty of a gross anachronism," and committing a "great error." Early petitions, such as that of the Stamp Act Congress, had couched their grievances with phrases such as "a loyal and dutiful address to his majesty, and a humble application to both houses of parliament." There existed a tendency among many to assume that errors, committed by bad or ignorant ministers, had misled the judgment of the King and Parliament, but by 1774, few Americans were willing to be so charitable. Jefferson had all of the actions of the past ten years to use in his essay to argue that a consistent misapplication of power evinced the design of a malevolent will; in terms of precedent for such an indictment, he had a whole corpus of documents from English history to draw upon.[38]

This was a history well-known to Whig historians of Jefferson's time, ever vigilant to point up the failures or transgressions of government, and it was to these works that Jefferson and his compatriots turned for examples. The Magna Carta, the Petition of Right, and the Declaration of Rights set forth the various abuses of power committed by certain kings against the essential rights of their subjects. The last document possessed an especially powerful influence on the thoughts of the revolutionaries, because it had not only delineated the charges against a deposed king, but secured the rights of subjects that a new king was required to uphold. After James II fled England, Parliament drew up in January of 1689 a Declaration of Rights that specifically charged the monarch with breaching the law. Initially, the Whig lower house had used the term, "original contract," but this was omitted by the Tory majority in the House of Lords in favor of simple reference to his abdication and his violation of the laws.[39] Nonetheless, the final version left intact the long list of charges against the King, and the enumerated rights he had abrogated. Upon assuming the throne, the Protestants William and Mary gave their approval to this new version, formerly ratified as the Bill of Rights in February of 1689. In that document, James' guilt was established by the enumerated crimes ascribed to his rule, delineating, in the minds of the Parliamentarians, his considered intention to undermine the ancient constitution of England. As noted earlier, the English Bill of Rights of 1689 grounded its case in the received law of the realm, as it was handed down through time and immemorial practice. Jefferson incorporated this same approach in what became his *Summary View*, but united it, as Bland had done, with the Lockean invocation of natural rights and natural law, creating a document close in spirit to the original Whig Declaration of Rights.[40]

Drawing up a list of grievances that would influence both the Declaration and Resolves of the First Continental Congress as well as the Declaration of Independence, Jefferson broke with the more conciliatory and charitable interpretations of British policy that were characteristic of previous writers. He wrote, "Single acts of tyranny may be ascribed to the accidental opinion of a day; but a series of oppressions begun at a distinguished period, and pursued, unalterably through every change of ministers, too plainly prove a deliberate and systematical plan of reducing us to slavery." Most notably, Jefferson began by divesting his address to the King of "those expressions of servility which would persuade his Majesty that we are asking favors, and not rights." Outlining ancient Saxon history, he observed that it was never presumed that the continent of Europe retained dominion over those Saxons who left their birthplace to settle Britain. The Americans had simply exercised the same basic right as their ancestors, a right "which nature has given to all men, of departing from the country in which chance, not choice, has placed them, of going in quest of new habitations, and of there establishing new societies, under such laws and regulations as to them shall seem most likely to promote public happiness." The essence of Jefferson's argument was a blanket denial of Parliament's legislative power over the colonies that wove together in typical Whig fashion the arguments from history and natural rights. From this standpoint, the King had the responsibility to restrain the power of one legislature within the empire from infringing on the rights of another. He was meant to be an executive with primarily defensive or negative authority, as revealed by the historical development of his office, to check the abuse of power—not to sacrifice "the rights of one part of the empire to the inordinate desires of another; but deal out to all equal and impartial right."[41]

Similar sentiments were published by a number of other writers around the same time. James Wilson's 1774 *Considerations on the Nature and Extent of the Legislative Authority of the British Parliament* made nearly identical points regarding the notion that the empire was essentially a confederation of distinct assemblies presided over by one sovereign. This would become the model accepted by the British in the twentieth century, but was not comprehensible to Englishmen of the eighteenth century who were still accustomed to defending the ultimate sovereignty of Parliament. Once again, the intriguing nature of the dilemma between Great Britain and her colonies showed in the way that each emphasized a different aspect of the Glorious Revolution of 1689. Parliament interpreted the historical outcome of the conflict with the Crown as the affirmation of its sovereignty throughout the realm and the empire. The colonists, however, turned to the writers of the period who argued against the arbitrary powers of the King on the basis of natural rights and ancient practices that upheld the people's right of consent in matters of legislation and taxation. These were mutually reinforcing sources of authority that drew from the experiences and understandings of the people as they lived life in society. Restraining power was thus an ultimate concern of the Old Whigs and their American heirs, relegating the authority of mere precedent to a tangential, secondary consideration of the larger issue of justice and liberty. As Wilson wrote, "the happiness of society is the First law of every government . . . It must control every political maxim: it must regulate the legislature itself."[42]

The Continental Congress listed grievances ranging from taxation to Parliament's attempt to dissolve colonial assemblies, overlapping in many instances with Jefferson's *Summary View*. It then announced in its Declaration and Resolves that the colonies had certain rights, including those to life, liberty and property, guaranteed "by the immutable laws of nature, the principles of the English constitution, and the several charters or compacts . . ." They concluded with the determination to press for these rights by entering into associations for nonimportation, nonexportation, and nonconsumption of British goods; by an address to the people of Great Britain and to British America; and by making a loyal address to His Majesty.[43]

The document was never accepted by the Crown and the whole assembly was considered by Parliament to be illegal. Matters continued to intensify to the point where violence broke out in the Massachusetts towns of Lexington and Concord when British troops attempted to seize American arsenals. As originally scheduled, another Continental Congress was seated on May 10, 1775, one month after the fighting in Lexington. Even this Congress, however, held out hope for reconciliation with Britain, though they could not deny that the battle had been joined. Observing the obvious, the Second Continental Congress issued yet another statement proclaiming its reasons for the appointment of a commander in chief of the armed forces of North America, entitled Declaration of the Causes and Necessity of Taking Up Arms. Like its predecessors, this document listed the familiar series of grievances. Yet in the fourth paragraph the argument was cogently summed up by reference to the Declaratory Act of Parliament: "But why should we enumerate our injuries in detail? By one statute it is declared that parliament can 'of right make laws to bind in all cases whatsoever.' What is to defend us against so enormous, so unlimited a power?" To the advocates of resistance, the apparent designs of Parliament were the root cause of all that had transpired, but to another group of Americans, the issue was far from being so obvious.[44]

X. The Loyalists Respond

With the escalation of tensions after 1774, those who longed for an ultimate reconciliation with England were finally compelled to address more boldly than in previous years the charges made in the official pronouncements of colonial governments and the First and Second Continental Congresses. These Americans were alarmed by what they perceived to be the dangerous tendency of colonial radicals to resort to arms and heated rhetoric that could serve no other purpose but the reduction of the colonies to either military rule or a potentially fleeting and chaotic independence. This group was composed of diverse elements within American society, from moderates (who disliked the intrusions of Parliament in colonial affairs, but feared separation from Britain more) to those who owed their status and positions to the empire, and steadfastly insisted upon loyalty at all costs. From 1774 onward, their voices increasingly united to offer alternatives to the pronouncements of the revolutionaries, who were quick to brand them Tories and traitors.[45]

A good number of loyalists had been initially opposed to Parliament's taxation of the colonies. Daniel Dulaney, as mentioned earlier, had written a strongly worded account against the Stamp Act, but he increasingly came to feel uneasy with the intensity of colonial opposition to Parliament. When the issue of independence arose, he declined to support it and retired altogether from politics. Among others who followed a similar path was Joseph Galloway of Philadelphia, who sat in the First Continental Congress and tried to moderate the dispute with England, proposing a new "plan of union" that would give to the colonies their own representative body to administer legislation jointly with the British Parliament. Eventually he became so alarmed by the seemingly unstoppable push towards separation from the Empire that he switched tactics and led an abortive attempt to unite with other loyalists to turn the tide of revolution.[46]

Daniel Leonard is yet another example. Writing first as an ardent opponent of Parliament's taxation of the colonies under the pseudonym, Massachusettensis, Leonard drew upon the argument from natural rights and the necessity for consent for taxation to be lawful, but his disposition was apparently ill suited to revolution. Like Hutchinson, with whom he conversed at length before abandoning the cause of the American Whigs, Daniel Leonard put his initial opposition to Parliament behind him, and proceeded, under the same pseudonym, to attack the positions of his former compatriots. How he came to his new position is instructive of the tenor and nature of the loyalist position.

Leonard's former associates did not take well to his apostasy from the cause, and both Mercy Otis Warren and John Adams attributed Leonard's change of heart to a love of luxury and status. It was not difficult to point to Leonard's privileged background, his attendance at Harvard Law School, his rapid rise after admission to the Massachusetts bar to the post of his county's King's Attorney, and his love of fine attire and carriages. But if we seek to make sense of Leonard's decision on his terms, we have ample evidence from his writings to indicate a fundamental change in the basis of his arguments, which highlight the essential differences between American Whigs and Tories. When Leonard wrote his first essay in 1773 against Parliament's attempt to tax the colonists, he employed the argument from natural rights, and did this with considerable verve: "That men have a natural right to retain their justly acquired property," he wrote, "or dispose of it as they please without injuring others, is a proposition that has never been controverted to my knowledge: That they should lose this right by entering society is repugnant to common sense and the united voice of every writer of reputation upon the subject." Only by the subject's consent, as determined by his choice of representatives in government, could property be justly taken by the civil power. "All demands upon our purse, on other terms," he went on, "are illegal; and put into execution robbery; if the demand be made with the sword in hand, the crime is still more atrocious; 'it is robbery with murderous intention!'"[47]

By December 19, 1774, several months after a long conversation with governor Thomas Hutchinson in the spring, Leonard did a radical about-face and openly declared himself a Tory. Now he would write exclusively from the position of precedent, without the reservations of natural rights and consent: "At first we [the colonists] did not dream of denying the *authority* of parliament to tax us, much less to legislate for us. We had always considered ourselves, as a part of the British empire, and the parliament, as the supreme legislature of the whole. Acts of parliament for regulating our internal polity were familiar. We had paid postage agreeable to act of parliament, for establishing a post-office, duties imposed for regulating trade, and even for raising a revenue to the crown without questioning the right, though we closely adverted to the rate or quantum." And with as much enthusiasm as when he opposed Parliament's rule, Leonard went on to assert, "We were happy in our subordination; but in an evil hour, under the influence of some malignant planet, the design was formed of opposing the stamp-act, by denial of the right of parliament to make it."[48]

Leonard went to great lengths to portray the disorder and violence of the revolutionaries in his historical account of colonial protest of parliamentary taxation. Continual upheavals, he contended, were caused by a seditious faction intent upon remaining in the public eye, noting that many of the faction's leaders would have fallen into obscurity "had these turbulent commotions" been allowed to subside. Leonard's view was typical of the loyalist concern with social instability. In his first essay opposing Parliament, he had referred to the philosopher Thomas Hobbes for the reasons that men enter into civil society, but it was, at that same moment in his career, to Locke that he owed his understanding of the rights men retain when they form government. For Hobbes, the transfer of sovereignty to the state was absolute—the subject retained no right of property, and certainly no right to resistance. To Locke, men retained their right to property upon entering society, and when those in power abused their authority and violated that essential right of ownership, resistance was legitimate. As Leonard first argued, "they have by their attempts upon our liberty, *put themselves in a state of war with us*, as Mr. Locke observes, and being the aggressors, if they perish, the fault is their own."[49]

What seems clearly to have happened, for whatever personal reason, was the tipping of the balance in Leonard's mind in favor of Hobbes' vision of the origins of government. Hobbes' "state of nature," or view of the condition of life prior to the formation of government, was "nasty, brutish, and short." To escape this condition, men consigned their individual liberty to a sovereign, who then ruled absolutely to maintain stability and order. In his later essays, Leonard seemed to believe that when men destroy government, for any reason, they abandon the law and consign themselves to the disorders of predatory mobs, to "fraud, violence, rapine, murder, sacrilege, and the long train of abuses that riot uncontrouled in a state of nature." In a revealing passage describing the conditions brought on by the revolutionaries, Leonard quipped, "This is what is called a state of nature. I once thought it chimerical."[50]

When Hobbes wrote his work on the origins of government, he attempted to temper the spirit of resistance sweeping England in those troubled times of Charles I, the Interregnum under Cromwell, and the restoration of the Stuart monarchy of Charles II in 1660. Tories in the kingdom portrayed the disorder and violence of these periods as the products of disloyalty and declining virtue. They predicted a general up-heaval if the traditional bonds of obedience to the King were undermined. Their alternative to Whig resistance, when they had one, was to invoke traditional feudal ties and restore old baronial privileges, as the Magna Carta had done. They were opposed, however, to any open denial of kingly authority. The sovereign was the source of social order, and no fundamental distinction was made between the state and society. This perspective persisted in England, and came eventually to characterize English Whigs after the Glorious Revolution. These new "Whigs" shared with their forerunners only the belief that Parliament should be the source of English legislation—they gave little thought to the Old Whig arguments against the corrupting nature of government power and its distinctive-ness from society. The Rockingham Whigs, who were also associated with William Pitt, continued a rear-guard defense of these earlier views. A similar division could be seen in America, where the loyalists' arguments on behalf of Parliament were of the same nature as those the new Whigs in England were making. In their defense of Parliament, they were Whigs of a sort, but in terms of their understanding of the role of government in the preservation of social order, they were very much the descendants of the Tories. Both the new Whigs of England and the American loyalists presented a Tory view of social calamity as the result of the resistance to power. Social chaos was the ultimate fruit of sedition. Unlike the Tories of the seventeenth century who had defended monarchical privilege against the Whigs in Parliament, they were now fully committed, by the course of history, to defend the supremacy of the King-in-Parliament over the whole empire. It was not to the King alone that they pledged their loyalty, but to the King ruling over the colonies *with* Parliament—precisely what the American patriots rejected. To make their case, the loyalists portrayed a frightening scene of social degeneration and chaotic violence should the revolutionaries be successful.[51]

Samuel Seabury, writing as a New York "Westchester Farmer," point-edly attacked the whole lot of American resisters as the real enemies of liberty, and asked, "Who induced this necessity [of protest]? Who in-volved the province in discord, anarchy, and confusion?" "We have," he warned, "so long paid attention to sophistical declamations about liberty and property, the power of government and the rights of the people, the force of laws and the benefit of the constitution, that we have very little of any of them left among us; and if we continue to support the mad schemes of our Eastern neighbors [Massachusetts] in the manner we have done, in a short time we shall have none at all."[52] In the same spirit, Daniel Leonard compared the leaders of the American Revolution "to a false guide, who, having led a benighted traveler through many mazes and windings in a thick wood, finds himself at length on the brink of a horrid precipice, and, to save himself, seizes fast hold of his follower, to the utmost hazard of plunging both headlong down the steep, and being dashed in pieces together against the rocks below."[53] Or as John Joachim Zubly, writing as Helvetius, observed:

> It was the universal and professed maxim of the day, "if we succeed it will be called a Revolution, and deemed a Rebellion if we miscarry." On this dreadful alternative, which with the greatest safety to themselves and their country they might altogether have avoided, they ventured blindfold, and like rope-dancers skipped on merrily, and frisked about with the highest unconcern while attempting to pass over the narrow and frightful precipice . . . Perhaps those who set their country in blood and flames, to have the pleasure of trying whether they could bring about a rebellion or revolution, would now be very loth to admit the authenticity of so hazardous a principle.[54]

Loyalists made the argument that history had given England the mildest government on earth. If Englishmen enjoyed liberty, it was only because of the fortuitous circumstances of their past and the beneficence of divine providence, not because of a willful disposition inclined to challenge authority. Thus Charles Inglis gibed "By liberties, I mean such as you formerly enjoyed, and such as are the portion of British subjects.— Frenchmen have what they call liberties—and even Turks—the staunch allies of France—have what they call by the same name. But I conceive you would not be content with such liberties."[55] By such reasoning, it was ridiculous to make appeals to natural rights or anything outside the historical process of judicial understanding and political evolution that gave rise to English liberties. Beyond this, as the maps of early explorers said, be monsters. It was from this vantage point that the specific charges levied against the empire in the Declaration of Independence were evaluated by that most eminent of loyalists, former governor Thomas Hutchinson. By treating seriously the loyalist evaluation of the Declaration, what loyalists discounted and what they felt important to refute, the nature of the Revolution itself becomes more apparent. Unlike their loyalist adversaries, the patriots did not fear chaos from resisting power, but drew from the wellspring of natural law and natural rights a different history and a different conception of the sources of social order and the proper foundations of government.

Chapter 2

"Let Facts Be Submitted to a Candid World": Power on Trial

When John Dickinson wrote his *Letters from a Farmer*, he argued the case against Parliament's right to legislate for the colonies on the basis of historical precedent. The relations between the colonies and the mother country, Dickinson believed, were part of an evolved institutional order crucial to limiting the abuse of power, and Dickinson was not eager to abandon the empire altogether. He continued to hold out hope for restoring the imperial constitution to its original foundations by attempting a reconciliation with England, even while he served as a colonel in the American cause. The King's repeated refusal to hear American petitions, especially petitions from Congress, did not dissuade him from trying again. For most Americans, however, the perception that the King was simply the dupe of malicious ministers or an overbearing Parliament was rapidly receding. It is significant that those most deeply committed to a historical mode of reasoning about law and politics also tended to find it hardest to break with received institutions, even when critical of them. As noted earlier, most loyalists fell into this camp, but so too did many patriots.

The English constitutional disposition towards historical precedent encouraged a cautious conservatism that could be roused to counter dangerous innovations such as Parliament's transgressing the chartered rights of the colonists, or the growing American enthusiasm for independence. So it was with Dickinson. While he feared the uncontrolled power Parliament was asserting over the colonies, he passionately contended for the last conciliatory petition, the Olive Branch Petition, issued by the Second Continental Congress in July of 1775. Dickinson expended what was left of his influence with Congress getting that petition passed, but like previous efforts, it was simply brushed aside. In December of that year the King approved the Prohibitory Act, closing off all trade and declaring the colonies to be in rebellion and outside royal protection.[1] Thereafter, events quickly intensified beyond any hope of reconciliation. The deployment of foreign mercenaries to assist the British military escalation was just one of many insults to American dignity that paved the way for the advocacy of total separation. Among the most influential essays in this vein was Thomas Paine's *Common Sense*, published on January 10, 1776.[2]

Paine presented a reasoned argument against the King and against the traditional ties of loyalty to the old imperial forms of government. He made little mention of history, save to condemn practices that had lost their relevance to the present. Unlike Jefferson's *Summary View*, there is no celebration of a glorious Saxon past. *Common Sense* was a strident litany of monarchical abuses, calculated to cut away at the last vestiges of nostalgia for the King, both as a person and as a system of government. "A government of our own," he wrote, "is our natural right; and when a man seriously reflects on the precariousness of human affairs, he will become convinced, that it is infinitely wiser and safer to form a constitution of our own in a cool deliberate manner, while we have it in our power, than to trust such an interesting event to time and chance."[3]

Most Americans would not see so radical a rejection of their history as a necessary consequence of the application of reason and natural law to a critique of the abuse of power, but Paine's was an inspiring polemic against any further effort towards reconciliation. The majority of revolutionaries, however, saw reason, natural law—even divine law—and the constitutional history of England and America as ultimately complementary. All of these strands of thought were brought together in the Declaration of Independence because they seemed to affirm the importance of limiting power, preventing its consolidation, and extending liberty. The loyalists, on the other hand, presented a case based almost entirely on historically evolved institutions.

The loyalist's critical interpretation of the American cause, and of the Declaration of Independence in particular, affords a clear window through which to discern the character and theoretical content of the Revolution.

I. The State Declarations and The Declaration of Independence

Recently, close attention has been paid to the "declarations of independence" that were issued at the state and local levels. These were of two sorts. The first were instructions to delegates from townships, districts, and states authorizing representatives to vote for independence. These often gave specific reasons why separation was necessary. The second form of "declaration" was by way of a preamble to a state's constitution. Most of the resolutions in favor of independence that preceded the declaration of Congress were in the form of instructions to delegates, with the exception of Virginia, where both a resolution and a new state constitution were issued before July of 1776. These declarations set the backdrop for what came later. Most reveal the centrality of the assumption that natural rights and history went together. The King and Parliament, by violating historically established limits, had breached basic rights founded also in nature. The most important of these was the right of the governed to prior consent to taxation of their properties. Connecticut's resolution on independence, for example, observed that the King and Parliament "claimed and attempted to exercise powers incompatible with and subversive of the ancient, just, and constitutional rights of this and the rest of the *English* Colonies in *America*." The instructions from Buckingham County in Virginia to its state delegates observed that Britain had "violated the faith of Charters, the principles of the Constitution, and attempted to destroy our legal as well as natural rights." The Bill of Rights as written by George Mason for the Virginia state constitution and adopted on June 12, 1774, noted, "all men are by nature equally free and independent, and have certain inherent rights, of which, when they enter into a state of society, they cannot, by any compact, deprive or divest their posterity; namely, the enjoyment of life and liberty, with the means of acquiring and possessing property, and pursuing and obtaining happiness and safety."[4]

Except for Virginia's constitutional preamble, few of the colonial governments, local or state, made extensive lists of grievances against the King, though they did provide a source from which the more comprehensive list in the Declaration was drawn.[5] Some, like Pennsylvania, which ratified its new constitution after Congress approved the Declaration of Independence, ended the old regime by simply noting the grievances "more fully set forth in the declaration of Congress."[6] More interesting is the fact that most of the colonies, now states, declared independence by making it clear that they did so not alone, but united in Congress. This was not a denial of their status as newly sovereign states, but an indication of the grave danger they were assuming. Having now explicitly denied the authority of England, the leaders of the American cause faced the ultimate penalty for treason, with little hope of leniency should they fail. Only together, in a united alliance, could the states hope to achieve their common defense. It was with this in mind that the former colonies issued instructions to their delegates to support the Congressional resolution of Richard Henry Lee in favor of independence on July 2, 1776. Thus the Declaration of Independence served the important and distinct role of affirming the *united* effort of all the colonies to effect their separation, and was crafted to be as representative of the many grievances afflicting all of the states as could be reasonably accommodated.[7] And, unlike Virginia's constitution of June 1776, it was intended solely to announce and justify the end of an older regime.[8]

Since the Revolution, commentators have suggested that the Declaration's long repetition of alleged wrongs raises more questions than it answers. It is fairly well accepted that each member of the drafting committee sought to include his state's main grievances, but what the specific charges against the King refer to is often left open to speculation. Perhaps, like the state constitutions and resolutions, only the most well-grounded complaints should have been put forward, because the more general complaints open the document up to the charge of being vague and insubstantial. Yet the opposite argument could be also made. Why not insist that every possible grievance be included so as to ensure the most comprehensive case? This was, and still remains, a time honored practice among attorneys, but then what of the lack of specificity? Why was reference to specific acts of the King and Parliament omitted?[9] These questions are best answered by putting the document in historical perspective.

The Declaration of Independence followed a long train of declarations in English history in which the reasons for changing the operations of a government or monarch were delimited. Like the Magna Carta, the Petition of Right, and the Declaration of Rights, the American Declaration presented a list of charges against an offending monarch, but beyond this similarity, three important distinctions should be noted. First, in the earlier documents the reference was always to a clearly understood abuse of power in violation of a customary right claimed by Parliament. The appeal was thus always satisfactory to Parliament, and always fairly specific. The Declaration of Independence, on the other hand, was an appeal from many distinct sovereignties and had to be inclusive of the experience of each state. With such an object in view, to be any more specific would have rendered the document tedious, but there is an even more fundamental difference.

The Declaration was also an appeal to the "opinion of mankind" through the invocation of the higher law tradition of the English Whigs. By invoking the "Laws of Nature and of Nature's God," the Declaration judged the King's actions against a higher standard of abuse than did the earlier English documents of public right. From the perspective of natural law, an act of Parliament, such as that banning paper money, might be good in its effects, but would still violate the right of a people to legislate on such matters for themselves. From this perspective, the inclusion in the Declaration of the specific act of legislation would have distracted the attention of mankind from the larger issue of proper authority and proper jurisdiction, as prescribed by the higher law.

Finally, the intention of the earlier documents was different. The English Declaration of Rights, for example, was intended to do more than give the reasons for ending the rule of James II; it was to outline the traditional rights of Englishmen, *and* to set the terms under which the new monarchy was to operate from then onward. In essence, it was to serve as a constitutional document, presenting both specific grievances and specific remedies. This construction was the model often followed by the state constitutions (for example, Virginia's) just prior to the Declaration, whose object was to secure the new state government. The Declaration of Independence, on the other hand, was simply to announce the reasons of an entire confederation of states for ending a regime of long standing by revealing the transgressions of imperial power. It was not intended to prescribe what the new regime should look like and could not get any more specific, either about the charges, or about the shape of things to come other than to assert the right of the colonists "to provide new Guards for their future Security."[10] That said, its focus on the abuse to which government power is prone was very much within the Whig understanding of politics and constitutional theory.

The Declaration represents the typically Whig, typically American synthesis of deference to historical developments and reverence for the natural law and natural rights tradition. Both the preamble and the list of grievances are therefore critical to what the revolutionaries would consider a balanced argument for ending a long-standing regime. Common law practice demanded a demonstration of the criminal intent of the accused, and this required a long list of charges. Yet the laws being violated, according to Americans, were not simply the chartered and inherited rights of Englishmen, as revealed by history, but were the reflections of a higher natural order. Jefferson and the drafting committee had both of these objectives in mind when they set about writing the Declaration, and it was for this reason that the grievances were cast in a more general than specific fashion.

II. Drafting the Declaration

On June 11, 1776, Congress resolved that a committee would be formed to draw up a declaration of independence in the event that Richard Henry Lee's June 7th motion for separation was passed. The members of the committee were Mr. Thomas Jefferson of Virginia, Mr. John Adams of Massachusetts, Mr. Benjamin Franklin of Pennsylvania, Mr. Roger Sherman of Connecticut, and Mr. Richard R. Livingston of New York. Except for Livingston, Jefferson was the youngest of the members, and not an active speaker in Congress, according to John Adams, but his *Summary View* had established him as a penman with an excellent capacity to present the American cause. Adams wrote some years later that Jefferson had initially deferred to him to write the first draft, but he declined for a number of reasons: "1 That he was a Virginian and I a Massachusettensian. 2 that he was a southern Man and I a northern one. 3 That I had been so obnoxious for my early and constant Zeal in promoting the Measure, that any draught of mine, would undergo a more severe Scrutiny and Criticism in Congress, than one of his composition. 4thly and lastly that would be reason enough if there were no other, I had a great Opinion of the Elegance of his pen and none at all of my own." In his *Autobiography*, Adams made explicit reference to Jefferson's *Summary View*: "Mr. Jefferson had the reputation of a masterly pen; he had been chosen a delegate in Virginia, in consequence of a very handsome public paper which he had written for the House of Burgesses, which had given him the character of a fine writer."[11]

When Jefferson set about his task, he had in mind, if not in actuality, a number of documents to serve as models for a first draft of the Declaration. One of these was his own *Summary View* with its well-rehearsed set of grievances. Another was the list of charges made against George III in the preamble to the draft constitution for Virginia, which he had written and which was subsequently inserted into the actual state constitution on June 22, 1776. The last document was the Bill of Rights to that same constitution, written by George Mason and adopted ten days before the inclusion of Jefferson's preamble. Scholars have pored over these documents through the years to determine how much of the spirit and substance of Jefferson's draft of the Declaration was owing to one or another of these three documents.[12] The *Summary View* gives the arguments behind many of the charges, but the essay was of an earlier vintage when Americans still blamed Parliament, as opposed to the King, for their troubles. The great change from 1774 to 1776 was in the switch from the pronoun "they" to "he," as the colonists came to accept that the King was more a willing participant in the "errors" of Parliament than a dupe of his ministers. The remaining two documents were of course more recent.

In a close reading of the texts, Julian Boyd concluded that Jefferson had actually copied from the Virginia preamble directly, but was less sure of Mason's Bill of Rights. Noting the similarity of Mason's paragraph introducing men's fundamental rights, Boyd observed that these were such commonly accepted ideas, imbibed as they were from Locke, Burlamaqui, and Vattel, as to be unexceptional. By comparing what Jefferson designated his rough draft of the corrected copy of the Declaration, as it stood just prior to its submission to Congress, with an earlier draft copied by John Adams, Boyd was able to come to what is thought to be a fairly good estimate of what the very first draft looked like before any of the committee members had seen it. At this early stage, the Jefferson version likely read, "We hold these truths to be sacred & undeniable; that all men are created equal & independent, that from that equal creation they derive rights inherent & inalienable, among which are the preservation of life, & liberty & the pursuit of happiness." Mason's Virginia Bill of Rights, by comparison, noted "That all men are born equally free and independent and have certain inherent natural Rights, of which they can not, by any Compact, deprive or divest their Posterity; among which are the Enjoyment of Life and Liberty, with the Means of Acquiring and possessing property, and pursuing and obtaining Happiness and Safety." The use of the term "independent" might indicate a direct connection, but the issue is really one of degree, because Jefferson himself admitted in a letter towards the end of his life that there was a link: "[B]oth having the same object, of justifying our separation from Great Britain, they used necessarily the same materials of justification; and hence their similitude."[13]

The question of originality in composition, as suggested by Pauline Maier, became an issue only during the political struggles of the first years of the nineteenth century, when the Declaration took on new significance as a contested symbol of nationhood. Federalists desired to downplay Jefferson's role in its composition because he was the leader of the Republican opposition. Jefferson's retort has been taken to be fairly conclusive on the matter: "Neither aiming at originality of principle or sentiment, nor yet copied from any particular or previous writing, it was intended to be an expression of the American mind. . .   All its authority rests then on the harmonizing sentiments of the day, whether expressed in conversation, in letters, printed essays, or the elementary books of public right, as Aristotle, Cicero, Locke, Sidney, etc." The fact is, both Mason and Jefferson were drawing from the same intellectual currents. Adams praised the Declaration precisely because it expressed what were the commonly held views of the day. The three documents that influenced its composition were models of the Whig synthesis, marshalling history, philosophy, and law to support the cause. If it had been otherwise, the committee would likely have intervened far more than it did.[14]

Jefferson recalled writing the first draft and making a few alterations according to the individual recommendations of Adams and Franklin before sending it on to Congress. Adams, on the other hand, recalled that the draft was submitted to the committee before going on to Congress; a letter from Jefferson to Franklin would seem to confirm Adams' memory, but the letter was undated, and the referenced document was not specified. Boyd noted that Jefferson might have been referring to any number of other papers being prepared by other committees on which he and Franklin served, so the issue remains one of interesting speculation. The studies of Hazelton, Becker, Boyd, and Maier all reveal the significant changes made to the Declaration along the way from the draft committee to Congress, but differ as to the details. The earlier studies tend to side with Jefferson's contention that the draft issuing from the committee was principally his own work, while Maier attempts to build a case for a more energetic committee based upon the controversial letter to Franklin. But even Maier, in the end, does not deny that the committee made only a few significant adjustments to Jefferson's original draft. Before its submission to Congress, the Declaration underwent some forty-seven modifications, mostly to tighten prose, and the majority of these (approximately forty-one) were made by Jefferson himself. Congress then made some thirty-nine changes by Boyd's count and twenty-five by Maier's reckoning. These were mostly in the form of deletions from Jefferson's more wordy constructions, but included a few quite substantive alterations as well. They eliminated his reference in the final grievance to the slave trade, in which the King was charged with encouraging the forced importation of Africans. They also added to the last paragraph an appeal "to the Supreme Judge of the World;" and the phrase "with a firm Reliance on the Protection of divine Providence."[15]

Still, in the final analysis, the essential meaning of the Declaration was preserved, and its expression actually enhanced by the alterations in style. At the heart of the argument for separation was a resounding confidence in a divine and natural order ("the Laws of Nature and Nature's God") that set bounds on the powers of government ("That to secure these Rights, Governments are instituted among Men"), and defined the nature of those transgressions that would justify revolution ("that whenever any Form of Government becomes destructive of these Ends, it is the Right of the People to alter or to abolish it"). The fundamental importance of this line of reasoning to the Revolution becomes even more evident, when contrasted with the loyalist argument against the Declaration. Only then is the sharp contrast between the Whig and Tory conceptions of social order brought out.

Maier has observed that most modern studies go directly to analyzing the opening paragraphs of the Declaration, but spend little or no time on the charges against the King. She is correct to focus attention on these neglected portions.[16] Their significance is not so much in that the grievances comprise the longest section of the document or because so much time was lavished on their composition, but that they present the ethical limits of power ("a long Train of Abuses and Usurpations, pursuing invariably the same Object . . .") and the essential case for the Revolution to friend and foe both at home and abroad ("To prove this, let Facts be submitted to a candid World"). Embedded in the grievances was the American Whig's understanding of what had been the proper imperial constitution, and it was against these sections of the document that loyalists aimed their biggest guns. By understanding better the perspective of the "King's men," we can more fully appreciate the radical Whig character at the core of the American war for independence, and why the revolutionaries possessed the degree of confidence they did against the greatest power then existing on Earth.

III. Governor Hutchinson's Critique of the Declaration

Who better to write a denunciation of the Declaration of Independence than the last civilian governor of the state of Massachusetts, the same individual who had been so shocked to learn from the assemblymen of his state that separation from England was not beyond their contemplation? After surrendering his position to General Gage and fleeing with his family to safety in England, Thomas Hutchinson consoled himself by vindicating on paper the loyalist cause of which he was the most prominent representative. In America he had occupied a position of eminence and respect, but in England he was just another colonial refugee. Only in writing to the few prominent sympathetic members of the House of Lords who were willing to give him an ear was he able to find some release from his sense of frustration and political impotence. He executed his task with great precision in his *Strictures upon the Declaration of the Congress at Philadelphia in a Letter to a Noble Lord*, published late in 1776 in London.[17]

According to Hutchinson, the vast body of the colonists "had been happy under it [Parliament] for an hundred years past: They feared no imaginary evils for an hundred years to come. But there were men in each of the principal Colonies, who had independence in view, before any of those Taxes were laid, or proposed, which have since been the ostensible cause of resisting the execution of Acts of Parliament." These factious men who desired independence initially argued on the grounds of natural rights, he asserted, but this "would not be sufficient to draw the people from their attachment to constitutions under which they had so long been easy and happy." So these evil men looked for imaginary wrongs and exaggerated small ones, drumming up trouble wherever they could. The speciousness of their claims, he believed, were easily proven. The General Assembly of Massachusetts, Hutchinson noted, had only opposed duties set by Parliament when it was convenient, but as late as 1762, they had filed suit against the officers of the customs to recoup what they considered their share of the proceeds from the enforcement of the Sugar Act. "Surely," Hutchinson averred, "they would not deny the authority of Parliament to lay the Duty, while they were suing for their part of the penalty for the non-payment of it."[18]

History was invoked to demonstrate, contrary to the preamble of the Declaration, that "There never has been but one *political* band, and that was just the same before the first Colonists emigrated as it has been ever since, the Supreme Legislative Authority, which hath essential right, and is indispensably bound to keep all parts of the Empire entire. . ." Parliamentary supremacy was what kept the empire together and in harmony. Parliament was the final arbiter and ultimate sovereign within the empire, just as Blackstone and other contemporary English legal experts had argued, and, as Daniel Leonard stated, it had served to preserve the peace and happiness of the people. This was a historically evolved relationship that the Americans had once been proud to recognize, but which was now, according to Hutchinson, being thrown off by a reckless faction bent upon self-glory.[19]

As a proper subject of the King, Hutchinson dismissed the assertions of natural rights, and declared it to be impertinent for anyone to presume to show "in what case a *whole people* may be justified in rising up in oppugnation to the powers of government . . . or in what sense all men are created equal; or how far life, liberty, and the *pursuit of happiness* may be said to be unalienable." These were matters only for the "sovereign," that is to say, the King-in-Parliament. In the same spirit as Thomas Hobbes, he contended, "this authority must be the sole judge." Besides, the fact that "the Delegates of Maryland, Virginia, and the Carolinas" deprived "more than an hundred thousand Africans of their rights to liberty, and the *pursuit of happiness*, and in some degree to their lives," was proof enough that these vaunted rights are not "so absolutely unalienable." Here then was the hard view of authority and order as taken from the received practices of the past, and in which everything politically just was considered determined by the context of existing institutions. Taking his bearings from this perspective, Hutchinson had little time for the theory of revolution presented in the preamble, but went on to what he considered to be really essential—the historical facts of the case. These, he asserted, had been falsely presented in the Declaration, and he would expose them, "for as soon as they are developed, instead of justifying, they rather aggravate the criminality of this Revolt."[20]

IV. The Grievances: Abuses of the Royal Negative

Modern examinations of the Declaration have analyzed the grievances by dividing them up into various categories, descending from the most general complaints to the most specific. Not as much attention, however, has been given to the text's own delineation of "abuses and usurpations." Abuses of power and usurpations are not the same constitutionally, though they often go together. An abuse of power can be within the letter of constitutional authority, but in violation of the principle of an equal or impartial application of the laws. It is, in other words, a misuse of power. Thus, for example, the King had the power to disallow colonial legislation, being the constitutionally recognized executive power in the empire. It was not the unconstitutionality of his disallowances that created problems for the colonists, but the fact that he seemed only too willing to exercise that power against the colonists' interests, and not against Parliament. He abused his trust by the partiality and favoritism with which he exercised his power. Usurpation, on the other hand, referred to an application of power not sanctioned by any constitutional provision. The King's cooperation with Parliament's attempt to tax the colonists was for Americans an example of such a breach of the constitution of the empire. Both abuses and usurpations can violate fundamental rights, but it was the latter sort of offence that most alarmed the revolutionaries; it was by no means accidental that Jefferson crafted the Declaration to begin primarily with abuses and end predominantly with usurpations. By doing this, Jefferson sought to provide a sense of the increasing severity of a monarchical tyranny in which abuses of authority gradually shaded into usurpations of power. It is important to keep this distinction between abuses and usurpations in mind when evaluating the loyalist critique, because it will highlight the different conceptions of what patriots and loyalists considered constitutional.[21]

The first charge in the Declaration stated a general complaint that issued from colonies with a royal charter and proprietary colonies (i.e.

colonies given to specific individuals or families such as Pennsylvania or Maryland) that were required in their corporate grants to send all laws made in their colonial assemblies to the King for approval. It read simply that the King "has refused his Assent to Laws, the most wholesome and necessary for the public Good." Jefferson's inclusion of this grievance obviously drew from his Virginia experience and appears first in *Summary View*, but it was also applicable to the states of Massachusetts, Pennsylvania, Georgia, the Carolinas, New York, and New Jersey. In his *Strictures*, Thomas Hutchinson claimed that this charge "is of so general a nature, that it is not possible to conjecture to what laws or to what Colonies it refers." The best he could surmise was that it referred to those laws for issuing "a fraudulent paper currency, and making it a legal tender." In fact, this was a good guess. The earliest controversies over the royal disallowance were precisely on that subject.[22]

Early in Massachusetts history, experimentation with a state land bank had angered British merchants because a number of colonists had sought to use the bank's notes in overseas transactions. The money could not be redeemed in England, and so the charge of fraud was not without merit, but in the colonists' defense, the rates of depreciation were generally low, and most colonial courts took the depreciation into account when settling a debtor's obligations. One historian has recently observed that the opposition to colonial currency was overblown and based more on the fear of potential danger than actual losses. Nevertheless, for English creditors, using these notes was inconvenient. The King did withhold his approval of such paper money, but this did not stop the colonists from issuing the currency, at least initially, and this formed part of the argument for requiring a suspending clause on colonial legislation that demanded that laws not yet approved by the King be suspended from operation. But as Hutchinson pointed out, the colonists finally relinquished their use of paper money when Parliament passed the Currency Act of 1751, banning such practices in Rhode Island, Massachusetts, New Hampshire, and Connecticut. In 1764 the act was extended to all of the colonies, "since which such laws cannot have been offered to the King for his Allowance." These acts were well known throughout the colonies, and it is not inconceivable that the early controversy over paper money was in the minds of the drafting committee when it considered the first grievance. Adams had noted in 1774 in his *Novanglus* essays that "the act to destroy the Land Bank scheme raised a greater ferment in this province than the Stamp Act did," and Adams was a member of the drafting committee.[23]

That Adams referred to the land bank as a "scheme" certainly indicates that he was not enamored of paper money, but it would be incorrect to assume that the first grievance was therefore illegitimate. The King's prohibition on paper money sent a clear signal that the King was more than willing to countenance a total ban on colonial projects for the benefit of Englishmen, without considering the possible benefits lost to the colonists and their governments. It was not that the King was being unconstitutional, even according to the revolutionaries. As the executive branch of colonial government, he clearly had the right to disallow, and even to suspend, the acts of colonial assemblies. Rather, the complaint was that he had exercised his power with partiality in favor of British interests, but never used that power to veto acts of Parliament, as was theoretically his constitutional prerogative, to defend *American* interests. As Jefferson remarked in *Summary View*, "It is now therefore the great office of his majesty to resume the exercise of his negative power, and to prevent the passage of laws by any one legislature of the empire which might bear injuriously on the rights and interests of another."[24] Currency was not the only source of this complaint.

Other laws disallowed by the King's refusal to endorse them—and implicated in Jefferson's *Summary View* as well—included laws to prohibit the importation of slaves or to impose a prohibitive duty on them. Indeed, the King had actually explicitly vetoed all such attempts at halting the slave trade. Clearly the King's ministry had ensured this to preserve a valuable source of revenue to the Crown from the commerce in slaves. Jefferson had hoped to include this complaint as a separate charge against the King in his original draft, but it was stricken by Congress. It was simply untenable for most of the representatives, not to mention embarrassing, to argue that slavery was solely a crime of the King, and not desired or fostered by the colonists in the South or the shipping merchants in the North who imported them.[25]

Additional examples of legislation disallowed by the Crown included acts to prohibit the exportation of convicts and other undesirable immigrants to America, or even to encourage desirable ones. The King and Parliament believed such acts to be in violation of their special prerogative. The fact that Parliament seems always to have been involved in the disallowance of colonial legislation raises some interesting points from both the loyalist and patriot perspectives.[26]

For Hutchinson, Parliament's passage of the Currency Act, and the colonists' compliance, was a clear precedent demonstrating the authority of Parliament to legislate the internal policies of America. For patriots it was not Parliament's "legislation," but the King's disallowance that was the reason for any degree of compliance shown by the colonists. It was when the King attempted to enforce legislation originating in Parliament that we see the later charge of his enforcing "pretended acts of legisla-tion." Indeed, the Declaration refuses to even mention the name of Parlia-ment, as if to say that body never had a recognized place in the American polity. Hence, the King, according to the constitutional theory espoused by Americans, was chargeable with assuming a power that belonged to the colonial legislatures, not simply of exercising an executive power poorly, such as in the case of the disallowance.[27]

The second grievance follows in the vein of the first and is the same sort of abuse charged against the King: "He has forbidden his Governors to pass Laws of immediate and pressing Importance, unless suspended in their Operation till his Assent should be obtained; and when so suspended, he has utterly neglected to attend to them." The policy of requiring a suspending clause was initially applied to laws of a constitutional nature where the Crown sought to protect what it considered its special preroga-tive, or where it believed a crucial economic interest to be at stake. The first instance of such a suspension requirement was a royal command sent by circular letter to all of the colonial governors on November 8, 1708, in direct response to an act of the Barbados assembly which allowed colo-nial debtors to make their payments to British merchants in colonial pa-per currency. As discussed earlier, such laws could be disallowed by the King when presented for approval, but the circular made certain that no such act could be enforced *until* it was officially approved by His Majesty. This was the meaning of a suspending clause.[28]

In the matter of currency regulation, precedents existed to support both monarchical supervision of the colonies and parliamentary regula-tion, but there was a longer history of the King's independent interven-tion. Prior to the Currency Act, it was the King who moved to restrict the colonial legislatures, and Parliament had appealed directly to him to con-trol the issuance of paper money, rather than passing separate legisla-tion. On April 25, 1740, when Massachusetts was in the middle of its experiment with paper money and land banking, Parliament issued a plea to the King, asking His Majesty "That he will be graciously pleased to require and command the respective Governors of his Colonies and Plan-tations in *America*, punctually and effectively to observe his Majesty's Royal Instructions, not to give Assent to, or to pass, any Act, whereby Bills of Credit may be issued in lieu of Money, without a Clause be in-serted in such Act, declaring That the same shall not take effect until the said Act shall be approved by his Majesty."[29] When considering the appli-cation of Parliament's legislative power in the form of the Currency Act, the distinction raised earlier by John Dickinson between laws regulating commerce and laws designed to tax could have been applied, but this was not the position being taken by the Declaration. Here the charge was against the King and the partiality with which he exercised power.

On March 12, 1752, the royal policy of requiring a suspending clause was extended to a wide variety of other laws dealing with colonial government and trade. Each of the colonial governments was asked "forthwith to consider and revise all and every the laws and statutes and ordinances which are in force." It then requested that the laws be revised and the representatives "frame and pass a complete and well digested body of new laws, taking especial care that in the passing of each law, due regard be had to the methods and regulations prescribed by our instructions to you, and that no law of any kind whatever, making a part of such new body of laws, be passed without a clause be inserted therein, suspending and deferring the execution thereof until our royal will and pleasure may be known thereupon." Both Massachusetts and Virginia protested this requirement, and, as Hutchinson reported, no Massachusetts Assembly ever passed a law containing such a clause. The edict was, however, the King's right, according to Hutchinson, and to "pass laws which must have their whole operation, or which must cause some irreparable mischief before the King's pleasure can be known, would be an usurpation of the People upon the Royal Prerogative." Such a delay of operation until the executive can take its bearings, he noted, "can never be charged as an usurpation upon the rights of the People."[30]

Hutchinson was correct to argue that making the requirement was an executive privilege, but the charge was not levied against the King's authority to require a suspending clause, or even against his giving instructions to his governors. It was, on the contrary, meant as an illustration of the abuse of his rightful authority rather than as an example of usurpation. There had been, in fact, several instances of laws detained by His Majesty for a number of years, including one that was suspended for twenty years.[31] Moreover, a large number of precedents supported the view that the King, and not Parliament, was to deal with the colonies. This was an important observation from the perspective of the patriots, because it tended to illustrate that the King was more than willing to exercise his executive powers over the colonial assemblies to protect his subjects in England from such enterprises as paper money, but he was not willing to exercise the same power over Parliament to protect his American subjects from attempts to collect taxes from them. This is what constituted, not so much a fundamental violation of "the rights of the People," as Hutchinson couched the complaint, but a "long train of abuses" as stated in the Declaration.

V. The Grievances: Abusing Colonial Legislatures

The next two grievances touched on a particularly sensitive issue for the colonists, regarding the very right for which they were contending as the foundation of free government: the right to consent to laws of their own making. These were a refusal "to pass Laws for the Accommodation of large Districts of People, unless those People would relinquish the Right of Representation in the Legislature, a right inestimable to them, and formidable to Tyrants only," and the calling "together of Legislative Bodies at Places unusual, uncomfortable, and distant from the Depository of their public Records, for the sole Purpose of fatiguing them into Compliance with his Measures." Both complaints had been experienced by Massachusetts, but the fourth charge of removing representative bodies to places "unusual, uncomfortable, and distant" almost certainly came from John Adams, of that state. According to Hutchinson both grievances were gross distortions of fact, but the third was nothing less than a "wilful misrepresentation made for the sake of the brutal insult at the close of the article."[32] In actuality, the truth was somewhere in between.

The King had indeed attempted to check the tremendous growth in the popularly elected branch of the Massachusetts legislature, which had grown from 84 in 1692 to over 180 by the time of the Revolution. The right to regulate the number of representatives elected from each "County, Town, and Place" was granted in the Massachusetts Charter to the general assembly itself, but in 1742, then-Governor William Shirley complained to the Privy Council (a royal body which represented the King's voice in colonial affairs and was a court of final appeals for the most important colonial cases) of the great inconvenience arising from the unchecked number of new townships electing representatives, while the Governor's Council remained at a paltry 28 members. The King found it agreeable for the governor to restrict the privilege of new townships to elect new representatives, so long as the government provided "all the officers necessary for their good government and security." Complaints were lodged against this practice as being contrary to the colony's charter; in 1761, the King admitted as much and abandoned the practice as far as Massachusetts was concerned, and looked for an alternative. Instead of denying the right of townships to elect representatives, the governor enjoined them to unite with nearby older towns to jointly elect their delegates and share in the expense. According to Hutchinson, this was enough to vindicate the Crown and demonstrate "that there never was the least intention to deprive a single inhabitant of the right of being represented." For the general assembly, this was interference enough, but outside Massachusetts, colonies did not possess even the limited protection of determining their own elections. Jefferson described similar efforts by the Crown to limit the number of representatives to the Virginia House of Burgesses by orders given to then-governor Martin in 1771. All of the remaining colonies struggled at various times with the King over the right to set their own rules governing elections. New York, for example, attempted to admit representatives from Cumberland County in 1766, and from Albany County in 1768, but was denied by the Crown in each case. Hutchinson was familiar only with the experience of Massachusetts, but it is interesting to observe again the criteria he applied to evaluating each grievance. It was a matter of past practice defining the King's prerogative, and always tending to uphold that power. Nowhere was it even mentioned that the King himself had withdrawn the original orders to restrict representation because it was in conflict with the charter of Massachusetts.[33] The grievance was not limited to that colony. It was a very real, ongoing controversy about the proper limits of regal executive power and it was in this light that the fourth complaint was added, bringing the charges up to more recent events.

Hutchinson had very little patience with this grievance because it implicated him directly, referring to his part in the decision to keep the legislature of Massachusetts in Cambridge, where it had been moved in 1768 by Governor Bernard. The complaint was also clearly the work of his old nemesis, John Adams, with whom Hutchinson had sparred innumerable times in the Massachusetts House of Representatives. Sending the legislature out of Boston had been a controversial action because of the vague motive given by Bernard, and the fact that precedent existed for such a transfer in times of emergency. It seems initially that the House of Representatives had themselves contemplated the removal from Boston because of fears that they might be intimidated by the presence of the King's troops, which had arrived to keep order. Then-governor Bernard, Hutchinson's patron, had informed the House that he had no authority to dismiss the troops, but he could and did move the House to Cambridge. It was shortly after Hutchinson assumed office, however, that the assembly complained that the removal was inconvenient and even illegal, citing the charter of the colony to insist that the House could not be convened anywhere but Boston. As Hutchinson noted, "He thought proper to adjourn them to Cambridge, where the House had frequently sat at their own desire, when they had been alarmed with fear of small pox in Boston; the place therefor was not unusual." Cambridge was also "within four miles of the Town of Boston, and less *distant* than any other Town fit for the purpose."[34]

Hutchinson was on fairly strong ground where the original removal to Cambridge was concerned. More likely, it was the decision of his successor, General Gage, to remove the House to Salem that was uppermost in the mind of Adams, but this signaled an additional grievance that was raised later concerning the King's subordination of the civil authority to the military. An early draft of the Declaration shows that the fourth charge was pasted to the list of complaints, so it was not one that had come most readily to mind for Jefferson. Nevertheless, Jefferson was no doubt sympathetic to the complaint, since Virginia had experienced something similar when Lord Dunmore had ordered the Virginia House of Burgesses to convene on the warship H.M.S. *Fowey* in June of 1775![35]

VI. The Grievances: Abusing Colonial Constitutions

The fifth and sixth charges sharply reveal the distinctions between the loyalist construction of proper constitutional authority and the patriot interpretation. Whereas the previous complaints focused principally on the abuse of the King's executive power, the next charges began to shade into the area of usurpation of powers not meant to be exercised by the King: "HE has dissolved Representative Houses repeatedly, for opposing with manly Firmness his Invasions on the Rights of the People;" and "HE has refused for a long Time, after such Dissolutions, to cause others to be elected; whereby the Legislative Powers, incapable of Annihilation, have returned to the People at large for their exercise; the State remaining in the mean time exposed to all the Dangers of Invasion from without, and Convulsions within."

The right of the King to dissolve legislatures was always a highly controversial issue in England. In the seventeenth century, the King had variously exercised his power both to dissolve Parliament or to extend it, in efforts to either control its proceedings or placate its members. Parliament, as we know, eventually won its struggle for supremacy over the monarch within England, though the King retained the formal tasks of calling the assembly together and excusing it at the end of its term. These became purely symbolic performances, however, and all knew where the real authority resided.[36] The colonial legislatures, on the other hand, were different from Parliament in their origins, having been sanctioned by royal charters or proprietary grants dating back, in most instances, to the years before the rise of Parliament to dominance in the Glorious Revolution. Consequently, the King and his representatives, the royal and proprietary governors, retained all of the constitutional powers of the supreme executive in the colonies in more than just theory. For patriots, this proved that their governments had a direct relationship with the monarch that admitted of no interference by Parliament. For loyalists, the fact that the King possessed real executive powers in America was fully consistent with his role as the keeper of the laws of the empire, in which his authority was subsumed by Parliament and designated by the term "King-in-Parliament."[37] In essence, his authority and that of Parliament were indistinguishable. Despite this crucial difference, note that both loyalists and patriots accepted the role of the King as an authentic executive, with all of the traditional powers to call assemblies together, pass or reject legislation brought before him, and dismiss the assemblies at the conclusion of their business. The real trouble began when the King exercised those constitutional powers. For loyalist Americans—even when opposed on policy grounds to Parliament's legislation—no action against the given hierarchy of authority could be sanctioned as constitutional, because it was the hierarchy itself that gave rise to and preserved social order. It was the King-in-Parliament's authority that maintained that order, and there could not be any countermanding of his will on constitutional grounds by the colonists or their assemblies. Simply put, the King was to execute the laws made by Parliament. For the patriots, who took their bearings from Old Whigs like Locke and Coke, however, not only was the King accountable when he exercised new and improper powers, but also when he used his given authority abusively. If the abuse was such that it defeated the legitimate objectives of the accepted constitutional order, such as preventing legislatures (in this case the colonial assemblies) from exercising their proper constitutional responsibilities, then such an act could be held to be an unconstitutional usurpation of power.[38] Such was the nature of the fifth and sixth charges according to American Whigs.

On three very recent and separate occasions, Jefferson's Virginia had experienced the executive dissolution of its House of Burgesses. No doubt this was in Jefferson's mind when he composed the sixth grievance, but it was also experienced by the other colonies. When Massachusetts issued its circular letter protesting the infringement of colonial rights, Lord Hillsborough informed then-Governor Francis Bernard that he should dissolve the House if it did not immediately rescind it. When the House resoundingly refused, Bernard dissolved it the same day—June 30, 1768. Other colonial legislatures were similarly dismissed when they refused to reject the Massachusetts letter. The governors then refused to reconvene the assemblies at their normally appointed times in the following years, requiring extralegal conventions of the people in eight colonies to elect representatives to the Continental Congress. The royal governors were then instructed to attempt to disband these assemblies, but to no practical effect.[39]

Hutchinson's reaction was a strong affirmation of the established hierarchy. "No Government," he wrote, "can long subsist, which admits of combinations of the subordinate powers against the supreme." This was justification enough for the governor to use his "prerogative in suppressing a begun Revolt." The view of the American "rebels" was quite different. They conceded that the King had the right to dissolve assemblies, but not for the purpose of foiling the proper business of legislation. The only reason he possessed such authority was to prevent a rogue legislature, unrepresentative of the people, from abusing its power. It was then incumbent upon the executive to call new elections so that the actual will of the inhabitants might be expressed. The King had authority over the assemblies not to abuse them, but to counter any abuse they might commit by their powers. Thus Jefferson could write in *Summary View*, "But your majesty or your Governors have carried this power beyond every limit known or provided for by the laws." The King had, in essence, defeated the very intentions of the imperial constitution.[40]

VII. The Grievances: Abusing Colonial Property Rights

Charges seven through twelve constituted similar transgressions entailing an abuse of constitutionally granted powers of such a magnitude as to negate the objectives of constitutional government. Rather than using his authority to restrain arbitrary power, according to American patriots, the King was himself being arbitrary. The seventh complaint returned to the subject of the King's disallowance of colonial legislation, but singled out those acts of the colonies that had been designed to encourage immigration to America. The Crown had guarded control over immigration jealously, issuing a royal command prohibiting all naturalization acts throughout the colonies on November 24, 1773. But there was a far more pressing concern: the question of ultimate ownership of land. After issuing an order to suspend the granting of patents on royal land in 1773, the King aggravated Americans further by decreeing in 1774 that land grants would again be available for purchase, but this time at public auction to the highest bidder—this opposed to simply acquiring a warrant of survey for "small sums and on reasonable rents." Moreover, not only would the grant go to the highest bidder, but the yearly quitrent for the use of the land was to be raised to a halfpenny sterling for each acre, and all precious metals that might be found thereon would remain the property of the Crown.[41]

Jefferson followed the lead, once more, of Richard Bland, who had written a treatise against a similar fee for land patents in 1753. Where Bland had argued primarily on the basis of precedent against the charging of fees in Virginia, however, Jefferson emphasized natural rights and the "allodial" (meaning unencumbered by feudal obligations) nature of land in America. In constructing his argument, Jefferson illustrated the American Whigs' proclivity for using arguments from both history and philosophy. Far back in England's Saxon past, he observed, all land was held with absolute right by the owner. Feudal dues to an overlord were unheard of until the time of William the Conqueror, but even then, not all land in England was placed under feudal vassalage, only that seized directly by the Normans. America was not a conquered land, however, and the King had no right to exact feudal dues. All land was allodial. That there was precedent to the contrary did not negate the patriot interpretation, and here Jefferson's argument illustrates a very crucial distinction between the patriot and loyalist views of precedent. When two constructions of the history of ownership were possible, the patriot would side with those precedents in line with natural rights, while the loyalist would cite the practices that upheld the established hierarchy. To the former, history was illustrative and instrumental. To the latter, it was primary and determinative. Thus Jefferson wrote, "Our ancestors however, who migrated hither, were laborers, not lawyers. The fictitious principle that all lands belong originally to the king, they were early persuaded to believe real, and accordingly took grants of their own lands from the crown. And while the crown continued to grant for small sums and on reasonable rents, there was no inducement to arrest the error and lay it open to public view." With the new purchasing requirements, however, it was time to "lay this matter before his majesty, and to declare that he has no right to grant lands of himself." The lands of America, he went on, are in the domain of the societies established by the colonists, and where they have not been allotted either by the colonial legislatures or the colonists collectively assembled, each individual "may appropriate to himself such lands as he finds vacant, and occupancy will give him title." Compare this with Hutchinson's rejoinder to the seventh charge: The King was purely within his constitutional right to refuse his assent to colonial acts to further encourage immigration, and in regard to restricting grants of land, "it certainly was justifiable, and nobody has any right to complain."[42]

VIII. The Grievances: Abusing
the Colonial Justice System

Hutchinson's response was nearly identical with regard to the following two charges, but a bit more ingenious. Charges eight and nine dealt with the American concern for the administration of the judiciary and the dependence of justices upon the purse strings of the Crown. In North Carolina, the King had refused his assent to the colony's act to renew its court system. This was for an assortment of reasons, but principally because he desired a change in the tenure of judges from life appointments on good behavior to the Crown's pleasure; demanded a reduction in the jurisdiction of the county courts; and opposed a clause that allowed the associate justices to conduct business in the absence of the chief judge. The legislature refused to make such changes and the dispute raged back and forth from 1759 to 1773, with the governor approving various provisional court bills with the stipulation of their being temporary until the King's pleasure could be reassessed. This did not appeal to His Majesty, however, and Governor Dobbs found himself in the unenviable position of being despised by both the assembly and the Privy Council. In 1773, another issue arose concerning a provision in the bill for establishing a judiciary, that permitted creditors to seize the property of bankrupts. This had been a common practice in the colonies and had been a standing law in North Carolina for some time. It was decided by the King that such a provision often worked to the detriment of distant creditors in England who were (naturally enough) usually the last to get paid, receiving only what remained after local colonial creditors had descended upon the estates of colonial debtors. The governor was ordered not to approve the new bill for restructuring the court system until the offending clause was removed. Again, the assembly refused, and again, the colony was without an officially sanctioned judiciary. This went on for more than a year, when out of desperation, the governor finally agreed to set up inferior courts. Realizing, however, that nothing further could be expected from the legislature, the governor refused to convene the House, and the colony was bereft of a superior court system until one was established by the revolutionary government, forming the basis of the eighth grievance against His Majesty for "refusing his assent to laws for establishing judiciary powers."[43]

The subject of judicial tenure and compensation in the ninth charge reached a far greater number of colonies, including New York, South Carolina, Massachusetts, and New Jersey. In England, the tenure of judges was life, with good behavior. This was a principle deemed necessary to ensure the impartiality of the judges and to insulate them from the political pressures of either Parliament or the Crown. They were also granted fixed salaries that could not be diminished by the government. The colonies had long practiced a similar policy of life tenure with good behavior, though most had not fixed the compensation of their judges, but instead held tight control over judicial compensation as a means of countering the power and influence of royal governors.

The King and the Privy Council had a different view of the situation in North Carolina. Holding fast to the executive prerogative, they insisted that the presence of unlettered justices in the colonies necessitated a means for removing them when more qualified candidates appeared, and that a fixed salary, paid by the Crown, if necessary, was essential for the enforcement of imperial regulations and laws.

In Massachusetts the situation was aggravated by an effort on the part of then-governor Hutchinson to pay his own salary, in addition to the judges', from the royal coffers. In the eyes of the colonists, this diminished their ability to check the power of imperial authority. From this perspective, it was not so much the independence of the judges or the governor that was being assured, but their undue influence by England. Hutchinson's response to both the eighth and ninth charges was to reiterate that these powers of disallowance and judicial control were perfectly within the royal prerogative. In the first case, he cited only the controversy concerning debtors' property to argue that it was an unjust law that demanded the King's negative. In the second case, however, Hutchinson took the colonial interpretation of the imperial constitution and stood it on its head.[44]

If the Americans wanted to claim that their allegiance to the King preceded the present claims of Parliament to supremacy in the empire, and instead took their authority directly from the person of the King, then they had no right to complain about the fact that the monarch, in certain instances, was reclaiming his right to dismiss judges when he pleased, or to pay their salaries. This was an interesting argument, because it was certainly the case that prior to the completion of the Glorious Revolution in 1701, the King did possess in England the power to appoint and dismiss members of the judiciary at his pleasure. This came to an end with the settlement, which established the new royal line of succession and ushered in a new policy for judges of life tenure with fixed salaries, on condition of good behavior. A number of colonies (but not all of them) successfully incorporated similar measures. New Jersey provided for good behavior as early as the 1730s. New York initiated the policy in the mid

1740s, and Pennsylvania recognized it in its Judiciary Act of September 29, 1759. "There has been a change in the constitution of England in respect of the tenure of the office of the Judges," the former governor noted, but "How does this give a claim to America?" His answer was the same in regard to all of the abuses charged against the King's royal prerogative: "This will not be allowed and until the King shall judge it so, there can be no room for exception to his retaining his prerogative."[45]

The patriot response to this controversy stands in stark contrast to Hutchinson and was outlined nicely in the debate between John Adams and Daniel Leonard. Writing as Novanglus, Adams, like Jefferson in his argument against the arbitrary dismissal of assemblies, contended that the British monarchy was always and anciently a limited monarchy. "[A]n English king," he wrote, "had no right to be absolute over Englishmen out of the realm, any more than in it; and they were released from their allegiance, as soon as he deprived them of their liberties." This was simply because those liberties were natural rights: "English liberties are but certain rights of nature, reserved to the citizen by the English constitution, which rights cleaved to our ancestors when they crossed the Atlantic, and would have inhered in them if, instead of coming to New England, they had gone to Otaheite or Patagonia, even although they had taken no patent or charter from the king at all." And once Englishmen had arrived in America, they "had a clear right to have erected in this wilderness a British constitution, or a perfect democracy, or any other form of government they saw fit." In other words, the King's prerogative was limited to protecting the rights and liberties of his subjects, of ensuring their protection from the abuse of power, but not to be abusive with his own. Just as the Crown was a limited monarchy in England, so it was limited in America. In essence, the King had entered into "a contract with his subjects . . . that they should enjoy all the rights and liberties of Englishmen for ever . . . made with all the colonies, royal governments, as well as charter ones," and once this contract was violated, the King was beyond the constitutional intent of his powers.[46]

IX. The Grievances: Abuses Against the Rule of Law

The next three charges dealt with the most recent events of the Revolution. These controversies were well-known and ongoing at the time of the Declaration's composition, and are repeated and expanded on in more detail in the nine subcategories of the thirteenth charge. But grievances ten, eleven, and twelve were meant to round out the indictment of the

King for the specific abuse of his executive powers. In republican political theory, the King had the responsibility to enforce the laws. Grievance number ten referred to the new inspectors of the customs and the Courts of Admiralty, which were established to apply the acts regulating American trade and the collection of revenues. The legality of these acts was disputed by Americans who considered only those bills passed by their own legislatures as representative of the people and therefore law. The King's commitment to sending new officials was, consequently, nothing other than an abuse of executive power.[47]

The eleventh charge was directly related to this and was connected to the King's duty to protect the realm from outside invasion and internal disturbances that threatened the public peace and safety. Whigs held that this was properly done by calling upon the people, their representatives, lords, and constituent authorities, to raise an army in times of crisis. In America, these forces took the form of colonial militias. In troubled times, such as frontier clashes with native tribes, they were called out by governors and assemblies under the King's authority. What was not acceptable to the Whigs of the seventeenth century and later American Whigs was the maintenance of a formidable army within the realm in times of peace. The presence of such a force was considered to be one of the telltale signs of tyranny. In the words of Cato, "Standing armies are standing curses in every country under the sun, where they are more powerful than the people."[48]

The basis for the twelfth complaint against the King for rendering the "Military independent of and superior to the Civil Power," was worse than any that preceded it. As commander in chief of the kingdom's defenses, the monarch was responsible, in Whig theory, for defending the constitutional order. But if he placed himself or his military officers above the civil laws of the realm, he made himself a tyrant. American patriots extended this argument to their colonial laws, which they considered on a par with the laws passed by Parliament. From this perspective, the King stood in the very same relationship to the colonial assemblies as he did to Parliament in England. The charge was levied directly against his appointment of General Gage as both military commander and governor of Massachusetts. This concluded, in order of ascending magnitude, the abuses of the King's executive powers.

Hutchinson's response to these charges powerfully illustrates just how "Tory" the conception of social order was among loyalists. Each of the protested actions was defended as a constitutionally recognized exercise of monarchical authority, sanctioned by Parliament and recognized by history. The so-called swarms of officers was dismissed as no more than thirty or forty out of some "three millions of people." To the question of maintaining a standing army, he noted that it was not necessary to gain the colonists' consent; the King needed only that which he already possessed— "the consent of the Supreme Legislature," by which Hutchinson meant Parliament. To contend otherwise, he asserted, was to beg the question of who the legitimate authority in the empire was. He ended by noting that "When the Subordinate Civil Powers of the Empire became Aiders of the people in acts of Rebellion, the King, as well he might, has employed the Military Power to reduce those rebellious Civil Powers to their constitutional subjection to the Supreme Civil Power." For Hutchinson, social order necessitated the preservation of the hierarchy wherein a "supreme" body presided over all "Subordinate Civil Powers." In the post-seventeenth-century sense, Hutchinson was a Whig because he defended Parliament; but in the *older* sense of Whig, in the sense of Locke, Sidney, and Cato, he was a Tory, using the same arguments to affirm the supremacy of the King-in-Parliament as were used by the defenders of monarchical supremacy.[49] This is borne out in the next charge, as we move from the abuse of constitutionally recognized powers to the usurpation of powers never meant to be exercised by the King.

X. The Grievances: Usurpations and Acts of War

The thirteenth charge introduces in greater detail the sorts of acts that finally compelled the colonists to seek separation. These were the usurpations of powers—actions without any basis in constitutional authority. They are, in fact, directed squarely against the presumption of Parliament to rule for the entire empire and all of its constituent parts. At this early date, Massachusetts was still experiencing the brunt of the offences which make up the nine categories under the thirteenth charge. They refer to the well-known policies reviewed in the previous chapter, but for our purposes here, the thirteenth charge summarizes the essential disagreement between loyalists and patriots. The patriots avoided even mentioning Parliament, so there would be no misreading their view of Parliament's legal relationship to the colonies: virtually no relationship at all. Here the King is accused of combining "with others to subject us to a jurisdiction foreign to our Constitution and unacknowledged by our laws; giving his assent to their pretended Acts of Legislation." Hutchinson's reaction presents a classic statement of the Tory understanding of empire that contrasts sharply with the views of such revolutionaries as Bland, Dickinson, Wilson, Adams, and Jefferson.

After the Glorious Revolution which concluded (or nearly so) Parliament's struggle for supremacy in the realm, Whig doctrine underwent a subtle transformation in England. Early Whigs had used both custom and natural right to argue for both the basis of government in consent, and against the abuse of power. Both nature and the ancient constitution were said to uphold English liberties, and precedent was invoked to illustrate when consent was given to the exercise of power and when it was not. After the settlement, English Whigs reduced the definition of "Whig" to mean supporting Parliament over the king, sometimes referred to as the "kingliness of Parliament." When Locke was mentioned in this context, it was only to refer to those aspects of his theory that he shared in common with thinkers like Hobbes. Thus when Hutchinson referred to Locke, it was to emphasize his argument for a supreme power in society, not for his justification of resistance to tyranny or his insistence that certain rights are retained from the state of nature.

American Whigs, on the other hand, retained the earlier Whig view of society and the critique of power. From their perspective, Parliament could not represent them, and in fact constituted a dangerous and alien power. Rather, they had only a customary constitutional relationship to the kings of England. Thus in John Adams' first debate with Governor Hutchinson in 1773, Adams made the point that the colonies had had their own "Glorious Revolution" against James II and had consented only to accept as their king whomever Parliament chose as the King of England. But they had never ceded the right to tax or legislate for themselves to Parliament, thus preserving the original contract with the monarchy.[50]

Some find this older constitutional construction puzzling because on the surface it seems to reduce American Whigs to defenders of the royal prerogative, while English Whigs remain the defenders of Parliament. In fact the American opposition to Parliament was even more authentically Whig, and based upon the wholly congruent fusion of customary and natural rights. Thus Adams could insist that "English liberties are but certain rights of nature," but such an argument was perplexing to those in the ascendancy in the empire who supported the "kingliness of Parliament." "This is a strange way," Hutchinson observed, "of defining the part which the Kings of England take in conjunction with the Lords and Commons in passing Acts of Parliament. But why is our present Sovereign to be distinguished from all his predecessors since Charles the Second? . . . And then, how can a jurisdiction submitted to for more than a century be *foreign* to their constitution?"[51] This was precisely the point under contention, and each legislative precedent was hotly contested and interpreted differently by both sides, reflecting their very different understandings of what happened in the Glorious Revolution. The nine subcategories of the thirteenth charge are perfect examples.

Most interesting from a constitutional perspective is Hutchinson's response to the fourth category, "FOR imposing Taxes on us without our consent." The idea that taxation could be distinguished from other forms of legislation was a point that Americans were once willing to make, he observed, but now they listed taxation as just one of many other grievances, and no longer the primary cause of their rebellion. No taxation without representation, he noted, was regarded by the Americans as a fundamental principle of government while it was useful, but they were now aiming at independence, or a ban on all legislation without representation. They forget, he argued, that their Whig forebears had contended against Charles II and James II for the sake of gaining Parliament's supremacy over the kingdom, fighting for the principle "that there were no bounds to the power of Parliament by any fundamentals whatever, and that even the hereditary succession to the Crown might be, as it since has been, altered by Act of Parliament."[52]

That was not the American Whig's reading. Just as the English king had always been a limited monarch, as Adams pointed out in his debate with Daniel Leonard, so too had the power of Parliament been limited by the principles of consent, by the laws of the land, and by natural right and natural law. It was a point raised by men like Richard Bland, James Wilson, and even John Dickinson. Parliament could not pass an act contrary to justice and expect it to be law. This was the argument of the original Old Whigs of the seventeenth century, like Coke and Locke: "For whereever the Power that is put in any hands for the Government of the People, and the Preservation of their Properties, is applied to other ends, and made use of to impoverish, harass, or subdue them to the Arbitrary and Irregular Commands of those that have it: There it presently becomes *Tyranny*, whether those that thus use it are one or many." [53]

Hutchinson resolutely refused to recognize this part of the Old Whig theory of the English constitution. He accused the colonists of confounding "Taxes imposed by the authority of the *King alone*" with "Taxes imposed, by the *King, Lords and Commons* . . . as if the latter case were analogous to the former." In reality, Hutchinson was not making a Whig argument, contrary to his own understanding. His argument for supremacy was not bounded by Locke's or Coke's insistence on a *limited* power to legislate. He feared the disruption of the empire and the dissolution of the order imposed by its hierarchy. "The people," he wrote, "have not observed the fallacy in reasoning from the *whole* to *part*; nor the absurdity of making the *governed* to be *governors*." In essence, his *was* a Tory argument much like Filmer or Hobbes might make, that evinced fear of chaos in the absence of a strong imperial sovereign—however constituted. It was simply that Parliament was now the ruler, not the King alone. English Whigs, with the exception of the Rockingham Whigs, were no longer Whigs at all.

The last six charges against the King in the Declaration went beyond the scope of even usurpation. They describe a state of war. The colonies were outside royal protection and were now open targets of the King's aggression. Hutchinson could only fume against such "consummate effrontery," and defend England's military campaign: "The Acts of a *justly incensed* Sovereign for suppressing a most *unnatural, unprovoked* Rebellion, are here assigned as the *causes* of this Rebellion." And that was being lenient. He continued, "To subjects, who had forfeited their lives by acts of Rebellion, every act of the Sovereign against them which falls short of the forfeiture, is an act of favour." War was the natural result of resistance to the sovereign, and social calamity was the rule of the day in the colonies. Those in America who defended the right order of the Crown, he noted, were "exposed to the rage and fury of the populace." So ended Hutchinson's commentary on the Declaration, underlining as it did the Tory perception of a society in "unnatural" rebellion. Without due subjection to a supreme sovereign, there was no society at all, but simply "the rage and fury of the populace."[54]

XI. Between Order and Chaos

"Unnatural" was not an uncommon perception on the part of loyalists and imperialists reflecting on the American Revolution. "Remarkable" was its more charitable counterpart among American patriots. Both responses evinced a profound astonishment at the causes that could have motivated resistance to English imperial authority, and ever since, historians have sought some ultimate rationale or explanation. It became an obsession with those Americans who remained loyal to Great Britain, and now found themselves aliens in England.

A dramatic example is found in Jonathan Sewall, a former friend of John Adams, a native of Massachusetts, and a Crown official, who fled to England in 1775. Like Hutchinson, he found the entire colonial resistance to be unnatural:

> It should seem astonishing, that a Country of Husbandmen, possessed everyone, almost, of a sufficient Share of landed property, in one of the finest Climates in the World; living under the mildest Government, enjoying the highest portion of civil and religious Liberty that the Nature of human Society admits, and protected in the Enjoyment of these, and every other desirable Blessing in Life, upon the easiest Terms, by the only Power on Earth capable of affording that protection—that a people so situated for Happiness, should throw off their rural Simplicity, quit the peaceful Sweets and Labours of Husbandry . . . and rush to Arms with the ferocity of Savages and the fiery Zeal of Crusaders!

The cause of this, he suggested, was deep within American culture, and was nothing "other than that ancient republican independent Spirit, which the first Emigrants to America brought out with them; and which the Forms of Government, unhappily given to the New England Colonies, instead of checking, have served to cherish and keep alive." Americans were acting "under the power of mere Delusion," but they were beyond reasoned arguments. "It is vain to think any longer of drawing them—to such a pitch is the Frenzy now raised, that the Colonists will never yield Obedience to the laws of the parent State, till, by Experience, they are taught to fear her power."[55]

At the height of the Revolution, loyalists saw "frenzy," "rage," and "fiery Zeal," but patriots saw something else—a perception of ordered liberty threatened by power. This was the image encapsulated in their Declaration of Independence. It was that "ancient republican independent Spirit." But what exactly did that mean?

Chapter 3

"Life, Liberty, and the Pursuit of Happiness": Jefferson and the Natural Social Order

Confidence resonates throughout the Declaration. The whole tenor of the document runs counter to the warnings and admonitions of Joseph Galloway, Samuel Seabury, Daniel Leonard, Thomas Hutchinson, Charles Inglis, John Joachim Zubly, and Peter Oliver, and the reasons for this have intrigued generations of scholars. Like Jonathan Sewall, they have undertaken to "search deeper for the Grand and hidden Spring which causes so wonderful a movement in the Machine," but their conclusions have differed widely. Sewall pointed to "that ancient republican independent Spirit," but just what that means has not been altogether clear.

The earliest histories, written by contemporaries of the great event, assume a familiarity with sources and concepts that are no longer common knowledge, and this has encouraged a wealth of modern theories. Early in the twentieth century, scholars looked to the natural rights philosophy of John Locke to contend that American Whigs were essentially Lockean individualists, but later writers thought they saw a more corporatist, communitarian republicanism reflecting the rhetoric of ancient thinkers on balanced government. For these writers, individual sacrifice for the common good—not individual liberty—was the central moral and political virtue. Still others have stressed the central place of Christian moral teachings and the essentially covenental nature of American politics going back to the Puritans. Then there are those who simply insist that Americans agreed to disagree about fundamentals, or accepted basic contradictions, fudging the distinctions in an effort to unite against a common foe. Each of these perspectives has its advocates, and as one important recent contributor to the conversation has noted, each has grasped a fundamental part of the American political tradition; but there is another perspective from which to view all of these strands.[1]

The Old or Real Whig tradition, as noted earlier, united the perspectives of natural law and history to form a conception of the human social order distinct from the purely historical and hierarchical political view of the Tory tradition. For the Whig, human social interaction had a natural capacity for attaining a flourishing and highly complex order independent of political governance. This is not to say that political institutions were unnecessary, but only that large portions of human life owed their mainspring to a basic social impulse aside from the political drive for power. Whigs differed about the source of that social impulse. Some looked to the workings of rational self-interest, others to a moral compass hardwired in the human being in the form of a "moral sense," or capacity for sympathy and fellow feeling. Still others looked to custom and the received wisdom of the common law. Most Whigs borrowed variously from all of these sources, but what united them as Whigs was a belief that human order was not fundamentally the product of political mediation. Politics was necessary to protect the natural social order that arose spontaneously from the basic impulses to sociability, but it was not their source; in fact, government could endanger social life through the violence and corruption of arbitrary power.[2]

What the opening paragraphs of the Declaration represent is a synthesis of all these various perspectives, which was exactly the intention of its author. The confidence expressed in the Declaration is to be found in the history of the Whig tradition that Jefferson drew upon. It was that tradition that gave the charges against the monarch their persuasive power, and imparted to the idea of self-government a far more profound meaning than simply the ability to participate in political decisions. Americans thought of self-government as predominantly all of the nonpolitical means by which human society is capable of ordering itself spontaneously through custom and the common law, through rational self-interest and the law of nature, and through the human capacity for moral understanding and sentiment. We should begin with the first of these to explore the origins of Whig political thought in the development of English constitutional and common-law history. This will give us a better sense of how Whigs used the past, conceived historically the problem of power, and understood the role of custom and precedent in politics. From there, it becomes possible to trace the development of natural-law thinking, the influence of scientific thought, and the complementary developments of political economy and moral sense theory.

I. The Whig View of Law and the Ancient Constitution

The seventeenth-century contest between Parliament and the king over political supremacy in England had its origin in the very complex cultural and political landscape of late medieval Europe. In England, as on the Continent, power was distributed unevenly among numerous local lords and magistrates with a nominal claim of supremacy by the king. Prior to the Norman Conquest of 1066, according to Whig historians, an elected monarch, deemed to be distinguished by experience and wisdom, was chosen by a high council of local authorities. After the defeat of the Saxon King Harold by William, Duke of Normandy, at the Battle of Hastings, the pretense of intellectual merit was replaced by an explicitly feudal system where heredity was the principal claim to membership in the high council, and the council's purpose was not to elect, but to advise a monarch who ruled by right of birth. It was common among Whigs to speak of Saxon liberties and Norman yokes and manacles, but while the Norman lords and the remaining Saxon leaders pledged an oath of fealty to their sovereign and his heirs, there was actually little central control. The local powers were jealous guardians of their privileges, and subsequent monarchs found it difficult to complete the process of consolidation begun by William. This was the source of the great charter of English rights, the Magna Carta, which was forced upon King John on the banks of the Thames at Runnymede in 1215. The essential requirement was that John respect the traditional rights and privileges of his barons if he wanted to remain king. The monarch was thus never permitted to become an absolute ruler over his subjects.[3]

The constitutional history of England is a story of competing powers. This is reflected in the evolution of its legal system, which arose from the blending of many different traditions. Over the course of the Middle Ages, the Old Saxon laws and the Norman feudal claims were woven together to form a set of rules negotiated among the various contending authorities. The king, seeking to gain some foothold over the justice system, instituted his own royal courts in the thirteenth century, but the judges reserved for themselves the power to discover law, and built up a formidable body of general rules based upon precedent and custom. These came eventually to embrace the rules of the rapidly expanding commercial centers, originally under the adjudication of private "law merchants." In time, the entire fabric of English law came to reflect the complexity of negotiated understandings of the various components of English society, whether they were great or petty lords, rich or middling merchants, or

small- or large-scale peasant land owners. This system of evolved customary and negotiated rules came to be called the English common law.
Parliament was itself the result of the same historical forces that shaped
the customary practices and negotiated rights and privileges of the realm.
Those who defended Parliament against the power of the king looked to
this history to find relevant precedents and the source for their claim that
the monarchy was limited in its power by the rights of Parliament and the
individual's rights in common law. Ironically, the strength of these claims
was only enhanced by the king's continual quest for revenue and power.[4]

With the expansion of commerce and agriculture in the late Middle
Ages, the increasing number of petty lords and ignoble men of wealth
afforded the monarchy new potential sources of taxes. The great barons
and prelates of the Church had long insisted upon their right to consent to
the taxes imposed by the sovereign, and had often effectively resisted the
kings' more ambitious projects. In 1295, for example, Edward I was compelled to reaffirm the rights proclaimed in the Magna Carta in exchange
for revenues he initially sought to raise by arbitrary exaction to finance his
war with France. The growing wealth of the lower orders, of small
proprietorships and commercial centers, provided the king with the opportunity to expand his revenues independently of the greater lords. Increasingly the kings summoned representatives from the towns to par-
take of the honor of being represented in the great council. This history is
a complicated one, but in general terms, the enlargement of the representative body resulted in the formation of a lower House of Commons,
distinct from the House of Lords, which quickly became a primary force
in the struggle against monarchical supremacy. In the ongoing power play
between king and aristocracy, both sides sought the support of the lower
nobility and the inhabitants of the towns and commercial cities, collectively known in England as the commons. The initial hope of the king was
to raise revenues by circumventing, in part, the authority of the higher
nobility, but it soon became clear that the commoners would insist, with
equal vigor, on exercising their substantive right to consent. The House of
Commons finally coalesced into a permanent component of the constitution by the end of the fourteenth century, and was soon the source of
some of the loudest voices in favor of limiting power. By the middle part
of the seventeenth century, its most radical members could be heard advocating republican forms of government and even the abolishment of
hereditary monarchy, giving rise to the first "radical Whigs," initially called
Petioners, of the English Civil War period (1642–51).[5]

The history of Parliament, together with the development of the common law and the appeal to history and custom, thus formed the first basis

of political "whiggery." The authority of the common law drew from received custom and the wisdom of negotiated legal understandings in the community, and not from the arbitrary power of the monarch. The classic expression of common-law judges was to refer to practices and rights of immemorial origin, expressed through the ages by the practices of the whole kingdom, rather than to the power of monarchical decree. Thus Blackstone defined the common law as

> Distinguishable into three Kinds: 1) General customs; which are the universal rule of the whole kingdom, and form the common law in its stricter and more usual signification. 2) Particular customs, which for the most part, affect only the inhabitants of particular districts. 3) Certain particular laws; which by custom, are adopted and used by some particular courts, of pretty general and extensive jurisdiction. . . . All these are doctrines that are not set down in any written statute or ordinance, but depend merely upon immemorial usage, that is upon common law, for their support.[6]

Tories accepted the notion of custom and precedent as necessary parts of the law, but for them the ultimate source of authority rested with the sovereign, whether that was the king in the seventeenth century, or the King-in-Parliament in the eighteenth. The authority of history thus embraced more than custom as shaped by the community, but also precedents as shaped by royal prerogative, however composed, which could trump customary practices. Whigs likewise looked to the history of political institutions, but not to support the prerogatives of power. Rather, they looked to the history of political institutions to uncover means of limiting power.[7]

II. The Whig View of Power and Republican Government

The Whig approach to ancient constitutional history and the common law was additionally informed by another line of inquiry that sought to explain the corrupting nature of political power and the need to balance authority among executive, legislative, and judicial branches of government. This was the civic republican tradition and it took its bearings from ancient classical sources as well as late Renaissance scholarship, providing a broader, complementary perspective wherein to situate the legal history of England. Like the study of the common law and the ancient constitution, civic republicanism looked back into history to find examples of the well-ordered society. Classical analogies and references to ancient writers like Aristotle, Polybius, Tacitus, and Cicero typically appeared alongside references to ancient Saxon liberties in the works of both English and American Whigs.[8]

According to the republican writers of antiquity, society was composed of basic social orders, or classes of men, who possessed distinct virtues and weaknesses. These orders were the common people, the talented few, and the great leader or king. Each class produced its distinctive form of government, capable in its ideal political form of great and virtuous actions. Democracy was government by the people, aristocracy was by the few, and monarchy by the one. Each of these, when tempted by power, could be corrupted into its opposite—anarchy, oligarchy, and despotism, respectively. During the High Renaissance of Italy, scholars focused on the means of mixing the three virtuous forms of government so as to balance them against each other and thereby prevent corruption and assure the preservation of virtue, or the common good. The great merit of the ancient English Constitution for Whigs was precisely the happy accident of its having evolved a mixed polity, capable of holding at bay the abuses of those in power.[9]

Writing against Robert Filmer's defense of absolute power in the monarch, Algernon Sidney observed that the only acceptable kingships are limited ones "which are mixed and regulated by laws, where diets, parliaments, assemblies of estates or senates, may supply the defects of a prince, restrain him if he prove extravagant, and reject such as are found to be unworthy of their office, which are as odious to our author [Filmer] and his followers, as the most popular governments, and can be of no advantage to his cause." He went on, "if I should undertake to say, there never was a good government in the world, that did not consist of the three simple species of monarchy, aristocracy, and democracy, I think I might make it good." Evils in such a mixed polity were supposedly moderated by the virtues of the parties in government who made up for the deficiencies of those who might be corrupted. Rivalry in this context would lead to the best outcome, representing the common good as it "did in Rome for above three hundred years after the expulsion of Tarquin."[10]

This tempering quality of a mixed government, wherein power is pitted against power, was made necessary by the corrupting nature of political authority. Individuals of avaricious ambition would always seek to overturn even the soundest constitutions, and they would do so typically through the formation of factions created by the use of patronage or wealth. Wealth at the disposal of the politically powerful was thus a great menace to liberty and required the constant vigilance of the good citizen. Alliances between commerce and power were especially suspect. Thus Sidney observed that "corruption will always reign most where those who have the power do most favor it." It was not wealth from trade, but wealth allied with power, amassed by fraud and theft, that alarmed Sidney. Drawing from another classical source, he remarked that "Eutropius when he was a slave, used to pick pockets and locks; but being made a minister, he sold cities, armies, and provinces. . . . And when the power is in the hands of base mercenary persons, they will always (to use the courtiers' phrase) make as much profit of their places as they can." It was power itself that attracted corrupt appetites and invited bribery. "Many seem to be modest and innocent in private fortunes," he noted, "who prove corrupt and vicious when they are raised to power. The violence, pride and malice of Saul, was never discovered till the people had placed him in the throne. But where the government is absolute, or the prince endeavors to make it so, this integrity can never be found." This is precisely why the limited nature of mixed polities was favored over absolute monarchy and why the Whigs cherished the virtue of self-restraint. A virtuous regard for the common good was not sufficient in itself to prevent the abuse of power, but it was one of many helps to be employed in the preservation of a free society.[11]

Later Whigs took the same position. John Trenchard and Thomas Gordon, writing in the early eighteenth century, continually raised the tragedy of the corrupting nature of power. "Unlimited power is so wild and monstrous a thing, that however natural it be to desire it, it is as natural to oppose it; nor ought it to be trusted with any mortal man, be his intentions ever so upright: For besides that he will never care to part with it, he will rarely dare. In spite of himself he will make many enemies, against whom he will be protected only by his power, or at least think himself best protected by it." That power, moreover, will be by its nature "ever encroaching, and converting every extraordinary power, granted at particular times, and upon particular occasions, into an ordinary power to be used at all times, and when there is no occasion; nor does it part willingly with any advantage." What was their solution? "The Romans," they observed, "who knew this evil, having suffered by it, provided wise remedies against it; and when one ordinary power grew too great, checked it with another." "Only the checks put upon magistrates make nations free; and only the want of such checks makes them slaves." American Whigs were familiar with both Sidney and the *Cato's Letters* of Trenchard and Gordon, and echoed time and again the same sentiments.[12] In an essay published in Philadelphia in 1776 on *The Genuine Principles of the Ancient Saxon or English Constitution*, to which was appended a copy of the Declaration of Independence, an anonymous writer (very likely the radical American Whig, George Bryan) wrote imploringly, with the history of the ancient republics in mind, that

> Our new Republics should use the utmost caution to avoid those fatal errors; and
> be supremely careful in placing that dangerous power of controlling the actions of
> individuals, in such manner that it may not counteract the end for which it was
> established.
>
> Government may be considered, a *deposite*[sic] of the power of society in
> certain hands, whose business it is to *restrain*, and in some cases to take off such
> members of the community as disturb the quiet and destroy the security of the
> honest and peaceable subject. *This government* [Pennsylvania's constitution of
> that same year] *is founded in the nature of man, and is the obvious end of civil
> society;* "yet such is the thirst of power in most men, that they will sacrifice
> heaven and earth to wrest it from its foundation; to establish a power in them-
> selves to tyrannize over the persons and properties of others."[13]

From the Whigs' understanding of power was derived their admiration
of certain ancient virtues. Men who resisted the corruption of power and
wealth, who could relinquish their posts when the time came and return
to their private estates—these were the models of great leaders, but no
Whig ever trusted to such virtues alone, because they understood all too
well the nature of power. Sidney contended with sincerity that he "who
could rise from the plow to the triumphal chariot, and contentedly return
thither again, could not be corrupted," but it was to a government of
divided powers with frequent rotation of office that he assigned his primary defense of liberty.[14]

Some authors have tried to make more of such virtue by placing it at
odds with an earlier interpretation of liberty that stressed a liberal, or
Lockean, individualism. The Revolution, by their estimate, was a flight
away from commerce and modernity back to an older ideal of a political
community of selfless virtue. Such a reading places in opposition modes
of reasoning that are, in fact, quite compatible. It ignores the instrumental
nature of history in the early liberal program, or what Bolingbroke called
"philosophy teaching by example," that informed the first English opponents of absolute government and their American descendants.[15] Republican ideas about power formed one of the essential "harmonizing sentiments of the day" at the root of the Declaration, and expressed, according
to Jefferson, in such "elementary books of public right, as Aristotle, Cicero,
Locke, Sidney, etc."[16]

III. Jefferson and the Whig Use of History

Jefferson was drawn to the study of history early in his youth. It formed a
substantial part of his readings, and when he went to study with William
Small and George Wythe in Williamsburg, he was introduced to the clas-

sics on the English constitutional system, republican government, and the origins of the common law. As the foregoing quotation indicates, the influence of these works remained with him for the rest of his life. By 1771, as indicated in his letter to Robert Skipwith, he had read Sidney's *Discourses*, Coke's *Institutes*, and Blackstone's *Commentaries*. All of these gave him the standard Whig account of the ancient Saxon laws and the origins of Parliament, along with many classical allusions to Rome and Greece as observed especially in Sidney. Other sources, less known today but acclaimed in Jefferson's time, were Henry Home, Lord Kames' *Historical Law Tracts*, John Sommer's *Rights of King and People*, Sir Henry Spelman's *Works*, Obadiah Hulme's *An Historical Essay on the English Constitution*, and Sir John Dalrymple's *Essay on Feudal Property*. Along with Blackstone, all of these sources were quoted and discussed at length in relation to the history of the common law and Parliament in Jefferson's Commonplace Book (an informal journal, or notebook, of favorite citations and observations on various subjects), establishing the basis for his historical arguments about allodial property rights and the ancient right of representation and consent to taxation in his *Summary View*. They were also works well-known to the other members of the Declaration's drafting committee, most notably John Adams. Indeed, if the lists of books kept in the libraries of the leading founders are to be credited at all, these were texts with which the entire generation was deeply familiar.[17]

The essential lesson of this history for the Whigs was summed up nicely by Adams when he wrote in an article for the *Boston Gazette* in 1763, "the liberty, the unalienable and indefeasible rights of man, the honor and dignity of human nature . . . and the universal happiness of individuals, were never so skillfully and successfully consulted as in that most excellent monument of human art, the Common Law of England." The historically evolved customs of the common law provided one means by which the people of the Anglo-American world could come to understand and realize the "unalienable and indefeasible rights of man." The past was not the ultimate source of moral authority for Americans of the Whig tradition, but it was an essential mode of discovery. It provided examples of how past generations gave form and substance to their natural rights, and so could aid men's reason in the attainment of liberty. Thus Adams could also write in his response to the Tory Daniel Leonard, "English liberties are but certain rights of nature, reserved to the citizen by the English constitution, which rights cleaved to our ancestors when they crossed the Atlantic."[18]

History proved its usefulness when tyrants were threatening those essential rights. Jefferson encapsulated well the American Whigs' conception of English history and its relationship to the liberty of the colonies when he reminded the King in *Summary View* that feudal holdings were "but exceptions out of the Saxon laws of possession, under which all lands were held [by individuals] in absolute right. These therefore still form the basis or groundwork of the Common law, to prevail wheresoever the exceptions have not taken place." He concluded with the satirically obvious, but quite meaningful, observation that "America was not conquered by William the Norman, nor its lands surrendered to him or any of his successors. Possessions there are undoubtedly of the allodial nature." Later in his *Notes on the State of Virginia*, he would make explicit the need for an instrumental historical perspective to guard against tyranny: "History by apprising them [the people] of the past will enable them to judge of the future; it will avail them of the experience of other times and other nations; it will qualify them as judges of the actions and designs of men; it will enable them to know ambition under every disguise it may assume; and knowing it, to defeat its views." It was this instrumentalist view of the past in conjunction with the common law need to prove criminal intent, that necessitated the listing of the grievances against the King in the Declaration: "The History of the present King of Great Britain," the document reads, "is a History of repeated Injuries and Usurpations, all having in direct Object the Establishment of an absolute Tyranny over these States." But if history as the story of law and custom was useful in realizing the natural rights that inhered in men and in guarding against tyranny, history was not the ultimate source of those rights. While it could reveal the capacity of human beings to govern themselves in an orderly fashion by custom and practices outside the King's control, it was not ultimately the source of that order. That source was the people's "rights as derived from the laws of nature, and not as the gift of their chief magistrate." The Lockean conception of rights was thus very much a consistent part of the Whig perspective—an absolutely essential part.[19]

IV. Science, Society, and the Evolution of Natural Law

The evolution of English common law was illustrative of the ability of human beings to govern themselves without the interventions of despotic power, but customary law by itself was not a sufficient guide. Customs and precedents could be—especially when perverted by power—wrong. Consequently, custom pointed to yet a deeper source for the extended order seen in civil society. Republican and constitutional history both provided clues about the nature of power and how it could or should be restrained, but by themselves they could not account for the confidence with which Whigs contended against the abuse of power. If power is corrupting, and even virtue is ultimately an insufficient protection against its influence, what real answer could a Whig make to Filmer or Hobbes if he did not have some deeper sense of the capacity of human beings to do good and lead meaningful lives apart from coercive political relationships? If power served any end for the Whigs, it had to be something other than simple participation in its exercise, which they seemed ever so eager to restrain. The missing component is supplied in the concept of natural law and the various understandings of society derived from that idea.

The history of natural law dates back to the classical philosophers of ancient Greece, but its historical evolution produced profound changes over the centuries. The most influential strains of classical natural law philosophy sought to develop those potentialities in human nature that were deemed to separate man from the animals.[20] The capacity for social life and reason were considered the highest attributes of humanity, and their fulfillment either in politics or the life of the mind was thought to be the ultimate end of natural law. The city, for both Aristotle and Plato, was the primary political unit, and its laws and institutions were expected to be ordered so as to allow for the fullest development of these noblest qualities. With the advance of the Roman empire, the ancient city receded in importance, but the emphasis on reason persisted, establishing the basis for a more universal conception of the natural law as a guide to individual ethical behavior.

The Stoic understanding, as interpreted by such Roman statesmen as Cicero, looked to reason as the means by which the individual could perceive the true and the good and thereby resist enslaving himself to worldly passions. Such a course provided the virtuous citizen with the fortitude necessary to endure the ever shifting and uncertain fortunes of imperial power. Christianity built upon this earlier foundation but united it with a concern for the individual's spiritual salvation. As a consequence, it strengthened the philosophical concern with the individual by emphasizing the very personal nature of his relationship to God. Natural law was thus made a component of divine law, which embraced all of the known rules governing human nature, the natural world, and the laws revealed in scripture. Natural law governed the earthly, fallen city of man and was considered to be the expression of the divine law in conformity with reason. The fact that the natural world evinced an orderly construction proved the

existence of a higher power, whose superior reason was only dimly reflected in men, creatures made in God's image. According to this scholastic
tradition, man could apply his reason to study the orderly construction of
the world and thereby gain a deeper appreciation for his place in the great
chain of being. In sum, mankind could come to know God through both
faith and reason. Though the aim of this approach to natural law was the
fulfillment of the individual's spiritual nature, it opened up for legitimate
inquiry the entire natural universe. Increasingly, as European society pros-
pered commercially at the end of the thirteenth century through the growth
of trade, attention to the world became more secularized, to the extent
that the laws governing nature were studied more for their own sake than
for the sake of salvation. This process was set back about a century with
the onset of the Black Death and the Hundred Years War, but with the
passing of these calamities, commercial and social life recovered. The
expansion of trade and the opening of new markets in Europe and the
New World saw a resurgence of intellectual inquiry, first in Italy and later
in northern Europe. By the seventeenth century, England was making its
own contributions to science, and the consequences for thinking about
the natural law were profound.[21]

Sir Isaac Newton and Francis Bacon were among the luminaries of the
early years when modern science conceptualized its methods and objectives. What united those who endeavored to expand man's understanding
of the natural world was a belief that reason could explain the order of the
universe through the discovery of basic laws governing its operation. Such
a view, though not in contradiction with the Medieval Scholastic conception of the natural order, was far more mechanistic, and gave little consideration to the role of revelatory understanding and divine intervention.
The new science of Newton found its sustenance in the developing commercial order, where craftsmen and merchants, concerned with practical
solutions to everyday challenges in the market, applied a mechanistic and
highly analytical rationality to their world. This social development had
been underway since the end of the Middle Ages, and as one scholar has
observed, "if one pauses to consider the utilitarianism and practicality
that pervaded the outlook of the new scientists, one can hardly help being
reminded of the effects of a social environment in which merchants, pro-
fessionals and craftsmen had been for a long time the most vigorous and
dynamic group."[22]

It was that social environment, where men were looking for rules governing the physical world, that prompted others to look for an equivalent
natural order in the relationships governing human associations. John

Locke was among the most prominent philosophers to do just this. Far more than a political theory of natural rights, he developed a sophisticated understanding of a natural economic order that vindicated the individual's exercise of those rights. He developed this understanding of the economy from his initial participation in England's political debates over interest rates and money. It was from this conception of a natural social order that the preamble to the Declaration derives its most significant meaning.[23]

V. John Locke and the Science of Political Economy

The Declaration offers a convenient starting point to illustrate the Lockean influence on the American Revolution, if for no other reason than the similarity between certain terms and phrases in that document and Locke's writings. Yet that interpretation has not gone unchallenged. Along with the civic republican view of early America, a few have asserted that Jefferson's "Life, Liberty, and the Pursuit of Happiness" was a dramatic break with Locke's triad of "Life, Liberty and Estates," with its reference to property. These writers see a deeply communal meaning in the term "Happiness" that subordinates property to a greater social good; happiness is made an instrument in the hands of government. Gary Wills has drawn attention to the influence of the Scottish Enlightenment and ideas about an other-regarding moral sense that supposedly modifies the drive of self-interest found in Locke, and gives to government a wider mission to act on behalf of the greater good. Others have taken a different but complementary approach, depicting a radical Jeffersonian program where democratic government promotes equality of happiness by at times actively altering the order of property relations in society. Both views, like the republican interpretation mentioned earlier, posit a deeply rooted tension between the American Revolution and the commercial character of early classical liberalism. But such a view again assumes opposition where none exists, by conflating community or society with politics and setting them against the market. By examining afresh the liberal idea of a natural social order, it becomes clear that society and markets are intimately related and reinforcing conceptions. The attribution to Locke, and to liberalism generally, of an atomized understanding of individualism in which the individual is portrayed as fully capable of existence outside of society, is a present-day interpretation, alien to the understanding of seventeenth- and eighteenth-century Whigs. Thus, even though most historians now accept the direct influence of Locke on the Declaration, the debate over the meaning of happiness continues, and cries out for a closer study of Locke's understanding of social order.[24]

John Locke occupied a position in English society near the top of the skilled crafts and professional classes that first rose to prominence in the late medieval period. Trained to be a physician, he was familiar with the healing arts and a man of science. As was typical of such a person, he took a deep interest in all aspects of human life, including the speculative pursuits of moral and political philosophy. His real interest in these latter topics, however, did not reach its zenith until his association with Anthony Ashley Cooper, first earl of Shaftesbury in the late 1660s. Cooper pulled Locke into the debate raging over government regulation of interest rates in the 1670s, and it was on this topic that Locke began in earnest his investigations into the underpinnings of social order. Though he did not publish his first effort in political economy, he continued to develop his ideas to the end of his life, and eventually did produce an essay for publication entitled *Some Considerations of the Consequences of Lowering of Interest and Raising the Value of Money*, in 1692. His initial approach demonstrates an early desire to discover the ordering mechanisms of trade, just as one would study the bodily functions to understand physiology or the movement of the stars to comprehend the heavens. Reason, applied to the social condition of man, would produce a science of social order: political economy. Locke did not invent this pursuit, but as an early contributor to its development, he provides a central link between the political and economic conceptions at the heart of the liberal—or as it was called then—the Whig tradition.[25]

At the core of Locke's argument is a fundamental point about the nature of human social interaction: it is, in certain very important areas, orderly and essentially noncoercive. Considerable energy has been expended by scholars to determine what Locke meant when he referred to mankind in a state of nature. Some interpret this literally, to mean that Locke believed humankind once lived without government. Others have contended that this was a purely heuristic device to put the role of government in its proper perspective: government is an instrument used to protect the rights of individuals, as opposed to being a separate creature with its own ends. The latter view allows for a much richer understanding of Locke when placed alongside the theories of absolutist government as formulated by Thomas Hobbes in *Leviathan* and Robert Filmer in *Patriarcha*.[26]

Hobbes and Filmer set about to justify government on different grounds, but ended up with very similar results. Hobbes first formulated the notion of a state of nature to illustrate the depravity of man and the necessity of a strong government to mediate disputes, enforce the peace, and allow for the flourishing of an advanced society. Government was the mechanism that made all good things possible, and rebellion against its authority was unconscionable, for "men have no pleasure, (but on the contrary a great deal of grief) in keeping company, where there is no power able to over-awe them all." Filmer, on the other hand, dismissed the whole idea of reasoning from some imagined state of nature. He contended that men were forever born unequal in station and abilities, and likened the established power relations of society to the natural inequalities found in the family. The family, he argued, was the historical basis for the power of kings, and resistance to a king's authority was as unconscionable as rebellion within the family: "There is, and always shall be continued to the end of the world, a natural right of a supreme father over every multitude, although, by the secret will of God, many at first do most unjustly obtain the exercise of it." Though different in their theoretical starting points, both Hobbes and Filmer viewed life without government at some ultimate level of control as an irrational step into social chaos and anarchy.[27] Locke disagreed.

Rather than rejecting the idea of a state of nature, Locke saw it as a valuable explanatory device to aid in the conceptualization of the proper role of government, much as Hobbes did. Unlike Hobbes, however, Locke had a deep appreciation for all of those ways in which human life is structured by voluntary commitments quite distinct from political engagements. This was precisely because of his study of market relations, first in the controversy over interest rates and later over the recoinage debates. The first of these concerned the proposal to lower the legal rate of interest to four percent throughout the kingdom as a means to stimulate economic growth. Locke took the position that interest reflected the voluntarily negotiated deals made by individuals to achieve their particular ends. Government's interference with those arrangements, he argued, would set off a series of unexpected consequences that would disrupt investment decisions and the patterns of trade. The market responded to its own laws, and these were akin to the laws of nature; in fact, Locke equated them with natural laws governing human social order. This was brought out in an even more striking manner in the debate over the proposal to remint British silver coins with twenty-five percent less silver to increase the circulating medium and replace the older clipped coins in circulation. Locke's point was that further interference with the coinage would not answer the country's need for a stable circulating medium. Instead, he argued, money responds to the market transactions of individuals, and to interfere with them would be futile at best and ruinous at worst. Debasement introduces deception and breaks contracts, for "men are absolved from the performance of their legal contracts, if the quantity of silver under settled and legal denominations be altered." Money was governed by the natural laws of trade, and government would have to constrain itself within the limits of those laws.[28]

It was this perception of human life as being composed of significant ordering forces outside the control of government that structured Locke's conception of the state of nature, his definition of natural law and natural rights, and his notion of the proper role of government. He set that conception of political economy to work at the heart of his political theory in the *Second Treatise on Government*. Locke concedes to Filmer that government might well have begun historically with the patriarchal father of an extended family or tribe, but he does not admit that this fact gives unlimited dominion to political rule. Indeed, the whole point of the *First Treatise* was to argue that paternal authority, from its very beginning with Adam, was itself a limited power. Rather, Locke conjectures that the source of human flourishing had an altogether different source. Historically, man first bartered products for products, but eventually came to fix a certain value upon rare items that were durable and could be stored without diminishing their worth. Gold and silver came to serve such a purpose as the favored medium of exchange. It was this development of money that allowed the accumulation and diversification of property. To illustrate the nonpolitical aspect of this development, Locke placed the discovery of money in the state of nature, or as he wrote, "out of the bounds of Societie." It formed a stage just prior to the establishment of government, representing an advanced level of human organization far different from the chaotic condition found in Hobbes' state of nature.[29] Locke was very careful to emphasize that point. Humans entered the political stage when the complexities of their property relations reached a point where it became too cumbersome to protect life and estates by individual means, but it was not because life in the state of nature was hopelessly antithetical to human association and order. Hence for Locke,

'tis not every Compact that puts an end to the State of Nature between Men, but only this one of agreeing together mutually to enter into one Community, and make one Body Politick; other Promises and Compacts, Men may make one with another, and yet still be in the State of Nature. The Promises and Bargains for Truck, etc. between the two Men in the desert Island, mentioned by *Garcilasso Del la vega*, in his History of Peru, or between a Swiss and an Indian, in the

Woods of America, are binding to them, though they are perfectly in a State of Nature, in reference to one another. For Truth and keeping of Faith belongs to Men, as Men, and not as Members of Society.[30]

It was because men, in economic life, exhibited a profound capacity for orderly exchange (i.e., "The Promises and Bargains for Truck"), promise keeping, and good faith, that Locke's state of nature could not be as bad as Hobbes' war of all against all. It was precisely for this reason that government for Locke could not even possess the claim, let alone the practical assertion, of power over every aspect of human society. It was to Hobbes that Locke referred when he noted that "some Men have confounded" a state of nature with a state of war, which "are as far distant, as a State of Peace, Good Will, Mutual Assistance, and Preservation, and a State of Enmity, Malice, Violence, and Mutual Destruction are one from another." The state of nature was left behind because a few men preyed on the rights and properties of their fellows. These men were the "quarrelsome and contentious;" they were not the majority of men. If we take Locke's concession to Filmer as sincere, that political life might well have begun with a patriarchal figure, then we must accept the heuristic quality of Locke's state of nature. It does not describe an actual historical moment, but serves as an illustration of mankind's continuing capacity for "Truth and keeping of Faith." Consequently, for Locke, government must limit itself to the protection of that natural order from which men take their natural rights to "Life, Liberty, and Estates." Such order was evident in the operations of simple trucking and bargaining and of commerce in a more highly advanced state of society, and is more properly termed "parapolitical," by today's reckoning, than "prepolitical."[31]

Locke attributed this capacity for human sociability to man's rational self-interest, though he was perfectly aware of the unequal capacity of men to reason well. Reasoned self-interest was what motivated men to enter into economic association, but it was their inability at times to be impartial in cases of justice that necessitated entrance into political society. Moreover, some men were simply disposed to using force and violence to attain their ends. It was to ensure that justice would be consistently and objectively meted out, and protection given against the "corruption, and vitiousness of [these] degenerate Men," that government was instituted. Government's purpose, therefore, was not to obliterate those good things that came from man's capacity for reasoned intercourse, which were everywhere evident, but to enhance and preserve such capacity by discouraging violence. Thus certain basic rights are retained by individuals when they enter into political association. Natural law, which for the ancients prescribed an active cultivation of certain virtues, became in Locke the recognition of orderly association outside political compulsions, governed by scientifically knowable laws of economy that derived from humanity's inherent capacity for reason. The capacity for nonpolitical social order underscored the necessity for limited government and the reason why men could be trusted with the retention of their natural rights to life and liberty in political association, while surrendering only the instrumental right of exacting justice and wielding coercive violence on their own.[32]

Locke was troubled, however, by the degree of emphasis he had placed on reason in the *Second Treatise*, and in his other works he attempted to draw out further the basis for human morality. He consigned, in other writings, considerable importance to divine revelation and faith, but the influence of Christianity on Locke, and its compatibility with his political theory, have been topics of considerable debate among scholars.[33] This was not the case at the time of the American Revolution, and Jefferson's approach to Locke demonstrates that it is a mistake to assume a necessary conflict between Christianity and the natural law/natural rights idea found in Locke. The focus, again, should be on the Whig conception of "happiness."

VI. The Happiness of Society and the Divine Order of the Universe

In the *Second Treatise*, Locke uses the term "happiness" to describe the proper aim of civil society and to question the propriety of establishing an absolute monarchy to attain it. The condition of happiness is thus related directly to the condition of civil society, which is properly instituted when it protects the rights of individuals as carried over from the natural order. In his *Essay Concerning Human Understanding* (1690), Locke actually used the phrase, "*pursuit of happiness*," though it is not certain whether or not Jefferson had actually read this work prior to the time he composed the Declaration. Nevertheless, Locke's usage is instructive of the thinking of early Whigs. Here Locke ascribed happiness to a state in which individuals were free to pursue the good. Thus he wrote, "the highest perfection of intellectual nature lies in a careful and constant pursuit of true and solid happiness, so the care of ourselves, that we mistake not the imaginary for real happiness, is the necessary foundation of our liberty." Such liberty could exist only in a society properly constituted so as to protect the ability of individuals to care for themselves; such a society could only be called a civil society. This was common usage among Whigs, contemporary with Locke and later.[34]

Algernon Sidney described just such a state of civil society, in which the liberties and rights to property of the individual are protected from tyranny by the proper balance of powers in government. Thus Sidney wrote, "all nations have been, and are more or less happy, as they or their ancestors have had vigour of spirit, integrity of manners, and wisdom to invent and establish such orders, as have better or worse provided for this common good." Trenchard and Gordon, as Cato, gave even clearer expression throughout their essays forty years later. The opposite of a happy society is a miserable one wherein a tyrant preys upon the lives and property of the people, robbing them of their sustenance, depriving them of meaningful association, and wherein "The very hands of men, given them by nature for their support, are turned by tyrants into the instruments of their misery." In contrast to such misery is "happiness," which appears frequently throughout the essays. A happy country is a free country, because "liberty is the divine source of all human happiness." And the definition of liberty was not ambiguous. "To possess, in security, the effects of our industry, is the most powerful and reasonable inducement to be industrious: And to be able to provide for our children, and to leave them all that we have, is the best motive to beget them. But where property is precarious, labor will languish. The privileges of thinking, saying, and doing what we please, and of growing as rich as we can, without any other restriction, than that by all this we hurt not the publick, nor one another, are the glorious privileges of liberty; and its effects, to live in freedom, plenty, and safety." But those who are corrupted by power understand none of this: "That wealth, which dispersed amongst their subjects, and circulated in trade and commerce, would employ, increase, and enrich them, and return often again with interest into their coffers, is barbarously robbed from the people, and engrossed by these their oppressors, and generally laid out by them to adorn their palaces." Thus tyrants show "every-where such constant and strong antipathy to the happiness of mankind, that if there be but one free city within their ken, they are restless in their designs and snares against it." Happiness in society was the product of man's capacity for orderly social interaction, untainted by force or coercion. Misery was the product of man's corruption by power and his physical abuse of others for personal gain. Happiness affirmed the orderliness of God's creation, while misery illustrated man's limitations, and it is here that we see just how compatible the early liberal voice and Christianity could be.[35]

Jefferson, as many have observed, was himself unconventional in his beliefs about the deity and man's nature. Traditional Christianity stressed the "fallenness" of humankind and man's inability to achieve perfection, whereas Jefferson is seen to uphold the idea of progress and perfectibility. This is correct up to a point. Jefferson believed in man's capacity to improve himself intellectually, technologically, and socially within the realm of society and its many voluntary associations. Thus, in writing to John Hollins of the spread of knowledge through scientific associations, he could celebrate the fact that "these societies are always in peace, however their nations may be at war. Like the republic of letters, they form a great fraternity spreading over the whole earth, and their correspondence is never interrupted by any civilized nation. Vaccination has been a late and remarkable instance of the liberal diffusion of a blessing newly discovered." He could also encourage Sir John Sinclair in his efforts to form an agricultural society in England, noting that "Our agricultural society has at length formed itself. Like our American Philosophical Society, it is voluntary, and unconnected to the public, and is precisely an execution of the plan I formerly sketched to you." But, like most Whigs, Jefferson was profoundly disturbed by the corrupting influence of power on human nature, and here there was a clear convergence of Whig political thought with Christian belief. Cato, for example, could write with perfect clarity to his Christian readers, "Why should not the knowledge and love of God be joined to the knowledge and love of liberty, his best gift, which is the certain source of all the civil blessings of this life? And I have shown that religion cannot subsist without it. And why should not the dread and hatred of Satan be accompanied with the dread and hatred of tyrants, who are his instruments, and the instruments of all the civil miseries in this life?" Reflecting the observations of Sidney, Cato elaborated that "There is something so wanton and monstrous in lawless power, that there scarce ever was a human spirit that could bear it; and the mind of man, which is weak and limited, ought never to be trusted with a power that is boundless." Such power has "defaced creation, and laid the world waste."[36]

Happiness and tyranny were incompatible, and as unalterably opposed as good and evil, for tyrants "could not erect one great city, and make it flourish, without renouncing in a great measure their power over it." Thus, Cato argued, "all civil happiness and prosperity is inseparable from liberty . . . Nor is there one way in the world to give happiness to communities, but by sheltering them under certain and express laws, irrevocable at any man's pleasure." Samuel West said nearly the same in his sermon in Boston in 1776. After citing Locke on the natural law and "the appeal to Heaven," he noted that "idolatrous reverence has ever been the inseparable concomitant of arbitrary power and tyrannical government; for even Christian princes, if they have not been adored under the character of gods, yet the titles given them strongly savor of blasphemy." He then went on to interpret scripture to reveal that "tyrants are the ministers of Satan, ordained by him for the destruction of mankind."[37]

Though not explicitly religious in tone, Jefferson's perception of the corruptibility of human nature by the temptations of power was very much the same. Jefferson wrote in 1774 that "History has informed us that bodies of men as well as individuals are susceptible of tyranny," and in 1784 he warned against the concentration of power in an "elective despotism," stating that "Human nature is the same on every side of the Atlantic, and will be alike influenced by the same causes," and "The time to guard against corruption and tyranny, is before they shall have gotten hold of us." But the danger of tyranny would always exist because, "In every government on earth is some trace of human weakness, some germ of corruption and degeneracy, which cunning will discover, and wickedness insensibly open, cultivate, and improve."[38] These sentiments were retained in his later years. Writing to Joseph C. Cabell in 1816, he asked,

> What has destroyed liberty and the rights of man in every government which has ever existed under the sun? The generalizing and concentrating all cares and powers into one body . . . And I do believe that if the Almighty has not decreed that man shall never be free, (and it is a blasphemy to believe it,) that the secret will be found to be in the making himself the depository of the powers respecting himself, so far as he is competent to them, and delegating only what is beyond his competence by a synthetical process, to higher and higher orders of functionaries, so as to trust fewer and fewer powers in proportion as the trustees become more and more oligarchical.[39]

The Christian concept of imperfect and fallen man had become the man of limited capacities who served society well when contained within the bounds of law and voluntary association, but who became perverted by the temptations of power when removed from the immediate consequences of its exercise. In other words, the less accountable and more arbitrary the power, the more corrupting its influence. In this light, whether Jefferson himself was orthodox or not in religion is of little consequence in interpreting the Declaration. Its readers could readily identify the corruption of power with the fallen state of sin, and share in the view that happiness is to be found in limiting power and its capacity to inflict harm, and by voluntarily associating and covenanting with each other. It was to protect the nonpolitical forms of association in society from the imperfect natures of men that politics needed hard and set limits. Thus Pastor Samuel Sherwood of Weston, Connecticut, could preach in *A Sermon Containing Scriptural Instructions to Civil Rulers* in 1774,

> [God's] authority and power over us is unlimited and uncontrollable, and cannot be denied, or opposed without our being guilty of the highest crime of rebellion. But no created being is invested with such absolute, unlimited power, nor qualified for the exercise of it. Error and imperfection belongs to every individual of the human race. The brightest character that was ever justly drawn among mortal men, has this dark shade to it: So that the will of none, is infallibly right in all things, and cannot therefore be complied with in all instances, consistent with a good conscience, and the superior obligations we are under to the sovereign Ruler of the world; who still maintains this rightful authority over us, and has not given it by delegation, to any one among created beings: all of whom were originally made free-agents; and considered as in a state of nature, previous to their uniting as members of society, have their liberty and free choice to agree upon such a form of government, and mode of administration in their civil and temporal affairs, as they judge most conducive to their happiness and good.[40]

VII. Happiness in the American Context

Such sentiments about the happiness of society permeated American thinking. Minister and revolutionary Daniel Shute of Boston noted in a sermon given in 1768 that "Civil government among mankind is not a resignation of their natural privileges, but that method of securing them, to which they are morally obliged as conducive to their happiness." Or, as Simeon Howard, also of Boston, noted in 1773, when he briefly described the origins of civil society: "In this state, the liberty which men have is all that natural liberty which has been mentioned, excepting what they have *expressly* given up for the good of the whole society; a liberty of pursuing their own happiness governing their actions, and disposing of their property and persons as they think fit, provided they transgress no law of nature, and keep within those restrictions which they have consented to come under." To cite the Reverend Samuel West, yet again, "a state of nature is properly a state of law and government, even a government founded upon the unchangeable nature of the Deity, and a law resulting from the eternal fitness of things." Government was justified only insofar as it preserved that natural state of liberty by restraining "Men of unbridled lusts" who would "betray us into actions injurious to the public and destructive of the safety and happiness of society." Another example comes from Richard Bland, who was so much admired by

Jefferson: "yet [men] retain so much of their natural freedom as to have a Right to retire from the Society . . . for their Engagements to the Society, and their Submission to the publick Authority of the State, do not oblige them to continue in it longer than they find it will conduce to their Happiness, which they have a natural Right to promote." Happiness was thus a very common turn of phrase within the Whig (and we might say Christian Whig) tradition, and far from signaling a break with Locke or with the traditional concept of a divine order in the Declaration, it underscores a profound consistency.[41]

George Mason, a representative from Fairfax County to the Virginia Convention, the revolutionary government of the state, composed a draft of his state's Declaration of Rights which Jefferson likely had in hand before writing the Declaration of Independence. Mason's choice of words demonstrates even more clearly the consistent association of happiness with the retention of natural rights in civil society, the crux of the entire Lockean argument. So close is the wording of the revised committee version to Jefferson's own, that the influence has never been denied: "all men are by nature equally free and independent, and have certain inherent rights, of which, when they enter into a state of society, they cannot by any compact deprive or divest their posterity; namely, the enjoyment of life and liberty, with the means of acquiring and possessing property, and pursuing and obtaining happiness and safety." Civil society was composed of that portion of liberty found in the state of nature which conduced to the voluntary association of men, minus the right to exact personal justice. The state was thus an instrument of civil society used to further man's natural sociability by curtailing his capacity for violence, but government could itself become corrupted by power and prey on its own citizens. For civil society to be happy, it had to allow for the flourishing of the natural order of human sociability by guarding against violence and restraining the government from overstepping its intended purpose. This conception was well developed by the eve of the Revolution, and was enhanced by another philosophical tradition that sought to explain further man's capacity for self-government through the existence of an inborn moral sense. It was by the application of this sense that humanity experienced happiness in a far more direct fashion than was suggested by the more abstract concept of rational self-interest. Rather than displacing the earlier idea, however, moral sense theory supplemented it to form a far stronger case in favor of the presumption of man's capacity for social order independent of political power. This was the central contribution of the Scottish Enlightenment.[42]

VIII. The Influence of the Scottish Enlightenment

Reality suffers when nuance is sacrificed to "clarity" in historical argument, but the risk emphasizes, again, the importance of continuous and vigorous participation in our civil discourse. The influence of the Scottish Enlightenment on America is one of those topics in which reality has been obscured by hyperbole. When Gary Wills set out to demonstrate the influence of the Scottish moral thinkers on the Declaration of Independence, he was tempted to deny altogether the *direct* influence of John Locke. Finding a similarity of phrase between Francis Hutcheson's work and the Declaration, he made Hutcheson's version of Lockean liberalism the filter through which Jefferson received his revolutionary ideas. Challenging this view, Ronald Hamowy demonstrated with little difficulty that Jefferson probably did not read Hutcheson with any care, until well after 1776, and that Jefferson's words had far more similarity to phrases in Locke's *Second Treatise* than to Hutcheson's works. Both Jefferson and Hutcheson, Hamowy argued, got their Locke from the source. Unfortunately, so resounding was Hamowy's refutation that some scholars have simply assumed that the Scottish influence on the Declaration was itself refuted. In fact, Hamowy made no such claim, but argued for a more balanced understanding. "What makes Wills' thesis so startling," he wrote, "is his assertion that these thinkers alone provided the framework for Jefferson's thought on politics and morals before he drafted the Declaration and that Locke's treatises on government can be dismissed as having no influence on Jefferson's views." Nevertheless, Hamowy observed, it would be surprising if Jefferson were not "closely acquainted with the Scottish moral philosophers."[43]

Wills' hyperbole was doubly unfortunate because it detracts from some of his most important insights about the Scottish Enlightenment's conception of social order and its relationship to the Whig understanding of happiness. Wills makes the discerning observation that for "Hutcheson 'faith in commerce' arises directly from the moral sense. Men are already associated in families, and in the exchange of goods and ideas, before it becomes necessary for them to form civil government. We begin in society, which is our state of nature." This is precisely the same conception that Locke was attempting to portray, and which was common among Americans, but Wills makes the usual misstep of associating Locke with Hobbes, because of their common use of the concepts of a state of nature and self-interest as the motives for human association. But to reiterate the difference, self-interest for Hobbes drives men into government because self-interest is incapable of producing any good in the absence of a supreme controlling power. For Locke, it is a broader understanding of self-interest which gives rise to the capacity to "bargain" and "truck" and keep "faith" independently of government, and which unites men in their various associations. Government and human association is not synonymous for Locke, and consequently, he cannot be tarred with the same interpretive brush as Hobbes. Wills casually portrays Locke as positing the autonomous individual who enters into government by compact with other autonomous individuals. "Autonomous" is his word, however, and not Locke's.[44] Locke employed rational self-interest to explain why men were social before the institution of government, and continued to be so afterward. From Locke's perspective, God "made Man such a Creature, that, in his own Judgement, it was not good for him to be alone, but put him under strong Obligations of Necessity, Convenience, and Inclination to drive him into *Society*, as well as fitted him with Understanding and Language to continue and enjoy it." It was because of this natural sociability that an energetic or intrusive government was unnecessary and could be limited to just the basic functions of meting out justice and providing for the common defense. The compatibility of Scottish thought and Lockean liberalism is thus manifest in the evidence marshaled by Wills. In fact, the complementarity of Hutcheson and Locke, particularly with regard to their conceptions of a just society, is even more profound than he suggests.[45]

In Hutcheson, despite his own perception of his work as displacing that of Locke, we have a strong affirmation of Locke's original idea of man's sociability, with the added ingredient of the moral sense to supplement rational self-interest. Locke himself was troubled by the difficulties of founding a moral system on reason alone, but the Scottish notion of a moral sense, or inborn sentiment, left room for an immediate sense of what is right, good, and proper by nature; or as Hutcheson wrote, "each man has not only selfish desires toward his own happiness and the means of it, but some tender generous affections in the several relations of life."[46] Thus man was indeed moral and sociable before the institution of government and this made the pursuit of happiness both social and private, but not essentially political. Hutcheson went to great lengths therefore to spell out the limits of political society by conveying the profoundly nonpolitical means by which human beings acquire happiness through voluntary association:

> Nay, no confidence of a wise distribution by magistrates can ever make any given quantity of labour be endured with such pleasure and hearty good-will, as when

each man is the distributor of what he has acquired among those he loves. What magistrate can judge of the delicate ties of friendship, by which a fine spirit may be so attached to another as to bear all toils for him with joy? Why should we exclude so much of the loveliest offices of life, of liberality and beneficence, and grateful returns; leaving men scarce any room for exercising them in the distribution of their goods? And what plan of polity will ever satisfy men sufficiently as to the just treatment to be given themselves, and all who are peculiarly dear to them, out of the common stock, if all is to depend on the pleasure of magistrates, and no private person allowed any exercise of his own wisdom or discretion in some of the most honourable and delightful offices of life? Must all men in private stations ever be treated as children, or fools?[47]

The consistence with Locke is clear, but Hutcheson's is a far more sophisticated refinement of Locke's argument about the need to contain political power. Men must be given the freedom to exercise those capacities, both selfish and generous, that are in their nature, and it is a failing to see all of human life as subordinate to political control. Thus according to Hutcheson, "it seems arrogant . . . to attempt an overturning the manifest constitution of the Creator, and to root out what is so deeply fixed in the human soul; vainly presuming to contrive something better than the *God* of nature has ordered." Wills' argument fails to convince because of a profound confusion of government with community, and the political with the social. When Jefferson spoke of the pursuit of happiness, he had both its private *and* social meanings in mind. What was private was also social. "Happiness" contained all of the voluntary associations and commitments found in society. Government was involved only to the extent that it protected society as it arose from men's natural sociability. But the direct influence of Hutcheson, as Hamowy has pointed out, is difficult to discern in Jefferson's writings.[48] There are other intriguing (and more obvious) influences, however, from other Scottish Enlightenment thinkers with dispositions very similar to Hutcheson's.

IX. Political Economy and the Moral Sense

Early speculation about the source of Jefferson's decision to use "happiness" rather than "estates" concerned a particularly interesting pamphlet published in 1774. Entitled *Considerations on the Nature and Extent of the Legislative Authority of the British Parliament,* it was written by the Scottish émigré and eminent American lawyer and founder, James Wilson. A graduate of St. Andrew's College in Scotland, Wilson was steeped in the philosophy of the Scottish Enlightenment. As both Carl Becker and Gilbert Chinard pointed out years ago, certain paragraphs of Wilson's

Considerations appear startlingly similar to the Declaration. Of these, two appear in Jefferson's Commonplace Book, but Jefferson did not copy the most striking of all: "All men are, by nature, equal and free: No one has a right to any authority over another without his consent: All lawful government is founded on the consent of those, who are subject to it: Such consent was given with a view to ensure and to encrease [*sic*] the happiness of the governed above what they could enjoy in an independent and unconnected state of nature. The consequence is, that the happiness of the society is the First law of every government." The similarity with Hutcheson, and the clear assumption of man's increasing a happiness he possessed before the institution of government, powerfully suggests the Scottish influence. Jefferson obviously read this passage, but exactly when and why he chose to omit it from his book is a mystery. The best that can be determined is that perhaps the paragraphs cited were copied some time in 1776, after, rather than before, the composition of the Declaration. Some speculate that Jefferson, having already written the Declaration, was unimpressed by Wilson's statement. Others think it very possible that the sentiments regarding happiness were so commonplace that they did not need to be copied. More interesting for our purpose is to analyze what he did use from Wilson. The passages Jefferson thought particularly noteworthy are interesting precisely because they give the context of the debate in which the idea of happiness is deployed.[49]

Wilson set out to counter the claims of Tory loyalists that the right of the King-in-Parliament to govern the colonies was grounded in the need of every state to have "a supreme, irresistible, absolute, uncontrolled, authority, in which the *jura summi imperii*, or the rights of sovereignty reside." Opposing the absolute nature of the claim, Wilson qualified it as operative only insofar as it furthered the aim of society. "But if the application of it," he wrote, "would, in any instance, destroy instead of promoting that end, it ought, in that instance to be rejected: For to admit it would be[to] sacrifice the end to the means, which are valuable only in so far as they advance it." The fact that Jefferson saw fit to draw attention to these paragraphs is an indication of how deeply impressed he was with the Whig conception of order or happiness in society as antecedent to government. But we can only infer the Scottish influence from these passages. Far more direct is the connection with the works of Henry Home, Lord Kames.[50]

Though not the first to draw attention to the influence of Kames, Allen Jayne's work has most recently elucidated this strand in Jefferson's thought. Jayne quite explicitly argues that Kames' conception of the moral sense provides the missing piece to the puzzle of Lockean social order. As noted earlier, Locke himself was troubled by the capacity of rational self-interest to carry forward the moral self-governance that he saw operating in human society. The moral sense argument, however, provided a crucial ingredient to Whig thought, supplementing their political economy with the idea of an inherent individual capacity to know right from wrong. This was a robust sense of natural social order that vindicated further the Whig idea of self-government and lent to the Revolution an added dimension of confidence.[51]

Whereas none of Hutcheson's works figured in Jefferson's 1771 letter of recommended books to Robert Skipwith, as noted by Hamowy, three of Kames' works appear. Moreover, in the religious category, Jefferson listed Kames' (Jefferson spelled "Kaims"), *Principles of Morality and Natural Religion*, which was first published in 1751. This work developed most fully Kames' conception of a moral sense that operated very much like the other senses of the human body. Not everyone possessed that faculty as fully as some (and a few were devoid of it altogether, just as some men were blind), but the vast majority did possess an inherent sense of justice. The closeness of phrase and terminology used by Jefferson in the Skipwith letter and a later piece of correspondence to Jefferson's nephew, Peter Carr, illustrate, as Jayne points out, the powerful influence of Kames' thought. Where Kames noted that men's capacity for morality is improved by use, "for the mind acquires strength by exercise," Jefferson noted in his letter to Skipwith that "every emotion of this kind is an exercise of our virtuous dispositions; and dispositions of the mind, like limbs of the body, acquire strength by exercise." The origin of this (and other parallel thoughts) was confirmed explicitly in a 1787 letter to Peter Carr in which Jefferson observed that God would have "been a pitiful bungler if he had made the rules of our moral conduct a matter of science . . . Man was destined for society. His morality, therefore, was to be formed to this object. He was endowed with a sense of right and wrong, merely relative to this . . . The moral sense, or conscience, is as much a part of man as his leg or arm." Allen Jayne has taken his interpretation of the Scottish influence further than most by interpreting both *Summary View* and the Declaration in its light. Thus when Jefferson implores the King to open his breast "to liberal and expanded thought," he is interpreted to mean that inborn sense of right and wrong. And when, in the Declaration, he invoked the "opinions of Mankind," he is seen to be appealing to the innate understanding of the common man for what is true and good. This understanding is also supposed to inform his thoughts on what is self-evidently true.[52] But there is another way in which to see the essential congruence of the Lockean and Scottish strands in Jefferson's work.

As Wills noted in connection with Hutcheson, "'faith in commerce' arises directly from the moral sense."[53] Men's capacity for moral behavior was seen to reinforce Lockean rational self-interest as a cohesive ingredient of and an explanatory tool for understanding the natural social order. Both Locke and the Scots (Hutcheson, Hume, Kames, and Adam Smith) celebrated the refinements of modern society brought on by an advanced development of commerce. Not only were agriculture and the mechanical arts improved, but so too were the manners and mores of the people. Just as Locke reflected upon the natural laws ordering the market, so too did the Scots contemplate the harmonious operations of commercial forces, culminating in Smith's masterful synthesis, *An Inquiry into the Nature and Causes of the Wealth of Nations*. Kames provided a succinct summation of the complementary relationship between the moral sense and self-interest in society when at the end of his *Essays on the Principles of Morality and Natural Religion* he presented a hymn of praise to the Creator that observed,

> What various and complicated machinery is here! and regulated with what exquisite art! While man pursues happiness as his chief aim, thou bendest self-love into the social direction. Thou infusest the generous principle, which makes him feel for sorrows not his own: nor feels he only, but strange indeed! takes delight in rushing into foreign misery; and with pleasure goes to drop the painful tear over real or imaginary wo.[sic] Thy divine hand thus formed the connecting tye, and by sympathy linked man to man; that nothing might be solitary in thy world, but all tend to mutual association.[54]

Here, then, is a powerful depiction of the hand of "Nature and Nature's God" forming the order of man's physical and social world, and the idea runs like a torrent through the intellectual channels of Jefferson's thought.

In the *Summary View*, Jefferson explicitly invoked the natural order of the Whig conception of economic life when he declared that "the exercise of a free trade with all parts of the world, possessed by the American colonists as of natural right, and which no law of their own had taken away or abridged, was next the object of unjust incroachment." The theme was returned to time and again to be embellished and reworked. In 1804 he wrote to the economist J. B. Say, observing that "So invariably do the laws of nature create our duties and interests that whenever they seem to be at variance, we ought to suspect some fallacy in our reasoning." In 1813, he wrote "To take from one, because it is thought his own industry and that of his fathers had acquired too much in order to spare others who, or whose fathers have not exercised equal industry and skill, is to violate arbitrarily the free principles of association, the guarantee to everyone a free exercise of his industry and the fruits acquired by it." Jefferson developed this notion further in a remarkable letter to P. S. Dupont de Nemours on April 24, 1816, in which he related his concepts of society, property, republican government and justice explicitly to self-government. "We both consider the people as our children," he wrote, "and love them with parental affection. But you love them as infants whom you are afraid to trust without nurses. I as adults whom I freely leave to self-government." He explained his conception of society by observing that "morality, compassion, generosity, are innate elements of the human constitution; that there exists a right independent of force; that a right to property is founded in our natural wants, in the means with which we are endowed to satisfy these wants, and the right to what we acquire by those means without violating the similar rights of other sensible beings." This moral principle constituted the "the fundamental law of society." Even the will of the majority could not violate this right without disrupting the natural order and morality that constituted society. As he continued, "the majority, oppressing an individual, is guilty of a crime, abuses its strength, and by acting on the law of the strongest breaks up the foundations of society." This was because civil society (properly conceived) was founded on the capacity of individuals to govern their own lives—"in affairs within their reach and competence." For the affairs of state, Americans chose representatives "removable by themselves," and this constituted "the essence of a republic." This idea of a just and natural order to civil society also explains Jefferson's profound respect and enthusiasm for the work of the French economist Destutt de Tracy, whose works he labored to have published in America. Jefferson personally devoted five hours a day for three months to de Tracy's *Treatise on Political Economy*, just to ensure a proper English rendition.[55]

Destutt de Tracy was a theorist who stated in no uncertain terms that "commerce is society," and who was revered by Jefferson as perhaps the most important thinker on political economy of his age—one who had written a more useful and succinct treatise on the operations of the market than had Adam Smith. Jefferson's only complaint with de Tracy was his grounding of social order on the single concept of self-interest. Over the course of the eighteenth and early nineteenth centuries, that idea had become synonymous among many classical liberals with Hobbes' political theory, where self-preservation drives men into contracts for mutual protection. By Jefferson's time, these liberals had been persuaded by the Scottish philosophers, whose notion of a moral sense softened, as it supplemented, the driving force of self-interest. Thus Jefferson could write in a letter to John Adams, "I gather from his other works that [Destutt de Tracy] adopts the principles of Hobbes, that justice is founded in contract solely, and does not result from the construction of man. I believe, on the contrary, that it is instinct, and innate, that the moral sense is as much a part of our constitution as that of feeling, seeing, or hearing; as a wise creator must have seen to be necessary in an animal destined to live in society." Still, he agreed with de Tracy's conclusions and noted that "however we may differ as to the foundation of morals, (and as many foundations have been assumed as there are writers on the subject nearly) so correct a thinker as Tracy will give us a sound system of morals."[56]

Happiness, to summarize, had a profoundly social meaning that was derived explicitly from the natural social order as it was conceived of by Whigs like Locke, Sidney, Trenchard, and Gordon, and refined by such Scottish philosophers as Hutcheson and Kames. It referred to a flourishing state of civil society, wherein self-government meant principally government of the self, and was given life, in Jefferson's words, by "the free principle of association." Happiness was not primarily or even essentially political, but operated parallel to government, without need of interference, only protection from violence, internal and external. Together, a government limited to defense and a society of voluntary associations constituted a civil society. That was the proper place of politics in Whig philosophy. To cite another source, Emerich de Vattel's *Law of Nations*, a textbook for statesmen like Jefferson, Madison, and Adams: "The end or aim of civil society is to procure for its citizens the necessities, the comforts, and the pleasures of life, and, in general, their happiness; to secure to each the peaceful enjoyment of his property and a sure means of obtaining justice; and finally to defend the whole body against all external violence."[57]

At the core of the idea of civil society was the crucial Whig distinction, so aptly drawn by Thomas Paine at the outset of *Common Sense*, between state and society. It is a distinction that historians writing today easily overlook in their expositions on the Declaration: "Some writers have so confounded society with government as to leave little or no distinction between them; whereas they are not only different, but have different origins. Society is produced by our wants and government by our wickedness; the former promotes our happiness *positively* by uniting our affections, the latter *negatively* by restraining our vices. The one encourages intercourse, the other creates distinctions. The first is a patron, the last a punisher."[58] These were the opening lines of the pamphlet that so gripped the attention of Americans and steeled them for independence. It expressed in a few words the ideas that infused the patriots with the confidence necessary to strike out on their own.

Early Americans could be so assured of their ability to go it alone apart from England because they were reasonably sure that their civil associations operated with no assistance from His Majesty the King or Parliament. The basis for social order was not the sovereign power, as they were told by their loyalist brethren, but was rooted in the very nature of man. It was an order confirmed by their historical experience, and informed by their understanding of the law and the history of political institutions. The pursuit of happiness was their liberty and their order. With his reputation established by *Summary View*, Thomas Jefferson presented the best prospect to succinctly draw together all the strands of Whig political thought, from the common law and the ancient Saxon constitution to the republican theory of power; from the Lockean notion of natural rights and the economic basis of order to the Scottish idea of a moral sense. It is from this vantage point, the perspective of the late eighteenth-century American Whig, that we can understand the philosophy of the Declaration.

X. The Declaration and the Harmonizing Sentiments of the Day

The opening paragraphs of the Declaration have been interpreted from a variety of standpoints. These have included the Lockean reading (most widely adopted), the Scottish moral sense reading, the democratic egalitarian thesis, the scientific rationalist point of view, and even a religious, deistic perspective. Each of these tells a part of the story, but when they are brought together, they reveal the coherent tradition unifying the arguments of the American cause.[59]

The opening paragraph is itself the very essence of the Whig synthesis of history and precedent, scientific rationalism and the order of a divine creation, natural rights and the moral sense. It succinctly expresses the Whig cosmology justifying the cause of independence. The first words, "WHEN, in the Course of human Events," invoke the history of abuses against the inhabitants of the colonies that make it "necessary for one People to dissolve the Political Bands which have connected them with another, and to assume among the Powers of the Earth, the separate and equal Station to which the Laws of Nature and of Nature's God entitle them . . ." The assumption of that station was not for arbitrary or capricious reasons, but was due to the violation of laws grounded in an orderly creation, laws which delimited the proper sphere within which a just government must be contained. The last phrase completes the argument with an appeal to the innate capacity of mankind to comprehend the good by virtue of the moral sense, as Allen Jayne has pointed out: "a decent respect to the opinions of Mankind requires that they should declare the causes which impel them to the Separation." This forms the thesis statement of the document, and what follows spells out the argument for separation.

The next sentence is the most intensely scrutinized of any in terms of the volume of interpretive literature: "WE hold these Truths to be self-evident, that all Men are created equal, that they are endowed by their Creator with certain unalienable Rights, that among these are Life, Liberty, and the pursuit of Happiness." From the vantage point of the Whig tradition, the meaning is both unoriginal and clear. Reasonable men, consulting both their intellectual and moral capacities, could agree on certain truths about the human condition—not all truths, but certain ones—and these were styled "self-evident." Self-evident not in the sense that just anyone would automatically recognize their legitimacy, but in the sense that one who honestly consulted his moral sense and right reason, without the influence of corruption or ignorance, would be readily able to assent to their validity.[60] The first of these is a basic equality in the eyes of God, because it was God who gave to man his essential character as a moral creature. The equality of man is therefore evident in certain basic moral claims, or natural rights. If not all rights can be positively identified and agreed to, certainly at least some can be established; "among these are Life, Liberty, and the Pursuit of Happiness." The intellectual debt to John Locke, as noted earlier, is clear, but what is less often noticed is the influence of Locke's skepticism. Locke had made it a point to emphasize the grave responsibility involved in the "appeal to heaven." The reasons for resisting government could not be light or transient abuses, but only the most glaring, consistent, and egregious violations of the most sacred rights, and the Declaration agreed with this. What we can know is limited by our nature as finite beings, so what is ventured by way of justification of so momentous a decision can only be the most basic of natural rights which must be acknowledged by all. The inclusion of the pursuit of happiness presupposes the individual's possession of the right to own property—the right to acquire or dispose of property through all sorts of voluntary arrangements. But "Happiness," as noted above, refers to the end for which society itself is formed. It is the liberty of individuals, as owners first and foremost of themselves, to associate freely for the realization of their hopes and aspirations. It moves beyond the right to own property to affirm that a society of individuals associating freely is orderly, good, distinct from relationships of political power, and free from the coercion of government.

This conception of the primacy of society over government is expressed in the next sentence, in which the classic Whig understanding of the limited purpose of government is made manifest: "That to secure these Rights, Governments are instituted among Men, deriving their just Powers from the Consent of the Governed, that whenever any Form of Government becomes destructive of these Ends, it is the Right of the People to alter or to abolish it, and to institute new Government, laying its Foundation on such Principles, and organizing its Powers in such Form, as to them shall seem most likely to effect their Safety and Happiness." Because some men are inclined towards aggression, the rights founded in nature cannot be effectively realized, as Locke argued, unless government is in place to guard against such "quarrelsome and contentious" characters. But government, as the depository of power, must use only those means which are just; when it goes beyond these limits, it defeats the purpose for which it was created. It becomes, in essence, one of the quarrelsome and contentious. At this point revolution becomes justified. The expression "Safety and Happiness" was a common refrain, heard in the sermons of Daniel Shute and Samuel West, and appearing in Virginia's Bill of Rights. The determination to overthrow government is not based on "light and transient Causes." The community will be assuming the reins of power, and how it does so will be critical for securing its members' safety and happiness. Only "the People" could arrive at such a decision—"to provide new Guards for their future Security." But nothing is said of the form of government—of the kinds of guards that should be instituted—though republican theory and colonial experience gave some idea of the basic outlines.[61] The governments of the various colonies had been, for the most part, republican in form, with the powers of government roughly separated into executive, legislative, and judicial functions, and it was through these independent state governments that the people expressed their authority—as a federation—in Congress: "Such has been the patient Sufferance of these Colonies; and such is now the Necessity which constrains them to alter their former systems of Government." Essentially, the alteration referred to was the removal of the imperial claim of the King-in-Parliament to ultimate authority over the colonies. Here then was the theory justifying resistance to England. It only remained for the American people to illustrate how their condition fit the criteria for revolution, and that was the role of history: "a History of repeated Injuries and Usurpations, all having in direct Object the Establishment of an absolute Tyranny over these States."

The assertion has frequently been made that the Declaration was geared mainly to an international audience to garner the support of foreign allies. John Adams had argued the wisdom of seeking such support when contending in Congress for separation, but there are excellent reasons to believe that this was not the sole function of the Declaration. Richard Henry Lee's resolution of June 7 (approved by Congress on July 2) could have served the international purpose well enough alone. Moreover, as a recent study of the composition of the Declaration has made clear, the document was composed with the intention of being read aloud, before an audience. The punctuation of the text was meant to create a sense of dramatic rhythm while the arrangement of the charges was in ascending order of severity. It was thus designed to be a popular instrument for an English-speaking audience. Moreover, Congress was slow in sending copies overseas, and the official communication with France of the Declaration did not arrive until some five months after the news had already reached the court, so that the American minister was somewhat embarrassed to present it. This indicates that America's chief supporter in the conflict was not the Declaration's primary target. It is most likely that the Declaration served a dual purpose, as an appeal to world opinion (to mankind, as was stated up front), and as an appeal to the American people, as demonstrated by its initial widespread circulation throughout the former colonies.[62]

The Declaration put into a few sentences the basic Whig suppositions in favor of separation. These were in essence a readily recognizable affirmation of what Whigs had always asserted about the nature of order in society. The fundamental difference between American Whigs and their true Whig counterparts in England was that American Whigs had experienced firsthand a large measure of self-government. This was not simply in the form of their state governments, though that was clear enough. Far more important were all of the nonpolitical and commercial associations that were the hallmarks of American culture even in colonial times. British restrictions before the 1760s had been ineffectually enforced, and even local government only lightly applied, yet commerce and the refinement of American life continued apace.[63] It was the rapidity of that progress, as noted at the outset of the first chapter, that so frightened the British imperial ministry. It was in America that the Whig theory of society and government, or what is properly called civil society, was lived experience. It was from this experience—the experience of individuals improving their lives without the interference of government—that the Whig theory at the heart of the Declaration drew its strength, lending the necessary assurance to the patriots to "Declare, That these United Colonies are, and of right ought to be, Free and Independent States," and for which they could "pledge to each other our Lives, our Fortunes, and our sacred Honour." It was that confidence which was ultimately lacking among loyalists, who still, for whatever reason, held to the essentially Tory idea that order depended upon the preservation of the governmental hierarchy of imperial institutions. Upon its reception in the states, the Declaration was roundly celebrated, not for any creative genius on the part of its author, nor as holy writ, but as confirmation of what was already a fact: American society was essentially independent of England. Its most important influence, however, was to come later. As a statement of the colonies' united effort at independence, it was among the chief documents expressing the common values and beliefs on which a young republic could build a national political tradition. But before that important development could take place, Americans had to confront the challenge of power. Power in its extant form was easy enough to criticize while it was being abused, but how one actually instituted the political safeguards to restrain it was an entirely different issue. The political debates that followed the realization of independence were precisely on the topic of how best to preserve the liberty and order of American society. The challenge for all Whigs was captured in the classic question on the problem of power, Who will guard the guardians? As it turned out, not all Whigs had the same answer.

Chapter 4

"New Guards for Their Future Security": The Declaration and the Constitution

In the early twentieth century, historians and legal scholars attempted to understand the founding era from the standpoint of progressive political theory. J. Allen Smith, Charles Beard, Herbert Croly, and Merrill Jensen, to name a few writers in this line, saw the American federal Constitution as representing a profound break with the egalitarian and democratic message of the Declaration. The 1780s were depicted as a time of con servative backlash in which the rights of property were asserted by wealthy elites who felt threatened by the poorer, less educated masses—masses who were supposedly asserting themselves during the Revolution and under the Articles of Confederation, the first constitution governing the proceedings of the Confederation Congress. Present-day progressive and social historians have carried forward this view, reciting the Declaration's preamble that "all men are created equal," often with a full stop at "equal," as if to suggest that the remaining phrases add little to our understanding of the document.[1] When the rest of the sentence is cited, it is to assert a radical break with Locke's conservative reference to "property" and put forward a supposedly more democratic "pursuit of happiness."[2] In an ironic twist, however, some modern conservative writers have arrived at the same conclusion, celebrating the Constitution as a bulwark of stability while excoriating the Declaration for its embodiment of radicalism and anarchy. Hearkening back not to the patriot Whigs, but to the loyalists with which they have more in common, these modern Tories assert that the Declaration's "ringing phrases are hardly useful, indeed may be perni- cious, if taken, as they commonly are, as a guide to action, governmental or private. Then the words press eventually towards extremes of liberty and the pursuit of happiness that court personal license and social disorder."[3]

The problem with both of these perspectives is that they juxtapose a democratic Declaration against a hierarchical, property-oriented Constitution that does not comport with the perceptions of Americans who lived through the period from 1776 to 1789. The essential point of the last chapter was to emphasize the nonpolitical conception of human social order that informed the Whigs' understanding of society and self-government in the late eighteenth century, and supplied the core principles of the Declaration of Independence. The corollary to this faith in a natural social order was a profound suspicion of the corrupting influence of government power. Once independence had been achieved, this suspicion of politics was turned inward, away from the old power that was the King-in-Parliament, towards the question of how power was to be situated within the former colonies so as to "provide new Guards for their future Security." What becomes apparent after independence is that Americans differed considerably about how they would distribute power within the confederation, but the essential underlying faith of the Declaration was preserved throughout the Constitutional Convention and the ratifying debates. The latter document was nothing if not an elaborate mechanism for containing the abuse of political authority so as to allow the flourishing of American civil society.[4]

I. The Articles of Confederation

Just a few days after Richard Henry Lee proposed independence in June of 1776, John Dickinson was appointed to head the committee charged with giving some formal legal shape to the government of the Confederation Congress. What came out of that committee was a set of recommendations that eventually became the Articles of Confederation in late 1777. That early document of union was officially put into effect with the ratification of the last holdout state of Maryland on March 1, 1781. The Articles reserved many important powers to the states, but also delegated certain responsibilities to the Congress that were considered appropriate to its position as the united voice of the confederation. In general terms, they gave to Congress the sole power to deal with foreign nations, settle disputes arising among the states, make war and peace, raise an army and a navy, and establish and regulate post offices from one state to another. What the Articles left to the states was the power to raise funds for the support of Congress, and all matters of civil law and internal policy, including the right to impose tariffs and duties on trade. In other words, each state retained every power "which is not by this confederation expressly delegated to the United States, in Congress assembled." One way of understanding the Articles is to see them as the formal expression of what had in fact already evolved over the course of the Revolution. It was also a fairly good approximation of what Americans had argued was the character of the old British imperial constitution. The states retained control of all internal legislative matters, including the power of raising revenue, while the federal Congress was to take charge of all matters of foreign concern.[5]

Traditionally, the Articles have not fared well in the estimation of historians. As Merrill Jensen pointed out in the mid twentieth century, this is largely because history is written by the victors. However, it is important to remember that the Articles carried the country through its final year of contest with what was then the most formidable power in the world, and not everyone was in favor of a wholesale abandonment of them when their failings became apparent. Discontent arose early in the 1780s around two main issues: the inability to effectively fund the national debt through a stable source of revenue or taxes, and the difficulty of presenting a coherent foreign policy to deal with the European powers. Both of these issues had wide and disturbing implications for the honoring of public and private debts and the ability to check foreign power and intrigue. The foremost concern was that of finance, because to a great extent, the ability to deal with other nations rested on the ability to pay for the confederation's defense, or so the nationalists argued. Consequently, the issue that persistently heads the list of complaints against the political order as instituted by the Articles of Confederation was its inability to halt "the rage for paper money" among the states and to secure a stable source of congressional revenue.[6]

II. The Rage for Paper Money

Current scholarship about the financing of the war for independence now tends to suggest that the emission of paper fiat money (i.e., notes not backed by gold or silver) by Congress and the states should be viewed more tolerantly than traditional economists have done. Rather than seeing so much bad debt in the form of depreciated notes, it is now argued that paper was a politically expedient and efficient form of taxation. Issued in various quantities over the course of the war and in various denominations by both the Confederation Congress and the state governments, paper notes lost value gradually over the course of their circulation. Inadvertently avoiding the need for more unpopular overt methods of taxation, the American governments actually implemented, "the taxation of the whole population via the depreciation of federal and state currencies, which were placed into circulation in vast sums during the war years to meet pressing military demands." While this description of the outcome may be true enough from today's vantage point, it was not the understanding of most contemporaries in Congress or the states. The paper notes were issued with the *expectation* that they would be made good through redemption in hard money and/or by making them applicable towards the payment of future state and federal taxes. From 1776 to 1781, Congress issued notes with a face value of some $227 million. At the end of this time, the whole amount was worth only $47 million in actual specie (gold and silver). State paper, by contrast, did slightly better, with approximately $210 million at face value equaling about $60 million in specie. With their ability to raise taxes, state legislators had greater success maintaining the value of their paper money by making their notes acceptable for use in payment of those taxes. But the record was uneven. Certain states did better than others—but to focus on this would be to miss an essential point from the Whig perspective: the fundamental importance of contract to the natural social order.[7]

The order of society for the Whig was one that depended upon the individual's following through with commitments. That order had its rules, and imposed strict constraints upon the individual once he had voluntarily engaged others in agreements, or, as Algernon Sidney argued, "Human societies are maintained by mutual contracts, which are of no value if they are not observed." Honesty in the fulfillment of contracts was a core value of early liberalism, and was seen as the very essence of what sustained a free market economy in an extended voluntary order. Thus Lord Kames wrote that "mutual assistance is the chief end of society; and to this end it was necessary, that there should be mutual trust and reliance upon engagements, and that favours received should be thankfully repaid." Adam Smith found it to be the distinguishing mark of humanity to "truck, barter, and exchange," for no animal ever shared its prey through "the effect of any contract." To exchange was distinctively human and the very expression of mankind's natural social capacities. Consequently, to tamper with the trust upon which a contract was based, whether for the simplest form of trade or the most complicated transactions, was to dissolve the essential glue of society. Even government, as discussed previously, was made contractual in Whig political theory because of the moral force that voluntary consent lent to the limited exercise of those few but necessary powers. It was the deleterious effects of paper money, as a solvent of contractual integrity in society, that aroused the anxiety of large numbers of American Whig patriots in the 1780s. Paper was issued to excess by both Congress and the state governments and for numerous Americans this meant that the power to issue paper currency had to be restrained, forming one of the very earliest bases for dissatisfaction with the Articles of Confederation.[8]

Late in 1779, and through the early 1780s, Pelatiah Webster, a former minister turned merchant and political economist in Philadelphia, authored a series of essays against the increase of paper money and in favor of a stronger federal union. In those pieces concerning paper notes, he hammered on the topic of their pernicious economic and moral consequences, observing that inflated paper issues, unlike taxes in the strict and usual sense, produce "a subtle and strong delusion in the depreciation as obscures the subject, and will almost cheat a man who views it under full conviction."[9] More onerous than the over supply of paper money was Pennsylvania's Tender Act of November 29, 1780, which made the state's most recent issue a legal tender; that is, the law required everyone to accept the state's notes for all transactions at face value. In response to this, Webster had even stronger words, noting that such a law, "which obliges a man to accept these bills instead of ready cash, obliges him to receive a *less* valuable thing in full payment of a *more* valuable one, and injures him to amount of the difference." Such legislation, he went on, is "a direct violation of *the laws of commutative justice—laws* grounded in the nature of *human rights*, supported by the most necessary *natural principles*, and enjoined by the most express authority *of God Almighty*." Against such basic natural rights, "it is not possible that any legislature on earth should *have right* to infringe or abrogate."[10]

It was legislation like the Tender Act that prompted Webster to look for some additional means to the standard separation of powers by which to further limit the interference of politics in the affairs of the community and the economy. He was not seeking to enhance power, but as a self-professed Whig, he was looking to find more effectual checks, because "It is a sad omen to find among the first effects of independence, greater restraints and abridgements of natural liberty, than ever we felt under the government we have lately renounced and shaken off." His first *Essay on Free Trade and Finance* noted at the outset that "FREEDOM of trade, or unrestrained liberty of the subject to *hold or dispose of* his property as he pleases, is absolutely necessary to the prosperity of every community, and to the happiness of all individuals who compose it." Direct taxes, as opposed to the deception of paper money, was an honest method and would sooner "*distinguish the Whigs from the Tories*" by revealing those who were willing to openly support the cause of independence. The depreciation of paper monies and the mess of the general finances, however, proved to him "beyond all contradiction the vanity of all recourse to the several assemblies of the states."[11] In one of the earliest published outlines of a plan for a new constitutional union of the states, Webster set forth the essential constitutional problem for American Whigs:

> I. The *supreme authority of any State must have power enough to effect the ends of its appointment*, otherwise these ends cannot be answered, and *effectually secured*; at best they are precarious.—But at the same time, II. The supreme authority ought to be *so limited and checked*, if possible, as to prevent the *abuse of power, or the exercise of powers that are not necessary to the ends of its appointment,* but hurtful and oppressive to the subject;—but to limit a supreme authority so far as to diminish its dignity, or lessen its power of doing good, would be to destroy or at least to corrupt it, and render it *ineffectual* to its ends.[12]

Having set out the problem thus, Webster went on to define how a properly constituted government would have an upper and a lower house composed of representatives chosen by the states. He thought that most representatives would be honest men, but "I believe it rarely happens that there are not *designing men* among them; and I think it would be much more difficult for them to unite their partisans in two houses, and corrupt or deceive them both, than to carry on their designs where there is but *one unalarmed, unapprehensive* house to be managed." He followed this traditional Whig approach with a novel proposal that a chamber of commerce be maintained, representing all of the various mercantile interests, small and great, to which trade and financial legislation would be referred for advice only. All of this, he noted "will prevent the hurrying a bill thro' the house without due examination." This was acceptable because "I think it much better in the main, to *lose a good bill* than to suffer *a bad one to pass* into a law." Such a government could be trusted with power to levy taxes directly on the states, "a dreadful engine of oppression, tyranny, and injury, when ill used," but it would be essential to grant such a power for it would be absurd to give the supreme authority "a power of making *contracts*, without any power of *payment*."[13]

III. Republican Tyrannies?

In a 1780 letter to Jefferson, James Madison, a fellow Virginian, longtime compatriot, and the future champion of the Constitution, observed, "if the states do not vigorously proceed in collecting the old money, and establishing funds for the credit of the new, that we are undone." He repeated his anxiety on this score in 1786, lamenting that there were too few instances of cooperation and good government among the states and "too many belonging to the opposite side of the account. At the head of these is to be put the rage for paper money. Pena. [Pennsylvania] and N. Carolina took the lead in this folly." He went on to observe that this was heightening tensions between the states, because the debtors of a state that issued depreciated notes would attempt to pay creditors residing in other states with their depreciated currency. The letter preceded his call for a convention in Annapolis, Maryland, to consider essential reforms of the Articles, noting that "Many Gentlemen both within and without Congress wish to make this meeting subservient to a plenipotentiary Convention for amending the Confederation. Tho' my wishes are in favor of such an event, yet I despair so much of its accomplishment at the present crisis that I do not extend my views beyond a Commercial Reform."[14] George Washington was another who gave voice to a similar concern for the public credit, noting in a circular to the state governors in 1783 that

> The ability of the Country to discharge the debts which have been incurred in its defence, is not to be doubted; an inclination, I flatter myself, will not be wanting; the path of our duty is plain before us; honesty will be found on every experiment, to be the best and only true policy; let us then as a Nation be just; let us fulfil the public Contracts, which Congress had undoubtedly a right to make for the purpose of carrying on the War, with the same good faith we suppose ourselves bound to perform our private engagements.[15]

This deep concern for the nation's credit, its inability to pay its debts, and the seeming anarchy of its circulating medium, formed the basis for the first hue and cry against the inefficacy of the Articles. Madison quickly took the lead in expressing the concern of those members of Congress who thought a change was necessary. In an outline to himself of the problems of the confederation done in the month prior to the Constitutional Convention, Madison listed some eleven fundamental defects. The most serious of these were the failure of the states to comply with constitutional requisitions, encroachments by the states on federal authority, violations of the law of nations and of treaties, and trespasses of the states on the rights of each other (which singled out the pernicious effects of paper money). He concluded his observations by setting out the classic Whig problem, much as Pelatiah Webster had done six years earlier: "The great desideratum in Government is such a modification of the sovereignty as will render it sufficiently neutral between the different interests and factions, to controul [sic] one part of the society from invading the rights of another, and at the same time sufficiently controuled itself, from setting up an interest adverse to that of the whole Society."[16]

Under the imperial constitution, Jefferson had argued that the King should apply his veto over Parliament, and not just the colonies, to ensure that the rights of one legislature did not invade the rights of another. This formed a part of the thinking about Congress' place in the union to be sure, and the Articles granted to that body the right to adjudicate disputes between the various states. Madison's ideas for a new constitution began to develop along slightly different lines. Not only would the national body (Congress) ensure justice between the states, it would discourage them from abusing the liberty of their own citizens. Thus he contended:

> In absolute Monarchies the prince is sufficiently neutral towards his subjects, but frequently sacrifices their happiness to his ambition or avarice. In small Republics, the sovereign will is sufficiently controuled from such a sacrifice of the entire Society, but is not sufficiently neutral towards the parts composing it. As a limited Monarchy tempers the evils of an absolute one; so an extensive Republic meliorates the administration of a small Republic.[17]

The fear that the state republics were themselves threatening personal liberty had its roots in Whig political theory. While much revolutionary rhetoric, including that of the Declaration, was levied against the tyrannical authority of the King and his accomplices (i.e., Parliament) during the fight for independence, Whig theory was as applicable to the abuse of power in a representative republic as it was in a monarchy. Even Algernon Sidney, who believed popular government to be the form least likely to harm liberty, recognized that the people could be misled by their representatives and through error, "hurt a private person, and that may possibly result to the public damage." Cato observed that "great bodies of men have seldom judged what they ought to do, by any other rule than what they could do. What nation is there that has not oppressed any other, when the same could be done with advantage and security?" And he offered the familiar Whig formulation of the problem: "And yet, thus formed and qualified, are the materials for government. For the sake of men it is instituted, by the prudence of men it must be conducted; and the art of the political mechanism is, to erect a firm building with such crazy and corrupt materials." He went on to note, "I think I may with great modesty affirm, that in former reigns the people of England found no sufficient security in the number of their representatives."[18]

By the mid 1780s, numerous Americans were evaluating their state legislatures in the same light. Thus Jefferson complained that Virginia's constitution was devoid of those "benefits which a proper complication of principles is capable of producing," and observed in his *Notes on the State of Virginia* that

> All the powers of government, legislative, executive, and judiciary, result to the legislative body. The concentrating these in the same hands is precisely the definition of despotic government. It will be no alleviation that these powers will be exercised by a plurality of hands, and not by a single one. 173 despots would surely be as oppressive as one. Let those who doubt it turn their eyes on the republic of Venice. As little will it avail us that they are chosen by ourselves. An *elective despotism* was not the government we fought for; but one which should not only be founded on free principles, but in which the powers of the government should be so divided and balanced among several bodies of magistracy, as that no one could transcend their legal limits, without being effectually checked and restrained by the others.[19]

While a number of people raised the issue of institutional checks to power, others were questioning whether Americans possessed the virtue necessary to restrain the lust for power. The Old Whigs like Sidney had emphasized the virtues of restraint and self-sacrifice necessary for a statesman to properly execute his charge, though they also stressed institutional checks on government, and never trusted to virtue alone. In this vein, Whigs saw the formation of political parties as dangerous factions serving more to inflame the minds of citizens than to encourage statesmanship. Pelatiah Webster provides another good example of this mode of reasoning:

> No form of government can preserve a nation which can't controul the party rage of its own citizens; when any one citizen can rise *above the controul* of the laws, *ruin* draws near. It is not possible for any nation on earth, to hold their strength and establishment, when the dignity of their government is lost, and this dignity will forever depend on the *wisdom* and *firmness* of the officers of government, aided and supported by the *virtue* and *patriotism* of their citizens.[20]

IV. Union of the States or the People?

Paper money and the unwillingness to make requisitions for Congress were the earliest complaints against the confederation, and brought into question the institutional forms of the state and national constitutions and the morality of the American people. The final straw for congressional representatives came when the states began to pass their own navigation acts in response to British and European restrictions on American commerce. Most Americans in 1776 believed that the world would quickly welcome the benefits of an open and free trade with an independent United States, but quickly became disillusioned when the old mercantilist powers closed ports to American vessels. In response, a clamor arose for retaliatory measures, but Congress had neither the resources nor the ability to enforce a general agreement among the many states. When each state consequently skirted the Articles to impose its own regulations on foreign trade, congressmen listened with greater sympathy to Madison's call for a convention in Annapolis to take place in September of 1786. The purpose of the convention was to reform the commercial powers of Congress, but too few representatives attended to form a quorum. The representatives who were there, however, passed a resolution for another convention to discuss more sweeping reforms of the Articles. Congress acquiesced and recognized the legitimacy of the new convention in February of 1787, after the incident known as Shay's Rebellion in Massachusetts. The Rebellion was an uprising against the higher taxes (relative to other states) imposed by Massachusetts to fund its war debts. The resisters organized themselves into militia units, but were quickly put down by volunteers from Boston and the surrounding area. Nevertheless, the incident produced a number of extreme accounts of the moral decline of the populace and its unwillingness to meet its obligations. These accounts, passed along in correspondence, induced state representatives to approve and send members to what became known as the Constitutional Convention in Philadelphia.[21]

The number of representatives from each state varied considerably, and attendance was uneven. In part, this was because of the unusually heavy spring rains that made travel to the Convention difficult. Those who did not travel by sea, slogged through the mud, and delegates dribbled in well after the official opening date of May 14. All told, business did not get underway until May 25, and of the 74 delegates chosen by the states, only 55 took part. It included some of the most eminent personalities of American politics, and none other than George Washington was selected to preside over the meeting as president. But many obvious leaders were absent—Thomas Jefferson and John Adams, for instance, were away in Europe. Further difficulties were internal to the Convention. While most who attended agreed that the Articles needed to be amended to form a stronger general, or what was also called a federal government, there was disagreement over how far the Convention could go towards that end. By the time the Convention finished its work on September 17, 1787, only

39 of the 55 participating delegates chose to sign the finished product—
the Constitution of the United States. And the disagreements were even
more severe among the public at large. The document was not approved
by a majority of the states until the following year, enduring a long period
of heated opposition and debate.[22]

Very early on in the Convention, two distinct views of what the union
should look like were formed. The representatives of the larger states put
their support behind a Virginia proposal mostly formulated by Madison,
while the smaller republics, concerned with the power of their more populous neighbors, championed a proposition put forth by New Jersey. The
former, known generally as the Virginia Plan, argued for proportional
representation by population, with democratic elections taking place in
large voting districts not necessarily corresponding to the states. New
Jersey's plan was for equal representation of the states. There were additional substantive differences in the details of the plans that revealed who
among the representatives feared national or state government the most,
but this was a relatively small matter among the delegates. Most of those
attending the Convention were committed to strengthening Congress,
and were self-selected by their interest in revising the Articles. Nevertheless, the subtle distinctions tell us something important about the delegates' thoughts on what constituted proper constitutional checks on
power.[23]

In addition to the direct election of representatives, the Virginia Plan's
most prominent features were to divide the national legislature into an
upper and lower house; provide for strong executive and judicial branches,
composed of unspecified numbers of persons; allow for a committee of
review, formed by a union of the executive and judiciary, with power to
revise or negate national legislation and the legislation of the states; and
give the national legislature the power to "negative all laws passed by the
several States, contravening in the opinion of the National legislature the
articles of Union." Those who objected to this plan wanted, for the most
part, a stronger constitutional role for the state governments.[24]

John Dickinson, the original drafter of the Articles and now a delegate
from Delaware, complained that the Virginia Plan was calculated to obliterate the states and remove an essential check to the abuse of national
power. But the inclusion of the states somewhere in the fundamental
political order (as he argued in the classic Whig mode) would "produce
that collision between the different authorities which should be wished for
in order to check each other." The Whig concern for checking power
animated both sides of the debate, but predilections about where the

threat to liberty originated were quite distinct. Those who advocated a stronger role for the state governments in the national government generally argued that democracy and the direct election of representatives were best reserved to the states. They distrusted representative democracy on the national scale as too removed from the concerns of the people and subject to no real check by its constituents. Here the delegates reflected the old arguments of Montesquieu's *Spirit of the Laws* concerning the proper size of a republic. By keeping the representatives close to their constituents in small jurisdictions, the people could better control an errant representative.[25]

The proponents of the Virginia plan, men like James Madison and James Wilson, feared democracy at the level of the states, but thought that democracy would work at the national level. Theirs was a novel break with the Montesquieuian argument. According to Madison and Wilson, better individuals would be filtered out from the mass of competing interests in larger national voting districts. Small districts, they reasoned, were more likely to be dominated by the passions of a few. The larger the voting area, however, the greater the number of interests would be in contention with one another and the less likely it was that any one interest would control government for any length of time. Interest would be made to check interest. Since no particular faction could dominate within a vast expanse of territory, only the general interest would be agreed upon in the selection of candidates. The result, supposedly, would work against the factions of party politics. Thus James Wilson responded to Dickinson, according to Madison's report of the debate, that he "did not see the danger of the States being devoured by the National Government. On the contrary, he [Wilson] wished to keep them from devouring the National Government." And within "their proper orbits," Wilson went on to say, "[the States] must still be suffered to act for subordinate purposes for which their existence is made essential by the great extent of our Country." Finally, he observed, the election of representatives directly by the people in large districts "would be most likely to obtain men of intelligence and uprightness." The central issue animating the two camps was, again, the issue of finance and paper money.[26]

On June 7, 1787, Madison noted that "The great evils complained of were that the State Legislatures run into schemes of paper money etc. whenever solicited by the people, and sometimes without even the sanction of the people. Their influence then, instead of checking a like propensity in the National Legislature, may be expected to promote it." Elbridge Gerry, a merchant and representative of Massachusetts from Marblehead, and a signer of both the Declaration and the Articles of Confederation,

responded in an interesting manner. Yes, the populations had been possessed by the rage for paper money, he argued, but their representatives
in the state legislatures had been opposed to it. They may have felt under
pressure at times to concede to the will of their constituencies, but the
state assemblies themselves would surely elect representatives to the national government that would not accede to such wishes and could therefore be counted on to check such evil. He insisted that "the commercial
and monied interest would be more secure in the hands of the State
Legislatures, than of the people at large. The former have more sense of
character, and will be restrained by that from injustice. The people are for
paper money when the Legislatures are against it." He also went on to
express concern that large voting districts that crossed state lines would
lead to conflict between the states as "small States forming part of the
same district with a large one . . . would have no chance of gaining an
appointment for its [their] citizens of merit." One who agreed with this
was Colonel George Mason of the Virginia delegation, author of his state's
1776 Declaration of Rights, which influenced Jefferson's composition of
the Declaration. Mason noted that "The State Legislatures also ought to
have some means of defending themselves against encroachments of the
National Government. In every other department we have studiously endeavored to provide for its self-defence. Shall we leave the State alone
unprovided with the means for this purpose?" A week later, on June 15,
the New Jersey delegates came forward with a far more federal plan of
union.[27]

The New Jersey plan was not so radical a break with the Articles of
Confederation. As with the Articles, the state legislatures would elect
representatives to Congress, but the authority of the national government
was enhanced considerably. This was done by granting Congress two
significant powers. First was the direct power "to pass acts for raising a
revenue" through import duties and postage rates. Second was the supreme power over the regulation of trade and the formation of treaties,
with the ability to "call forth the power of the Confederated States, or so
much thereof as may be necessary to enforce and compel an obedience
to such Acts, or an observance of such Treaties." The debate moved back
and forth between the proponents of the two designs. One group favored
the Virginia Plan for a national government that would operate from the
authority of the people directly so as to check the power of the states. The
other advocated the New Jersey Plan which derived the national government from the state governments, to create a mutual check of powers and
prevent the rise of a distant, centralizing tyranny. Both sides were essentially Whig. Some scholars find it curious that the Declaration was almost

never raised in these discussions, but there was little call to do so. The Declaration gave the reasons why separation from England was necessary. It reminded men of the essential principles of a just society, and judged the historical acts of Britain accordingly. What the delegates to the Constitutional Convention were seeking to do was find the right institutional mix to realize the stated ideal: allowing the pursuit of happiness in the natural order of society by restraining the power (or powers) of government. The fact that the Declaration was rarely mentioned in the debates is not surprising when one recalls that it was celebrated not for its uniqueness, but for its eloquent restatement of commonly held beliefs— the "harmonizing sentiments of the day." Nevertheless, it was raised once, and in a very important context.[28]

Luther Martin, a delegate from Maryland who had distinguished himself as attorney general by prosecuting Tories, was among the leading voices in favor of a strong role for the states in any constitutional plan and ultimately refused to sign the Constitution because it was not sufficiently confederate in nature. Early on in the debate, he contended that the states became separate sovereignties when they separated from the British Empire, placing them "on the footing of equality." James Wilson denied the contention and read aloud the Declaration, after which, Madison reports, Wilson asserted "the *United Colonies* were declared to be free and independent; and inferring that they were independent, not *individually* but *Unitedly* . . ." Alexander Hamilton, delegate from New York and General Washington's former aide-de-camp, made the interesting reply that in effect Luther Martin was correct, though he supported Wilson's objective: "He [Hamilton]," Madison reports, "admitted that the States met now on an equal footing but could see no inference from that against concerting a change of the system in this particular."[29]

The "system" referred to by Hamilton was the method of equal state representation that was operative under the Articles, and the change he and Wilson were advocating was the Virginia Plan's call for direct representation of the people based upon population, but between these two poles there was a third voice. John Dickinson first suggested the idea that the lower house be composed of representatives elected directly by the people, with representatives apportioned according to population, and the upper house be composed of members chosen by the state legislatures. He considered it, again as Madison reported, "essential that one branch of the legislature should be drawn immediately from the people; and as expedient that the other should be chosen by the Legislatures of the States." The idea was initially voted down, but the seed was planted in the minds of some important members of the Convention. Roger Sherman presented the motion from the Connecticut delegation to refer the problem of representation to a committee to fashion a compromise. It was in that committee that Benjamin Franklin championed Dickinson's notion of the mixed regime: a popularly elected lower house, and a senate or upper house composed of an equal number of representatives from each state, elected by the state legislatures. After a bit more wrangling, the compromise squeaked by on a five-to-four vote with Massachusetts divided, but that was sufficient to ensure that the proposed constitution would be both national and federal in character. A purely national government exercises power directly on the mass of the people with no interference by any competing or intermediate authorities. A federal government, on the other hand, is a government formed by a compact of distinct sovereignties. Each member of such a compact retains the fundamental claim to self-rule but gives to the federal, or general government, certain delegated powers over defense and foreign relations. The Dickinson/Franklin approach ensured that the American government would comprise elements of both. It was precisely because of the Whig predilection for institutional checks of power against power, stemming from the recognition of the salience for liberty of the divided powers of medieval England, that the compromise was even conceivable. In fact, its feudal pedigree was evident to all from the very outset. Dickinson had likened the Senate to the British House of Lords, but in America, where no such class of hereditary nobles existed, the states would fulfill the role of distinct territorial powers. The new plan would abolish the idea of voting districts that crossed state lines, and leave states free to draw their own. It also insisted that the number of representatives in the lower house be proportionate to a state's population.[30]

With that hurdle surmounted, another division arose between the delegates at the Convention—one that struck to the very core of the idea of liberty contained in the Declaration. This new division was between states that had a significant slave population and states that did not. How should population, in apportioning representatives in the lower house, be tallied? Should it include only the free white population, or the bound population of slaves as well?

V. Slavery and Representation

The issue of slavery in the states touched on all of the topics raised in the Revolution at once. It went to the heart of the question of representation, and neither northern nor southern states spoke comfortably on the subject. Some seemed ashamed and others embarrassed. Bound labor, by definition, could not vote, and that smacked strongly of British arguments about the "virtual representation" of the colonies against which the patriots had reacted so violently. Alexander Hamilton, the representative from New York and Madison's great ally in defense of a stronger union, "observed that individuals forming political Societies modify their rights differently with regard to suffrage," but he went on to note, "as States are a collection of individual men which ought we to respect most, the rights of the people composing them, or of the artificial beings resulting from the composition?" How did slaves fit into that equation? James Wilson moved for what had been the rule in Congress for dealing with the unfree when "apportioning quotas of revenue on the States." He moved that each slave be counted as three fifths of a person in the proportioning of representatives. The response was mixed. Elbridge Gerry put the question in a very unsettling light. If property was going to be part of the rule of representation, he wondered, "Why then should the blacks, who were property in the South, be in the rule of representation more than the Cattle and horses of the North?" Gerry was no great friend of proportional popular representation in the national legislature. Indeed, most of his comments upheld a strong role for the states in the plan for a new federation. Madison suggested another way around the problem. Early in the debate over the structure of representation, he suggested that the real division was not between large and small states, but "principally from the effects of their having or not having slaves." Admitting that "Wherever there is danger of attack there ought be given a constitutional power of defence," he recommended not the rule of three-fifths, but that one house should be represented according to the number of free representatives and another "according to the whole number counting the slaves as if free." In the end, the necessity for compromise prevailed, and the idea took hold that "We were partly federal; partly national." The three-fifths proposal was originally voted down for representation, but it was raised again in regard to apportioning federal taxes. It was then put forward once more in regard to the election of congressmen, and finally passed for both revenue and representation.[31]

Slavery came up once more in reference to the regulation of trade. Here the views were again mixed, and the embarrassment was just as palpable. Luther Martin was so worried that the inclusion of the three-fifths rule would encourage slavery that he felt it essential for Congress to have the authority to impose prohibitive duties or a general prohibition on the importation of further slaves. He raised the galling observation regarding slavery that it "was inconsistent with the principles of the revolution and dishonorable to the American character to have such a feature in the Constitution." To this, a number of observations were offered on the fate of slavery in the states. Charles Pinkney of South Carolina, reflecting on the proposal to end the slave trade, suggested that "If the States be all left at liberty on this subject, S. Carolina may perhaps by degrees do of herself what is wished, as Virginia and Maryland have already done." Roger Sherman thought that "the abolition of Slavery seemed to be going on in the U.S. and that the good sense of the several States would probably by degree compleat it." Colonel Mason did what Jefferson had done in his early draft of the Declaration. He blamed this "infernal traffic" on the "avarice of British Merchants." Another suggested that the Constitutional Convention not interfere. "As population increases," he insisted, "poor laborers will be so plentiful as to render slaves useless." In the end, the majority granted the national government its power over the regulation of trade, but agreed that no prohibition on the importation of slaves would be enacted prior to 1808. Again, these were not considered ideal solutions by anyone concerned, but the instrument of the Constitution was built upon compromise. The aim was to control power: both the powers of the national government and the powers of the states. It was partly federal and partly national. The southern states were fearful of the northern and vice versa. The small states were fearful of the big states, and vice versa. Each wanted, as Madison had observed, the ability to defend itself within the constitutional order, and what resulted was a formal instrument of checks and balances. The document did not embody a prescription of what natural rights and the higher law were all about, but established an institutional framework within which the competition of powers could be peacefully contained and regularized.[32]

This did not mean that the delegates to the Convention were unconcerned with natural law and natural rights. The Declaration recognized the rights to "Life, Liberty, and the Pursuit of Happiness," but how did this mesh with what the Convention produced? Early Whigs thought they detected the rise of liberty in the evolution of customary or common law and in the contingent historical development of political decentralization. Out of these circumstances, human beings proved their capacity for orderly existence through exchange and commercial intercourse, giving rise to an advanced stage of civilization in the late eighteenth-century English-speaking world. Americans added to this conception of society their own lived experience of self-government, in which politics played a minor role in relation to all of the other ways in which Americans associated for religious, commercial, and social purposes. Self-government in this wider sense of civil society was an experience that British Whigs could only theorize about, but which Americans put to the test by rejecting explicitly the competing claim of Tories that all order stemmed from the sovereign power, however constituted. Americans would trust to their pursuit of happiness, as they had always done, but the problem of power was real, and the question put to the people in 1787 was simply, Does the Constitution adequately address how power should be controlled?

Exactly what constituted all of our natural rights? What was moral and just? These questions could not be answered in the Constitution except for certain broad allocations of constitutional powers. The more specific questions had to be left to the same contingent historical forces and natural social capacities of mankind that had given rise to civil society in the first place. The decentralized units of political power in the states contained the competing elements of society. By assuring these boundaries and by limiting the abuses to which power could be put, the delegates to the Constitutional Convention hoped that a beneficial competition of views about the just and the good could be carried on among the states. Supposedly, within this federal system, the states could better approximate the higher law, in some abstract sense. Rights would be more perfectly realized, and justice more perfectly executed, if society could be left to work itself out with minimal interference from government at any level. This was the hope regarding slavery and why, tragically, the question was left to be worked out by the "good sense of the several states." The belief that things would eventually resolve themselves favorably towards liberty blinded the founding generation from seeing the irreconcilable differences arising among the regions that might better have resulted in not one, but two or even three republics.

The next phase in the struggle to answer how governmental power could be constrained in the formation of a stronger union was joined outside of the national convention in conventions of the several states. The parties in this debate were those who called themselves Federalists, in defense of the proposed Constitution, and those who came to be styled Antifederalists by their opposition.

VI. Whigs Divided: Federalists vs. Antifederalists

When the Constitution was circulated, the arguments presented on both sides were not unanticipated. Both the Federalists and Antifederalists were concerned with the same question of power, though they were deeply divided about where the threat to liberty originated. They were both Whigs. The Antifederalist writer Centinel challenged his countrymen to consider

"Whether [the Constitution] be calculated to promote the great ends of civil society, *viz.* the happiness and prosperity of the community; it behooves you well to consider, uninfluenced by the authority of names." He answered his own question emphatically in the negative. The confederation was not at a crisis, as the Federalists argued. The choice was not between "adoption of [the Constitution] and absolute ruin." That was "the argument of tyrants," and he concluded by imploring his readers to remember, "of all *possible* evils, that of *despotism* is the *worst* and the most to be *dreaded*."[33]

The Federal Farmer agreed. A series of letters signed simply "The Federal Farmer" were printed in the *Pough Keepsie County Journal* from November 1787 to January 1788. It has been speculated that the author was Melancton Smith of New York, or Richard Henry Lee, the author of the July 2 resolution for independence. These essays made a very sophisticated and able attack on the plan of the Convention. The states, the Federal Farmer conceded, had abused their powers "by making tender, suspension, and paper money laws," and "this very abuse of power in the legislatures . . . has furnished aristocratical men with those very weapons, and those very means, with which, in great measure, they are rapidly effecting their great object." He warned that should the proposed Constitution result in an "oppressive government . . . posterity may reproach not only a few overbearing unprincipled men, but those parties in the states which have misused their powers." It was very possible, he thought, to propose a plan which might "consolidate the states as to certain national objects, and leave them severally distinct independent republics, as to internal police generally." He would have "the general government consist of an executive, a judiciary, and balanced legislature, and its powers extended exclusively to all foreign concerns." Unfortunately, he believed, the Federalists had constructed a government so robust that it would "collect all powers ultimately, in the United States into one entire government."[34]

The Federal Farmer put the problem in such a way as to illustrate the central tension within the American Whig program:

> There are certain unalienable and fundamental rights, which in forming the social compact, ought to be explicitly ascertained and fixed—a free and enlightened people . . . will not resign all their rights to those who govern, and they will fix limits to their legislators and rulers. . . . These rights should be made the basis of every constitution.[35]

But there was a problem. "[I]f a people be so situated, or have such different opinions that they cannot agree in ascertaining and fixing them, it is a very strong argument against their attempting to form one entire society, to live under one system of laws only." To a limited degree the states' position in the debates held out the hope for compromise. Power, or what was also referred to as sovereignty, could be divided and each government given very specific domains, but the balance of power in the Constitution seemed tipped too far in the direction of centralization to suit Federal Farmer. "These powers must be lodged somewhere in every society; but then they should be lodged where the strength and guardians of the people are collected. They can be wielded, or safely used, in a free country only by an able executive and judiciary, a respectable senate, full, and equal representation of the people." Taxes formed a large portion of his concern because they would "fix themselves on every person and species of property in the community; they may be carried to any lengths, and in proportion as they are extended, numerous officers must be employed to assess them, and to enforce the collection of them." The proposed plan failed to delineate the powers granted and the powers retained in a fashion sufficient to prevent the national from swallowing up the federal aspect of the Constitution. The men who govern, he observed, "will in doubtful cases, construe laws and constitutions most favorably for increasing their own powers."[36]

This was a recurrent warning on the part of Antifederalist writers. Another Antifederalist writer who went by the name of Brutus noted that the "judges will be interested to extend the powers of the courts, and to construe the constitution as much as possible, in such a way as to favour it; and that they will do it appears probable." These concerns extended to every aspect of the proposal, and it was to the issue of power that the Federalists had to respond. While many in the convention, like Madison, Wilson, and Hamilton, wanted a union that was primarily national in character, the document they produced was "partly federal; partly national." In the debates that followed, they were compelled by the logic of the Whig argument to emphasize the federal nature of the compact they were proposing.[37]

The premier example of the Federalist defense of the Constitution is the essays of Publius, also known as *The Federalist Papers*. These essays were a cooperative effort of Alexander Hamilton, James Madison, and John Jay, with the first two being responsible for the vast majority of the writings. They were written over a seven-month period, appearing in newspapers from October 1787 to May of 1788 in the State of New York. They were also sent by Hamilton to Richmond, Virginia, where they were used as debaters' notes by the Virginia Federalists. The focus of Publius was the extent to which the confederation was exposed to external aggression, predatory commercial policies of other governments, and the internal abuse of the powers of the state legislatures. Without a strong union, they asserted, American society would quickly degenerate into hostile factions, of states against states, making the union easy prey to foreign aggressors. With their focus so entirely directed to the necessity of establishing a stronger union, the language they employed sounded at times not unlike what loyalists had argued about the fate of society should the empire be rejected. In the third essay, John Jay remarked that the loose construction of the confederation undermined the ability of the states to keep treaties, increasing the chances of war, and that "such violences are more frequently caused by the passions and interests of a part than of the whole; of one or two States than of the Union." He went on to observe that the new plan of government would "harmonize, assimilate, and protect the several parts and members, and extend the benefit of its foresight and precautions to each."[38]

This sounded eerily like the claims on behalf of Parliament and the British Empire offered by loyalists, who insisted that the order of society originated from the top of the political hierarchy. The similarity was not lost on the Antifederalists. Time and again they invoked the principles of 1776 or the Revolution, which in one sense referred to the Declaration, but in another sense asserted much more. The Declaration was a statement of general principles, affirming the capacity of Americans for self-government in the broader Whig sense of the term, and invoking certain generally agreed upon, unalienable rights. Specific delineations of rights, however, were to be found only in certain separate state constitutions of the polities that had seceded from the empire. The symbolism of 1776 encompassed both the common cause of independence *and* the idea that liberty was preserved in the decentralized condition of the separate and distinct states. It was not that the Declaration was ignored, as some would have it—it was simply assumed in the general invocation of 1776.[39]

VII. The Declaration and Ratification

When the subject of the Declaration was explicitly raised, however, the challenge was quickly and spiritedly joined. This was clearly so in Pennsylvania, where James Wilson once more pushed the idea that America was composed of a single people from which the Constitution derived its authority. Here Wilson developed what would become a standard argument among the Federalists; namely, that a bill of rights or similar instrument made no sense in a government established by the people themselves.

The Magna Carta and other such documents in British history were grants made to the people by a king; but in America, it was the people who retained sovereignty, and gave to government only what was granted in the written Constitution. John Smilie, an Antifederalist from Fayette County, responded that he was much disappointed in the gentleman from Philadelphia that he did not go further to explain how this was such a great advance. After all, the Pennsylvania Constitution contained an explicit declaration to the effect that men retained, in words handed down from Mason's draft of the Virginia Constitution, "certain natural, inherent, and unalienable rights." He then went on to "recur to the memorable Declaration of the 4th of July 1776," reading the entire preamble of the document to the Pennsylvania Ratifying Convention. He then challenged Wilson to try again to make the case "which induced the late Federal [Constitutional] Convention to omit a bill of rights, so essential in the opinion of many citizens to a perfect form of government." He suggested that Wilson's argument could not possibly be accurate since the Constitutional Convention gave explicit notice in the Constitution "that the writ of *Habeas corpus* and the trial by jury in criminal cases shall not be suspended or infringed. How does this indeed agree with the maxim that whatever is not given is reserved?"[40] Others amplified that concern.

Robert Whitehill of Cumberland County observed that "National freedom has been, and will be the sacrifice of ambition and power, and it is our duty to employ the present opportunity in stipulating such restrictions as are best calculated to protect us from oppression and slavery." He charged that the federal Constitution's opening, "We the People of the United States," clearly showed that "the old foundation of the Union is destroyed, the principle of confederation excluded, and a new unwieldy system of consolidated empire is set up upon the ruins of the present compact between the states." All of this constituted a departure from "the Union of 1776." Thomas Hartley, a Federalist, countered with the insistence that "As soon as the independence of America was declared in the year 1776, from that instant all our natural rights were restored to us," and this "truth, expressly recognized by the act, declaring our independence, naturally produced another maxim, that whatever portion of those natural rights we did not transfer to the government was still reserved and retained by the people." James Wilson followed but a few days later with another reading of the Declaration to insist that the Constitution was placed on the same "broad basis on which our independence was placed." All sovereignty was still with the people, and neither the state governments, nor the national government, received anything other than what the people delegated. The debate carried on long after the Pennsylvania state convention for ratifying the federal Constitution, and the Anti-federalists continued to hope that the state legislature might be induced to reject the Constitution. One unnamed Pennsylvania writer explicitly charged the Federalists with renouncing the principles of independence. "They maintain," he wrote, "that the *revolution* and the *declaration* of *independence*, however important at those periods, are now to be considered as mere farces, and that nothing that was then done ought to be any bar in the way of establishing the proposed system of arbitrary power." His verdict was to indict the entire plan as simply "the old *tory system* revived by different hands." Federalists, on the other hand, asserted that the framers of the Constitution were the same virtuous men "who had given proof of their patriotism in the declaratory act of independence."[41]

VIII. Publius and Power

Most of the essays of Publius were clearly focused on the disorders wrought by a lack of restraint on the part of state governments. It was still the abuse of power that structured the course of the debates. What Publius did was remind readers that men had both a political and a social nature, and that human nature was corruptible by power. "The latent causes of faction," Madison wrote in the tenth essay, "are thus sown in the nature of man; and we see them everywhere brought into different degrees of activity, according to the different circumstances of civil society." Human beings attach themselves to particular causes and form "an attachment to different leaders ambitiously contending for pre-eminence and power; or to persons of other descriptions whose fortunes have been interesting to the human passions." Such people "have in turn, divided mankind into parties . . . and rendered them much more disposed to vex and oppress each other than to cooperate for their common good." Envy was one such passion that motivated men to reach for the apparatus of government to take what was not justly theirs. Government must be so constructed as to guard against this evil through institutions that would allow for the best men, men with the common interest at heart, to govern. Madison went on to include the additional security of countervailing political institutions to check a misappropriation of power by any particular branch or institution of government. He did this by taking to heart that which he had originally opposed in the Convention: the partly federal and partly national character of the Constitution. Both government power and social interests would be pitted against each other at both the national and state levels.[42]

In a republican form of government, a minority faction bent upon attacking the common good could be effectively checked by the power of the majority to "defeat its sinister views by regular vote." If that majority were itself the faction, however, it could take the entire society down with it. Majority tyranny would thus infringe "both the public good and the rights of other citizens." Madison restated the Whig dilemma: "To secure the public good and private rights against the danger of such a faction, and at the same time to preserve the spirit and the form of popular government, is then the great object to which our inquiries are directed." A majority faction, Madison believed, was far more likely to form in a small republic. This countered the general wisdom of his day, which held with Montesquieu that a republic should not be too extensive in territory, because its governors would be too far removed from the people. Madison took a different perspective on the problem, and suggested that a larger expanse of territory would encompass so many different factions that no one group could dominate. "Extend the sphere," he wrote, "and you take a greater variety of parties and interests; you make less probable that a majority of the whole will have a common motive to invade the rights of other citizens." The only point of agreement between these views was the goal of electing representatives who were most in line with the good of all. For Madison, Congress could be entrusted with "the great and aggregate interests" of the whole, while the state legislatures would be confined to "the local and particular." Herein lay the real advantage of the federal character of the Constitution. "A rage for paper money," he began, "for an abolition of debts, for an equal division of property, or for any other improper or wicked project, will be less apt to pervade the whole body of the Union than a particular member of it, in the same proportion as such a malady is more likely to taint a particular county or district than an entire state." He expanded on this federal aspect in the thirty-ninth essay by positing that sovereignty was divisible. Americans were one people, as Wilson was arguing, but their sovereign will could be channeled into different offices. It could be divided by a specific enumeration of state and national objects. Thus the "local or municipal authorities form distinct and independent portions of the supremacy, no more subject, within their respective spheres, to the general authority than the general authority is subject to them, within its own sphere."[43]

The partly federal character of the proposed plan of union helped address Antifederalist concerns, but it did not go far enough for most of the opponents of the Constitution. Madison's structural protections against the abuse of central power were thought to be insufficient, and most writers continued to insist on a bill of rights like the ones many of the state constitutions possessed. The idea had been raised briefly towards the end of the Constitutional Convention, but was quickly voted down as inviting unnecessary controversy and delay. Yet, it was not a subject that would go away. James Winthrop, for example, warned that the Constitution made no provision for precluding the idea of legislative supremacy: "A legislative assembly has an inherent right to alter the common law, and to abolish any of its principles, which are not particularly guarded in the Constitution. Any system therefore which appoints a legislature, without any reservation of the rights of individuals, surrenders all power in every branch of legislation to the government."[44]

IX. Jefferson and the Constitution

On October 24 and November 1, 1787, Madison wrote to Jefferson (who was then representing American interests in France) to report to him the final product of the Convention and the reasons for its provisions. Of all the controversies, Madison reported, "the due partition of power, between the General and the local governments, was perhaps of all, the most nice and difficult." He was particularly disappointed that the delegates had decided by a bare majority to deny the national government a negative over the states. He explained that in all previous confederacies, ancient, medieval, and modern, local authorities eventually abused their powers to such a degree that the general authority had to either devour the local units or be itself destroyed. Without the general negative, he thought, the Constitution presented more of "a feudal system of republics, if such a phrase may be used, than of a Confederacy of independent States." The fate of feudal confederacies was "a continual struggle between the head and the inferior members, until a final victory has been gained in some instances by one, in others, by the other of them." Madison lamented further that a negative was necessary to "secure individuals against encroachments on their rights." In this, he said, "I am persuaded I do not err in saying that the evils issuing from these sources contributed more to that uneasiness which produced the Convention, and prepared the public mind for a general reform, than those which accrued to our national character and interest from the inadequacy of the Confederation to its immediate objects." While the Constitution removed from the states the power to coin money and regulate its value, the rage for paper currency was only one of many evils perpetrated by the states. They still possessed an "infinitude of legislative expedients" by which to oppress their citizens. He then outlined his general theory of representation whereby an extensive territory with broad representation produced the least likelihood of a majority faction seizing the reins of government. Paraphrasing his earlier notes written just prior to the Constitutional Convention, he summarized, "The great desideratum in Government is, so to modify the sovereignty as that it may be sufficiently neutral between different parts of the Society to controul one part from invading the rights of another, and at the same time sufficiently controuled itself, from setting up an interest adverse to that of the entire society."[45]

Jefferson received the letter nearly two months later and responded with what he liked and disliked about the Constitution. What he approved of was a general government that could sustain itself without having to ask the states for money. He liked the "organization of the government into Legislative, Judiciary & Executive." He liked the fact that the lower house would originate all bills for raising taxes as consonant with the idea that the people should be taxed only with the consent of representatives chosen by themselves. He was also "captivated by the compromise of the opposite claims of the great and little states, of the latter to equal, and the former to proportional influence." He also concurred in the "method of voting by persons, instead of that of voting by states: and I like the negative given to the Executive [over Congress, not the states] with a third of either house, though I should have liked it better had the judiciary been associated for that purpose, or invested with a similar and separate power."[46]

What Jefferson disliked was even clearer:

> First the omission of a bill of rights providing clearly and without the aid of sophisms for freedom of religion, freedom of the press, protection against standing armies, restriction against monopolies, the eternal and unremitting force of the habeas corpus laws, and trials by jury in all matters of fact triable by the laws of the land and not by the law of nations. To say, as Mr. Wilson does that a bill of rights was not necessary because all is reserved in the case of the general government which is not given, while in particular ones all is given which is not reserved, might do for the audience to whom it was addressed, but is surely a gratis dictum, opposed by strong inferences from the body of the instrument, as well as from the omission of the clause of our present confederation which had declared that in express terms.[47]

He rounded out his discussion with the observation that "a bill of rights is what the people are entitled to against every government on earth, general or particular, and what no just government should refuse, or rest on inferences." Another concern was that there was no provision restricting the number of terms a president could hold office. He considered such a limit essential to prevent the presidency from evolving into an imperial office for life, and discounted the criticism that frequent elections were destabilizing: "experience shews that the only way to prevent disorder is to render them uninteresting by frequent changes." He believed that every foreign power with an interest in the outcome would attempt to influence the election of such a powerful supreme executive as the one provided for in the Constitution. Jefferson expressed his whiggish concerns nicely when he remarked just before concluding his letter, "I own I am not a friend to a very energetic government. It is always oppressive." In subsequent letters to other people, Jefferson restated these same points, noting to his old friend Alexander Donald, "I equally wish, that the four latest conventions, which ever they be, may refuse to accede to it, till a declaration of rights be annexed."[48]

What finally transpired was not exactly what Jefferson hoped for, but it was satisfactory. Eleven states ratified the Constitution by early 1789. The Federalists decided to meet their opponents partway with a promise to move for a bill of rights to be added to the document once it was approved by at least nine states. The new government began operation on April 30. In November, North Carolina joined, and Rhode Island followed more than a year afterwards. James Madison, in keeping with the Federalists' promise, moved for a bill of rights on June 8. These first ten amendments to the Constitution resulted from the debates in the First Congress, and were passed by that body on September 25. They were then turned over to the states, three-fourths of which passed the Bill of Rights into law on December 15, 1791.[49]

The core of Jefferson's constitutional thought was purely Whig. Some scholars have argued for a sharp distinction between an older conception of balanced government among the early Whigs and the separation of powers doctrine common to later liberal theorists, but this misses a common connecting tie. A balanced constitution was one in which the powers of government corresponded to real social classes in society. Each supposedly represented a different source of authority and wisdom that would serve to check and balance the others in the exercise of political power. Separation of powers, on the other hand, meant the channeling of the authority of the undifferentiated mass of the people into distinct branches of government with clearly defined objectives. The balanced constitution was often called a mixed government, in which the common people, the nobility, and the monarch possessed similar and competing powers to make law and check the proceedings of the other houses of government. Sidney was an early exponent of such a mixed constitution to limit the power of the King. M. J. C. Vile has observed that the doctrine of the separation of powers grew out of the same notion of using power against power. Both were institutional attempts to limit government, and in this respect, were not, at their core, necessarily irreconcilable, as the American Constitution would show.[50]

Sidney's mixed constitution was the *early* liberal's attempt to constrain the abuse of government *given* the institutions that were retained from an earlier feudal Europe. Separation of powers was its refinement in light of the democratic tendencies of the eighteenth century. Sovereignty was conceded to be derived from the people, but its exercise still required the cautionary constraints of institutions to protect the people in their social, non-political relations—to protect certain basic rights possessed even by a minority. In the case of the American Constitution, elements from both constitutional views were combined in a novel way that further underscores the basic compatibility of balanced and separate powers. The new Constitution did not adhere to a strict separation of judicial, legislative, and executive powers, but allowed for some mixing of authority. For example, an executive veto power was retained that gave the president a role in the legislative process. Technically, according to the purist's understanding of the separation of powers, the executive branch should have been entirely limited to the enforcement of law, but the founders saw a clear role for the mixing of powers as an added barrier against the abuse of authority. Nonetheless, each branch retained predominant power in its respective sphere, and all power was ultimately, in theory anyway, derived from the people, consonant with the idea of the separation of powers. Joined with the decentralized federalism of the states, where each state produced its own variation on the republican theme, the overall structure was a masterful synthesis of Whig ideas on limited government.[51]

When one includes the Bill of Rights, it becomes clear that the Constitution was directed to establishing all of the various limits then conceived for hemming in and restraining the use of government in society. It separated out the powers of government in the classic format of executive, legislative, and judicial offices; mixed some of those powers to an extent that would allow for the mechanism of checks and balances; ensured, in theory anyway, the viability of federalism as it had evolved out of American experience; and then set to paper the rights which government would not be allowed to violate. Though highly controversial in its particulars, the theoretical and practical aspects of the constitutional structure were well understood by all parties. Nearly everyone, from the most consolidating Federalists to the most decentralizing Antifederalists, accepted the essential principles of the Whig proposition that society had to be protected from the abuse of power by dividing up political institutions. The disagreement was over the level of government posing the greatest threat and how the institutions of protection should be constituted. Pelatiah

Webster, James Madison, James Wilson, and Alexander Hamilton all contended for their own particular brands of limited government, as did William Findley, John Smilie, Robert Whitehill, Richard Henry Lee, James Winthrop, and Thomas Jefferson. The constitution that resulted from that far-flung debate was a massive set of compromises within the Whig parameters of discourse. It produced a very limited national government, but left certain issues unresolved and certain powers ambiguous. As it turned out, those issues would eventually undermine the original plan.

The first such issue has already been touched on. No other single factor would do as much as slavery to cause a separation between the political cultures of the North and South, bearing out the Federal Farmer's warning that fundamental moral disagreements between communities made "a very strong argument against their attempting to form one entire society, to live under one system of laws only."[52] The great unanswered question with regard to power was the question of the central government's relation to the states. How far could the national government go to enforce its will? How far could the states go to retain their integrity as distinct political communities? In one sense this was never really meant to be definitively answered. Both the central government and the states were to coexist with a necessary tension maintained between them—the essence of the Whig idea of setting power against power—but containing that tension within peaceful limits was perhaps too much to be hoped for in an environment of such deep moral discord.[53]

Even before the momentous issues separating North from South became particularly evident, other problems with the Constitution made themselves painfully obvious. Most disturbing of all was the realization that there were serious differences of judgment over how the Constitution should be interpreted once it had been written and ratified. This issue was the basis for the very first heated political controversy that gave rise to parties, or factions—the very thing Madison had hoped the Constitution would discourage. It was in this turbulent atmosphere that attention was focused once more on the Declaration of Independence to attain some guidance as to the purpose of the American Revolution and, inferentially, of the United States.

X. Reading the Constitution:
The Question of a National Bank

The Antifederalists had predicted that the new Constitution would be interpreted so as to amass ever more power to the central government, but James Madison appears to have been under the impression that the

Constitution would be read in the same fashion that common law had dictated a written statute should be interpreted—strictly according to the letter of the law. This seemed to be Madison's thinking as early as 1780 when he was a member of the Congress under the Articles of Confederation. In that year Congress chartered the Bank of North America to assist in the financing of the war. Madison pointed out that Congress had no such power, making the act purely symbolic. To legitimately incorporate, the bank would have to seek articles of incorporation from the states. It eventually did just this, and when the Articles of Confederation became defunct, the Bank of North America went on to become a purely private bank under a charter from the state of Pennsylvania. The issue of national or federal powers to grant corporate charters, however, did not end here. It was brought up again at the Constitutional Convention, and here Madison moved explicitly to have the power to incorporate lodged in the federal government. The Convention decided that such a power would be confused with the creation of monopolies and would detract from the document's appeal. Consequently, when the issue came up again in Congress in 1791, Madison remained consistent with his earlier views and reminded his distinguished colleagues that the power was moved for, and rejected, leaving no room for the incorporation of Hamilton's new Bank of the United States.[54]

Hamilton believed that a national bank was necessary to the financial integrity of the government, for its defense, and for the economic well-being of the country; he argued that the power to incorporate a bank was implicit in Congress' power to regulate commerce and to raise taxes. Jefferson viewed it in the older Whig light of a mercantilist instrument of government, capable of encroaching on the liberty of the people. Hamilton's position seemed to deny the Tenth Amendment provision that "all powers not delegated to the United States by the constitution, nor prohibited to it by the States, are reserved to the States respectively, or to the People." Jefferson wrote to President Washington, "It has been much urged that a bank will give great facility, or convenience, in the collection of taxes. Suppose this were true, yet the constitution allows only the means which are 'necessary,' not those which are merely convenient for effecting the enumerated powers." Revenue could be had by other means. The Bank of the United States was not necessary. The power to incorporate was reserved to the people.[55]

Both Madison and Jefferson argued that the bank would violate the federal principle, and this went to the heart of the "partly federal; partly national" character of the document. If the power to incorporate, as Jefferson insisted, was derived from the power to regulate commerce, "it would be void, as extending as much to the internal commerce of every State, as to its external; for the power given to Congress by the constitution does not extend to the internal regulation of the commerce of a State." Jefferson's opinion expressed the same essential skepticism that had informed the federal understanding of the place of rights in the Convention. The states were left with broad powers over internal matters, reflecting a pragmatic recognition of their very different circumstances and political understandings. The natural rights and the natural law foundations of political association were real, but imperfectly understood. States were left with the power to do any number of things, even evil things, but the evil would be contained within their borders. The federal government regulated their external commerce and assured the free flow of citizens and goods between states, but guaranteed only that a citizen of one state, moving to another, would enjoy the same privileges and immunities of other citizens *in that state*. It did not presume to tell the people of the states what to do with slavery, police powers, internal taxes, internal regulations, and other powers that directly impacted the liberties of citizens. These were the responsibility of the residents of each state, as it was their responsibility to fight and defend their bills of rights within the contexts of their own local governments. This was an essential aspect of the federal compromise which had been worked out in the national and state conventions, and what was generally meant by states' rights. The national bank, as Jefferson pointed out, violated those rights, if the regulation of commerce was its primary object; and it violated the spirit of the Constitution, if it was taken by way of an *implied* power, because that denied implicitly what the Federalists had explicitly asserted in the past, that this was a government of delegated powers only, and what was not given, was reserved.

Hamilton contended that the power was one implied by the power to raise revenue and regulate commerce, observing that "every power vested in a government, is, in its nature SOVEREIGN, and includes, by *force* of the *term*, a right to employ all the means requisite, and not precluded by restrictions and exceptions specified in the constitution, or not immoral, or not contrary to the essential ends of political society." Madison, on the other hand, forcefully argued in the House that the powers to raise revenues and regulate commerce were limited to those instruments "necessary and proper." "The power of granting charters," he contended, "is a great and important power, and ought not to be exercised without we find ourselves expressly authorized to grant them."[56]

Jefferson concurred with Madison and presented his opinion, as Washington's secretary of state, that such a broad construction would reduce the Constitution to a blank page. The passage of the Bank bill served to sharpen political divisions in the republic, and gave rise to the formation of various political associations. Those backing the Hamiltonian understanding of a broad or implied powers interpretation of the Constitution assumed the name of Federalists. By taking up this designation, they hoped to benefit from the recent victory of the Constitution and underscore their connections to the document's original champions. The fact that Hamilton was one of their leaders lent credibility to the claim. Those who took Jefferson's position in favor of a more limited construction of the document came to be called Republicans. They too had a distinguished list of former champions of the Constitution (Madison among them), but they also counted among their ranks a large number of the old Antifederalists.

Madison was so put off by Hamilton's conception of the doctrine of broad construction that he sided with his Virginia colleague and the Republicans, and embraced the federal principle of states' rights as a necessary check to the power of the national government. The growing political divide was exacerbated by the international picture. Federalists, eager to reestablish commercial relations with England, desired to downplay the issues of the recent war. Republicans were eager to support the French in their revolution. The politically ascendant Federalists initially avoided mention of the Declaration in their Independence Day celebrations, but the Republicans quickly rejoined by celebrating it. Now the issue of the Declaration would be raised in the Federalist and Republican presses, and the entire discussion would take on even more dramatic proportions with the attempt of the Federalists to squelch debate through the Alien and Sedition Acts near the turn of the century.[57]

XI. The Declaration: A Fight for Possession

Pauline Maier has noted that the modern reputation of the Declaration was born in the political turmoil of party conflict in the 1790s. The inference made is that a relatively unimportant statement of political ideas prior to the adoption of the Constitution became a political football when it was expedient, especially for Jefferson's Republicans, to make it so.[58] This study leads to a different construction.

The Declaration was a document that expressed a synthesis of certain views consonant with the Whig understanding of political history, philosophy, and society of late eighteenth-century America. Until passage of the Constitution, the Declaration was largely, though not completely, taken for granted. Americans *had* celebrated it for its expression of the cause of independence, and nothing much more was made of it. Philip F. Detweiler noted as much in his own study when he wrote, "The goals set before them and the political axioms supporting these goals accorded with the general body of the Declaration's theory, but in no sense were they particular to it."[59] The political conflicts that followed ratification, however, resulted from the soul-searching of those who tried to make sense of the "partly federal; partly national" character of the union created by the Constitution.

In the debates that preceded the ratification of the Constitution, the problematic nature of power and its deleterious effects on society were a given. No one presumed to deny the dangerous nature of political power that formed the broad basis of understanding on which the Declaration was founded. They differed over what was the most egregious source of such threatening power, and that prompted a discussion about specific institutions and mechanisms for containing it. The debates over the Constitution and the Bill of Rights dealt with the nuts and bolts of politics and looked into the specifics of state constitutions and the historical examples of republics and confederations. But once the vaunted mechanisms for the containment of power were in place, then every exercise of power by the new government was open to a general evaluation of its appropriateness. Citizens were now in a similar position, relative to the national government, as they once had been, relative to the imperial government. Every power could now be evaluated in light of the general principles of the Declaration. In the early republic, party politics became a primary vehicle for political discourse. It was only natural, in such an environment, to expect the Declaration to take on a much bigger role in men's minds than was perhaps originally intended. It would now serve as a primary text in the debate about the purpose of America, with each side claiming the right to interpret the reasons for American independence and relate them to their particular understandings of the Constitution. If that is the modern tradition, it serves to define a necessary conversation in American political and social life. The debates that took place in the last decade of the eighteenth century and the early half of the nineteenth took place in a formative environment where the character of America's political institutions was still very much open to debate. Americans celebrated, to be sure, invoking the symbolism of 1776 in their various causes, but they also argued about the content of those symbols. Thus Detweiler observed that in the years between 1790 and 1820 the "more mature reputation" of the Declaration was born, and the focus of discussion shifted from its justification of separation from England to its underlying principles.[60]

The Federalists dominated the first decade of American politics. In part, this was because they had successfully won the favor of Washington's administration and courted public perception that they were the original champions of the Constitution. Eager to restore the country's trade relations and satisfy their merchant supporters, Federalists sought to curry favor with British commerce, and were more than happy to downplay the significance of the Declaration as the 1790s wore on. The Declaration reminded people of the late unpleasantness with the empire. It was also a revolutionary document that underscored the role of consent in the justification of government, and did not sit comfortably with a broad construction of constitutional powers. Moreover, it carried too much of the flavor of the French Revolution, which had just experienced the executions and depredations of the infamous Robespierre. For all these reasons, the Federalist press sought to either negate the significance of the Declaration or of Jefferson's authorship. John Lowell's *The Antigallican, or The Lover of His Own Country*, published in Philadelphia in 1797, cautioned readers to beware of Thomas Jefferson, this "reputed framer of the Declaration of Independence," the "snake in the grass,—the more dangerous from the oily, wily language with which he lubricated his victims and applied his venom." The *Mercury and New England Palladium* published an attack on Jefferson's authorship, charging him with copying most of the work from the writings of John Locke![61]

Republicans, on the other hand, found the Declaration to be just what they needed to emphasize their construction of limited and reserved powers. It was, in the words of one newspaper, "the result of a rational discussion and definition of the rights of man, and the end of civil government." Unlike the Federalists, Republicans hoped to avoid war with France, believed that the United States owed the French a debt of gratitude for their assistance in the late war, and wanted to emphasize the dependence of government on the will of the people. The invocation of the "rights of man" was not an accident in the Republican effort to counter Federalist Francophobia. The Republican *Aurora* identified the Declaration as "This illustrious and immortal memorial of American wisdom and American virtue," and observed that "this grand and indelible register of Man's Right and of the wrongs of a nation at the hands of a tyrant gave at once a deadly blow to every class of meretricious distinctions and absurd titles— It established the right of men . . . to govern themselves."[62]

Thomas Paine's 1791 and 1792 essays, the *Rights of Man*, to which these newspaper sources made a less-than-veiled reference, were quite explicit about the meaning of that right to self-government. It was the original Whig view of society, but it was painted in bolder and more striking hues:

A great part of that order which reigns among mankind is not the effect of government. It had its origin in the principles of society and the natural constitution of man. It existed prior to government, and would exist if the formality of government was abolished. The mutual dependence and reciprocal interest which man has in man, and all the parts of a civilized community upon each other, create that great chain of connection which holds it together. The landholder, the farmer, the manufacturer, the merchant, the tradesman, and every occupation prospers by the aid which each receives from the other, and from the whole. Common interest regulates their concerns and forms their laws; and the laws which common usage ordains have a greater influence than the laws of government. In fine, society performs for itself almost everything which is ascribed to government.[63]

This was the conception of self-government and society that Republicans in the 1790s perceived to be under attack, and their fears appeared to be more than justified by certain unsavory acts of legislation.

XII. The Alien and Sedition Acts

Between June 18 and July 14, 1798, the Federalists decided to counter their adversaries in the public debates not with argument, but with the application of force. Because of the poor treatment received by America's ministers in France, anti-French sentiment was running at an all-time high, and the Federalists made good use of those negative feelings to attempt to secure their positions in the government. They would strike out against recent immigrants that took too prominent a part in Republican causes, and prosecute Republican newspapers for seditious libel under what became collectively known as the Alien and Sedition Acts.

President John Adams, Jefferson's compatriot on the committee charged with drafting the Declaration, was now deeply paranoid of French intrigue aimed at bringing America into an alliance with France. He concurred with the Federalist newspaper, *The Gazette of the United States*, that "Surely we need a sedition law to keep our own rogues from cutting our throats, and an alien law to prevent the invasion by a host of foreign rogues to assist them." Moreover, the same arguments used to justify the constitutionality of the Bank of the United States were now applied to the Alien and Sedition Acts. A flagrant violation of the first amendment prohibiting Congress from passing any law "abridging the freedom of speech, or of the press," the Acts seemed to prove the inefficacy of paper protections of rights, and put the lie to the Federalists' own original arguments that the federal government was a government of delegated powers. James Wilson had even invoked the Declaration in defense of that conception. Now the Federalists appeared all too willing to grant as much power to the general government as any imperial ministry had had under the empire, and more. In fact, a development similar to what had occurred in England after the seventeenth-century ascension to dominance of Parliament seemed to be occurring in the United States. Former Whigs appeared all too eager to forget their arguments about the corrupting nature of power once they held power themselves. Just like the parliamentarians after the Glorious Revolution, Federalists were asserting the power of the supreme legislature to enact any law thought necessary for the public safety. Thus a Federalist Congressman could argue that "The Government is bound not to deceive the people, and it is equally bound not to suffer them to be deceived. Delusion leads to insurrection and rebellion, which it is the duty of the Government to prevent. This they cannot prevent unless they have a power to punish those who with wicked designs attempt to mislead the people."[64] Here was as Tory a statement as one might find in support of government as the ultimate source of order in society. The Republican response was to turn back to the countervailing power of the states.

Madison and Jefferson worked together in secret to bolster the constitutional position of the states and awaken a general reaction against the Alien and Sedition Acts. Secrecy was essential because the very fact of countering the government could have been used to bring charges against the congressman and vice president. It was also essential that any actions taken be the actions of constituent authorities. It would be far more difficult to prosecute the state legislatures of Virginia and Kentucky than to take issue with statements of protest by particular government officials. Madison prepared the Virginia Resolution while Jefferson worked on Kentucky's statement of protest. In both, the line of argument rested on the mediating role of the states in the partly federal structure of the union, reminding Congress that powers not specifically delegated to it were reserved to the states. The Kentucky Resolution was the most extreme in its wording, actually declaring void the offensive acts in question. The general government, as the federal government was also called, possessed only certain delegated powers, and anything enacted beyond those powers was "unauthoritative, void, and of no force." Here was a powerful statement on the nature of the Constitution, addressed to all those who ever worried about the place of the states in the federal union. The general government was explicitly denied the power to legislate on freedom of speech, press, or religion. Matters of basic rights were left to the states "to retain to themselves the right of judging how far the licentiousness of speech and of the press may be abridged." Debate on these issues would be contained within the states; liberty would, perhaps, be defended in some states better than in others. Virginia had passed a law "on the general demand of its citizens" to keep "freedom of religious opinions and exercises" free from "all human restraint or interference." Other states might not take as keen an interest in this right, but in the long run liberty would still be safer among many jurisdictions than if all power were given over to the general government. This was a theme that Jefferson would return to time and again.[65]

The Virginia and Kentucky Resolutions incurred their own strong criticisms, and it appears that popularly, people feared the possibility of disunion as much as they did that of oppression from the general government. The Federalists held their own by a bare majority, and saved the alien and sedition laws from two nearly successful Republican campaigns to repeal them; in the end, the laws, set to expire on their own, were allowed to pass into oblivion during Jefferson's administration. Ultimately, the laws seemed to have the opposite effect of their intentions. Rather than quelling debate, the Republican newspapers became more emboldened to attack Federalist policies and officials. The balance was finally tipped just enough to ensure a Republican Congress and Jefferson's election to the presidency in 1800, but the debate about the nature of the union and how best to preserve liberty would go on. With the Republicans in power, constitutional fidelity would not be so well-preserved either, proving again the corrupting influence of power. The embargo imposed by Jefferson to compel France and England to respect American rights as a neutral trader would prove draconian in the extreme, and produce similar denunciations against Jefferson as the Alien and Sedition Acts had against Adams. Nevertheless, whether Federalist or Republican, there remained a common Whig language Americans could fall back on to express their concern with power.[66]

XIII. Jefferson on Power and Liberty in a Federal System

Writing to a friend in 1816, eight years after the end of his second term as president, Jefferson reflected on the problem of power and liberty. In that letter, he recommended the writings of de Tracy on politics and commerce. *The Federalist Papers* and Chipman's and Priestley's *Principles of Government* he thought comparable, but not quite as good as de Tracy's *Review of Montesquieu*. All of this was to say that he remained committed to his earlier understanding of the relationship of society to politics. Government formed a necessary part of the Whig notion of civil

society, but it was limited to protecting basic liberties. The only way to do
that with any certainty was to divide power against itself. "What has
destroyed liberty and the rights of man in every government which has
ever existed under the sun?" he asked. "The generalizing and concentrat-
ing all cares and powers into one body, no matter whether of the auto-
crats of Russia or France, or of the aristocrats of a Venetian senate."
Reflecting on his own presidency, he made the remarkable observation
that it was to the local governments that the citizenry owed its greatest
protection of freedom. In such little ward republics, where every man has
a clear stake in government, "he will let the heart be torn out of his body
sooner than his power be wrested from him by a Caesar or a Bonaparte.
How powerfully did we feel the energy of this organization in the case of
the embargo? I felt the foundations of the government shaken under my
feet by the New England townships."[67]

It seems odd to think that Jefferson would cite, as an example of an
institutional protection of liberty, an event that was directed against his
own policies. If we reflect, however, that at the heart of the Whig tradition
was the notion that liberty was born, not from politics but from the flourishing of society when power is constrained, it is not so difficult to fathom.
He could then observe with perfect consistency that "The elementary
republics of the wards, the county republics, the State republics, and the
republic of the Union, would form a gradation of authorities, standing
each on the basis of law, holding everyone its delegated share of powers,
and constituting truly a system of fundamental balances and checks for
the government." It was part of the system established to protect liberty,
and no one man should be left to act without the constraints of a
countervailing authority to temper his acts of political power. Not even
Jefferson.[68]

XIV. Conclusion

Checks and balances were institutional contrivances. They were designed
to do nothing more than keep power from interfering with society, and
this was consonant with the meaning of the Declaration. It was clear that
governments "should not be changed for light and transient causes."
Governments would err, and rights would never be perfectly realized.
Only the most basic liberties could be agreed upon by an enlightened
public, and even these would have to be violated consistently through "a
long train of abuses" to justify revolution. It was through setting up various institutional arrangements of power that Whigs hoped to minimize

the possibility of such a "long train of abuses." Then society, by way of man's natural capacity for social cooperation, stood the best chance of flourishing. The Declaration represented the liberty which men had in society, distinct from government. It drew from the Whig understanding of an orderly creation certain unalienable rights possessed from nature, and it appealed to the moral sense of the world to justify its revolution against the violation of those rights. The Constitution represented a reasoned response, within the Whig understanding of how to use power against power to protect that vision of society found in the Declaration. From this point of view, the two documents were wholly consistent. It was only later that it became apparent that the formal limitations to power established by the Constitution were not sufficient to contain and ameliorate the differences that would gradually arise from the deep moral disagreements among the states. Eventually the entire fabric of American society and politics would be rent by the basic contradiction of slavery, as would the federal idea of limited government and the Whig distinction between government and society. Just as Americans had taken so strongly to Whig ideas because they resonated with their experience of self-government, broadly conceived, so would Americans eventually loosen their grip on those conceptions when national power was successfully asserted over all federal limits. Until then, Jefferson's characterization of the Declaration seemed to hold out the best promise for dealing with the age-old Whig problem of securing liberty by limiting power. The Declaration was a synthesis of Whig views on society and government. The ancients, such as Cicero and Aristotle, and moderns like Sidney, spoke to the function of political institutions and the rule of law. Locke spoke of society and the origins of rights. Together they formed the essential basis for the Declaration and the Constitution. They were, as Jefferson wrote, "the harmonizing sentiments of the day."

Conclusion

The Declaration and Its Implications

The aim of this work has been to explain the political and social theory at the heart of the Declaration of Independence by drawing together the various interpretations of the American Revolution and showing how they fit into a single coherent tradition. The term used to describe that body of thought was "Whig"; but while many previous writers have relied upon that same designation, they have defined it in many different ways. Interpretations of the Whig tradition have emphasized varying aspects of seventeenth- and eighteenth-century thought and many of those theories seem, at least initially, to be at odds. Thus, the liberal versus republican debate has consumed a large amount of time and energy over the past three decades. Other controversies have raged over the influences of the Scottish Enlightenment, egalitarian democratic thought, and Christian theology. Each of these perspectives has been championed at one time or another as the dominant paradigm of 1776, but this work suggests that all can be contained within a single theory of politics and society. The unifying idea at the heart of that theory is the Whig distinction between government and society. It is that distinction that modern commentators have generally overlooked.

Politics, community, society, and economy are often used interchangeably because of a modern belief that all relationships are fundamentally power relationships, where hegemonies of class, race, and gender permeate the social fabric. Notions of voluntary interaction are looked upon as quaint ideals at best, and not descriptive of what is *really* happening. Consequently, the state/society distinction is passed over, and terms such as "the common good," "community," "society," "law," and "the pursuit of happiness" are given predominantly political constructions. And other terms used to describe essentially political relationships, such as "abuse of power," "corruption," and "oppression," are applied to all relationships in society, voluntary or otherwise.

A perfect example of this confusion is the long-running controversy between the historians who contend that early Americans were classical republicans, glorying in self-sacrifice for the common good, and those who insist that they were liberal individualists. After many years of debate, a consensus seems to have developed that Americans were "liberal republicans," and a number of the early advocates of the republican thesis assert that they were misinterpreted. Apparently, antimodern did not mean anticommercial, but anti public finance and government banks. On revisiting their earlier statements, however, the source of confusion is not so difficult to discern. In the definition of modern, historians had typically included the spontaneous developments of markets, price fluctuations, and money of all sorts, with the political creation of central banks, public finance, and mercantile regulations. By lumping together such disparate elements, they invited "misinterpretation"—the same sort of confusion that continues with regard to the Declaration—with profound implications for our understanding of liberty and self-government.[1]

But if the advocates of the republican interpretation can be faulted for not seeing the state/society distinction, their liberal opponents can be faulted for not developing that distinction far enough. In a more recent study of the Declaration and the Constitution, Scott Douglas Gerber observed that none of the advocates of the republican thesis mention the Declaration in their studies. According to his reading, however, the Declaration was the quintessential expression of Lockean liberalism, and the Constitution was the instrument by which it was to be realized. Republican institutions were designed to secure natural rights, not to promote a specific agenda of public virtue. Those rights, for the founders, were given by nature, not by government. As important as that observation is, it misses two essential points about the founding generation's conception of natural rights in society.[2]

The first point is a basic recognition among the founders of the epistemological problem posed by an assertion of natural rights. Locke was very cautious in discussing when a rebellion against government should be effected. Likewise, the Declaration observed that such resistance should not be undertaken for light or transient reasons. Only the most egregious violations of essential rights, those that were "self-evident," should be invoked to justify resistance. Further, when the founding generation spoke of government, it was invariably to stress the problematic and corrupting nature of power. Thus, institutional checks and divided government formed a means by which power could be restrained and rights realized in many different ways in the context of a decentralized confederation. They believed in natural rights, but they did not rely on government alone to secure them. They wanted to limit government, to keep it from invading the rights of society, and to ensure that it would confine itself to protecting property. In imposing these limitations on government, they trusted that society would evolve naturally towards the true and the good. Even when the advocates of a stronger national government spoke of the necessity for "energy" in government, they meant competence in the performance of the specific responsibilities delegated to each branch. They never contemplated the reformation of society by government in general. They hoped instead that certain evils would go away of their own accord. From the perspective of federalism, wrongs would be tolerated in states and local communities because there they would be isolated and contained, and would eventually wither and pass away by their own folly. Thus slavery was assumed to be in decline. The founders could trust in this to some degree because of their conception of what society was, and this brings us to the second point.[3]

Natural rights were given by nature, but man was peculiarly designed by nature to enjoy those rights. Whether by rational self-interest or a deep moral sense, men were not brutes, but were fitted for sustaining an order of existence through voluntary, cooperative interaction. The invocation of "Nature and Nature's God" was an affirmation of the faith in a benevolent creation in which individuals could govern themselves by rights given in nature, and where the meaning of self-government was much more than democratic politics. At the heart of this conception was the notion of promise keeping and good faith that Locke had described. The order seen in the market and in the development of custom and the common law underscored for the Whig—the American Whig in particular—the fact that society was composed of a natural order that drew upon a source other than politics. Political interaction was driven by the lust for power; but society, as Thomas Paine noted, united men by their "affections." The drive for power, the fact that some individuals were so malformed as to prefer violence to voluntary cooperation, meant that power would have to be employed to combat power, but it was never the source of the order found in society. Government and society were parallel phenomena reflecting the dual nature of man both as a divine and rational being and as a fallen creature of base passions. To some, steeped in today's politically oriented culture, that distinction may seem trivial. This is why the difference between Hobbes and Locke is often downplayed, but it is a crucially important distinction.

If all rights are ultimately dependent on an exercise of power by government, on the threat of violence, then no justification of resistance to power is ultimately tenable. If the order of society is principally political, then there is no appeal to any authority beyond power, and that is precisely what the Declaration was designed to reject. Loyalists and imperialists had predicted social chaos and anarchy if the Revolution was carried forward, but the Declaration attempted to assure men of their capacity to govern themselves. Human beings are not angels, so government would always be with us, but neither are we demons, so self-government in the broader sense of an orderly society of peaceful interaction and exchange would always be within our grasp. By obscuring or passing over this last point, many advocates of the liberal interpretation have made of the Declaration a grab bag of whatever natural rights they believe desirable. If the Constitution is seen to be the primary instrument for securing those rights, then it becomes constitutional to impose by force the realization of them. Thus Gerber moves from a very promising review of the scholarly literature and exploration of Lockean liberalism to a startling assertion that the pursuit of happiness "requires some degree of public-health regulation of the economy, especially in these times of environmental crisis." Such a leap illustrates precisely the problem of defining rights that the founders hoped to avoid. As Jefferson said in a different but still applicable context, "The constitution, on this hypothesis, is a mere thing of wax in the hands of the judiciary, which they may twist and shape into any form they please." It was to avoid this charge that the Constitution was initially portrayed by its champions as an instrument of delegated powers, and why the issue of strict construction was later raised by the Jeffersonian Republicans.[4]

The problem of natural rights jurisprudence is embodied in the variety of opinions concerning the content of natural rights, from libertarian to socialist views. Each has an idea of what the national court or courts ought to do. What they all lack is an appreciation for the formal arrangements of the original Constitution that left government divided up into many states and branches, each with its designated responsibilities and domains. The states were the realm in which men would contest the meaning of natural rights and give form to their conceptions—civil rights—through their local governments. The general government or federal government was to have very little to say in these matters. Thus Jefferson insisted, "Let the national government be entrusted with the defence of the nation, and its foreign and federal relations; the State governments with the civil rights, laws, police, and administration of what concerns the State generally; the counties with the local concerns of the counties, and each ward direct the interests within itself." Madison's initial wish for a federal veto over the state legislatures was explicitly rejected. Instead, limited powers of dealing with foreign nations, of making war, of taxation,

commerce, and the regulating of coin were given over to the federal government. And all this was done in the context of additional restrictions:
both state and federal governments were divided up into judicial, executive, and legislative bodies, each with the power to decide on the constitutionality of acts and policies within its jurisdiction. These were the formal arrangements by which society was to be protected from the
depredations of tyranny. It was by leaving society free, by keeping government local when it was dealing with such precious uncertainties as
rights, and by chopping government up into a system of checks and balances of delegated powers when granting it authority for general purposes, that Americans understood the pursuit of happiness. It was a happiness found in the voluntary associations and spontaneous orders of
society, not in the restricted and confined institutions of government.
Such happiness was both social and private in nature. And it seemed to
work spectacularly in some instances, and failed just as spectacularly in
others.[5]

When Alexis de Tocqueville observed American society in the 1830s,
he set about describing a people who affirmed a belief in the natural
equality of men. It was not an equality of material condition, but of rights
equally bestowed by nature. He feared the bad tendencies that such equality might have, of dividing men from one another and leaving them open
to tyranny, but in the United States he detected some hope in the development of its civil associations. He believed that this hope was reflected
in the distinction that Americans took for granted between politics and
society:

> In the United States, political associations are only a small part of the immense
> number of different types of associations found there.
> Americans of all ages, all stations of life, and all types of dispositions are forever
> forming associations. There are not only commercial associations and industrial
> associations in which all take part, but others of a thousand different types—
> religious, moral, serious, futile, very general and very limited, immensely large
> and very minute. Americans combine to give fetes, found seminaries, build
> churches, distribute books, and send missionaries to the antipodes. Hospitals,
> prisons, and schools take shape in that way. Finally, if they want to proclaim a
> truth or propagate some feeling by the encouragement of a great example, they
> form an association. In every case, at the head of any new undertaking, where in
> France you would find the government or in England some territorial magnate, in
> the United States you are sure to find an association.[6]

Tocqueville's observation of American society was the object of the
Declaration's pursuit of happiness. It had little or nothing to do with

government per se, and everything to do with the flourishing of civil society. The political order established by the Constitution, with its decentralized distribution of powers, seemed to be working. Americans were governing themselves, but in one very crucial respect it was failing.

Slavery was not going away—at least not in the foreseeable future for those living on the eve of the Civil War, and this created a moral divide that deepened with every new acquisition of territory by the United States. The cotton-exporting South felt it essential to match state for state in the Senate with the industrializing North to secure itself against those interests in the North that favored federal spending on internal improvements, such as canals, and high protective tariffs. Moreover, the rich tapestry of civil associations also included the development of vigorous antislavery societies that concentrated in the North and served to accentuate the cultural differences between the two regions. In response, the South made appeals to the Supreme Court and Congress to ensure that slavery would be treated uniformly—that is, tolerated throughout the territories of the republic—and fugitive slaves would be returned from the North to their Southern masters. Both North and South thus solicited the power of the national government to serve their particular purposes, whether for trade regulations or to protect slavery. In such an environment, the institutions of federalism and republicanism eventually began to crack; and how they fell apart had a devastating impact on the political tradition invoked by the Declaration.[7]

Federalism requires a necessary tension to exist between the states and the national government. It is a check to power, operating by the mutual constraints that the national and state governments place on each other. The ever-present, if often veiled, threat of secession serves to remind the parties to the national government that they ought not to push the states too hard in furthering their own agenda. When regional differences become too stark, that threat no longer restrains, and a decision must be made. Will the national government insist on having its way and attempt to force compliance, or will the "aggrieved" parties be allowed to exit?

William Lloyd Garrison had consistently advocated over the course of his abolitionist career that the North should secede from the South, and Horace Greeley's first response on hearing the news of Southern secession was to rejoice at the departure of such bad company. The idea that states could secede from the federal compact was not reserved to the South, but was a common assertion voiced at different times throughout the country. Some New Englanders had even entertained the idea in the

War of 1812, raising the possibility of two or more republics as had once been considered by some Antifederalists. Frequently, political leaders would stop just short of calling for secession, but would leave little doubt as to their ultimate intentions if their concerns were not addressed. Thus a young Daniel Webster, representative from New Hampshire, could argue in Congress on December 9, 1814, that the "operation of measures unconstitutional and illegal ought to be prevented by a resort to other measures which are both constitutional and legal. It will be the solemn duty of the State Governments to protect their own authority over their own militia, and to interpose between their citizens and arbitrary power. These are among the objects for which the State Governments exist; and their highest obligations bind them to the preservation of their own rights and the liberties of their people." The use of state power to counter power at the national level was thus part of the common store of political remedies available to the people in the early republic. It was that necessary tension between the general and state governments, however, that came to a final and ruinous climax after the decision by the North to compel the South to remain in the union. The consequences of this choice were farther reaching than appears obvious at first glance.[8]

The conduct of the war caused a rapid extension of the power and size of the national government; but, as many point out, the national government retrenched afterwards. Even though slavery was abolished, the South was quickly restored to self-rule, and returned to its exploitative ways regarding African Americans. In a recent work by Jeffrey Rogers Hummel, however, that conclusion is reevaluated and found wanting in several respects. Slavery was not the only casualty of the war—so too were the respectability of the states' rights argument and the foundations of the old federalism. There was some retrenchment in the size of the national government after the war, but the claim of ultimate authority was now firmly located in Washington D.C. Moreover, as Robert Wiebe has pointed out, reformers of the late nineteenth and early twentieth centuries increasingly appealed for assistance over the heads of local and state governments to the national government. The process of concentration was not instantaneous, but the post-Civil War supremacy of the national government created a vortex that has steadily drawn all power and responsibility to its center. Federalism today means that states will be indulged with managing funds distributed by Washington, and local governments are considered mere subdepartments.[9]

Rather than being a linear continuation of the Revolution as some would argue, the Civil War was America's nationalist conflict, equivalent in its glorification of the union with the unification of Germany.[10] One unfortunate long-run consequence of the War for the Union, as it was also called, has been the growing impersonalization of government's exercise of massive powers and a lessening of democratic participation. Government now seems something that is done to us, rather than something we participate in, and the implications of that have reached deeply into our intellectual life.

Historically Europe has always been shaped by its class prejudices and conflicts. The leading schools of thought after the Enlightenment tended to glory in government, and appealed to political means to achieve social and economic ends. Conflict was rooted in the conceptions of imperialists, socialists, Marxists, fascists, and the various other purveyors of "isms," and American social thought after the Civil War increasingly reflected that influence. Today the very idea of society as independent of government and with its own order, as opposed to its being a source of conflict demanding mediation, has been lost; with it has gone the notion of self-government at the core of the Declaration. Now scholars write, with little apparent embarrassment, that all rights flow from government, are not the gifts of nature or of the divine, and proceed to invoke the Declaration in support of this. The growth of victim-oriented political and legal reform movements is a wonderful example of how far we have moved from our political origins. We no longer take personal responsibility for such ordinary vices as the use of tobacco, but seek to make others share the burdens of our bad choices. Because we thus refuse to govern ourselves, we no longer accept that democracy depends on self-governing individuals. No longer Jeffersonian, we have become more European in our political outlook. It is the political and collective definition of self-government to which Americans now refer. Today we ask how people feel about the way the president or Congress is "running" the country, as if there existed a great tiller inside the Oval Office or the halls of Congress. The very question could not have been asked in 1776 by an American patriot because it implied the very thing he rejected. Government did not "run" the country; the people, through all their actions and associations did; and politics was a very tiny part of that equation. A loyalist might have been more inclined to see it the way we do now, and here is the real irony. Just as the loyalists could see only chaos beyond the bounds of imperial control, so today we can see nothing but conflict in society without the salvation of government. Politics has trumped society; and though America began as Whig, it has become Tory.[11]

Bibliographic Essay

Scholarly treatments of the Declaration of Independence can be roughly categorized into historical and theoretical accounts of the document, intellectual histories of the Revolution, biographies of Thomas Jefferson, and broader philosophical analyses of American political life. These lines cannot be sharply drawn for the most part, but the categories describe well the many intentions authors have brought to the study of the Declaration, and explain to a degree the great variety of interpretations. It was over the course of years of reading these various sources that the idea for this book developed. Faced with a bewildering array of perspectives on the ideology of the founding, historians appear to be surrendering to the temptation to ascribe all to "paradoxical premises," or "a profusion and confusion of political tongues," or "the notorious inconsistency of humans, who have always proven quite capable of holding contradictory views simultaneously."[1]

Certainly historians ought to be sensitive to the human capacity for contradiction and inconsistency. Treatments of the past that are too neat are legitimately suspect. It is no less true, however, that overt contradictions demand some explanation. If we assume that historical figures were at least as insightful as modern readers, then awareness of those contradictions must have been apparent and addressed at some level of discourse. Overt incongruities in ideas do not sit well in the human mind or else argument and rhetoric would serve no purpose. Consequently, scholars should continue to be concerned with how republican virtue fit with liberal self-interest, how commerce and a moral sense worked together, and what the meanings were of public versus private and social versus political. The review that follows tries to touch on those major works on the Declaration and its historical and philosophical context that have contributed to the complexity of our perception of early American politics. A great number of these studies have already been discussed in the notes to the text, so the project now will be to single out the most prominent contributions. They afford the interested reader or student a good place to begin a more in-depth investigation into the Declaration. With a few important exceptions, the primary attention will be on those studies in political theory and intellectual history that treat the Declaration directly, rather than biographies of Jefferson, which are so numerous that a brief survey is simply impossible.

Some of the earliest treatments of the Declaration are histories of its composition. These works tended to be fairly united in their assumption of the Lockean origins of the document, and while the discussions of its intellectual history are for the most part not very penetrating, they are usually very good concerning the details of the Declaration's creation. First and foremost in this category is John H. Hazelton's *The Declaration of Independence, Its History* (New York: Dodd, Mead and Company, 1906; Da Capo Press, 1970) which contains a very useful, line-by-line comparison of the various drafts of the document, and a discussion of the Declaration's reception in America. Another treatment is that of Herbert Friedenwald, *The Declaration of Independence* (New York: The Macmillan Company, 1904; New York: Da Capo Press, 1974). This work set out, in part, to discover the content of the various charges—a useful endeavor, but one which was more fully undertaken in an article by Sydney George Fisher, entitled "The Twenty-Eight Charges Against the King in the Declaration of Independence," in *The Pennsylvania Magazine of History and Biography* 31 (July 1907). Both of these works were superseded by Edward Dumbauld's *The Declaration of Independence and What It Means Today* (Norman, Oklahoma: University of Oklahoma Press, 1950). Nevertheless, details vary among all three accounts, so the reader would do well to take each into consideration.

Among the premier discussions of the historical evolution of the composition of the Declaration is the careful analysis of the text done by Julian P. Boyd, *The Declaration of Independence: The Evolution of the Text as Shown in Facsimiles of Various Drafts by its Author, Thomas Jefferson* (Princeton, New Jersey: Princeton University Press, 1945). Boyd did an extensive investigation of the various drafts, and pieced together what Jefferson's first thoughts on paper must have looked like. Overall, the work holds together well, but it should be supplemented with the useful correctives supplied by Wilfred J. Ritz in *"From the* Here *of Jefferson's Handwritten Rough Draft of the Declaration of Independence to the* There *of the Printed Dunlap Broadside,"* in *The Pennsylvania Magazine of History and Biography* 116 (October 1992).

Running parallel to the historical investigations of the writing of the text have been explorations of its intellectual background. In the early 1920s, Carl Becker came out with his classic study of the Lockean origins for the document in *The Declaration of Independence: A Study in the History of Ideas* (New York: Harcourt Brace and Co., 1922; reprint New York: Vintage Books, 1970). It was this work that initiated the scholarly infatuation with the opening paragraphs of the Declaration by declaring them to be the core of the text. With the noted exception of Dumbauld, historians would henceforth primarily debate the sources of Locke's influence, the origins of specific phrases in the preamble, and the texts used by its author. Becker's work was not original for its focus on Locke, but it was impressive for the definitive way in which he set about to confirm the Lockean thesis. Few questioned its basic conclusion, and the essential Lockean liberal thesis reigned supreme until the 1960s.

It was around this time that an entirely new school of historical interpretation of the Revolution began to unearth a political discourse with seemingly very different implications from Locke's individualist liberalism. This was the classical republican conception of American politics, which stressed the primacy of community and self-sacrifice and the need to balance the natural social divisions of men in the political order. Curiously, this school, which soon took on the appearance to some of a new historical synthesis, rarely made mention of the Declaration. Its major contributors, such as J. G. A. Pocock, Gordon Wood, and Lance Banning, made no study of the document.[2] The only one who came close was Stanley N. Katz, in his article, "Thomas Jefferson and the Right to Property in Revolutionary America," *The Journal of Law and Economics* 19 (October 1976), but this was only in passing, and most of the references were to the personal correspondence of Jefferson and his *Notes on the State of Virginia* which were written after the Revolution. It was this radical disconnect between the republican and Lockean perspectives that initiated the new series of studies (some by historians, but others by those in political theory) that pointed to the inconsistency of a Lockean Declaration produced in a republican world. While republican language certainly was evident in reference to the formation of political institutions and the corrupting nature of power, whole areas of liberal discourse were overlooked, both in the realm of politics and in economic thought, by the republican synthesizers.

Quick to defend the Lockean interpretation were political theorists whose concerns predated the debates among historians. Many of these scholars were first and second generation students of the work of Leo Strauss. Among the early works on the Declaration from this perspective are those by Harry V. Jaffa, that deal in particular with the relationship of a Lockean Declaration to the later republic of Lincoln. See especially his *Crisis of the House Divided* (Seattle: University of Washington Press, 1959), and his collection of essays, *The Conditions of Freedom* (Baltimore: Johns Hopkins University Press, 1975). In the latter work see particularly the essay, "What is Equality? The Declaration of Independence Revisited." A concise example of his thinking can also be found in his exchange with M. E. Bradford in the collection of articles republished in George A. Panichas, ed., *Modern Age: The First Twenty-Five Years* (Indianapolis: Liberty Fund, 1988). The study of the Declaration's relationship to the early republic is an important connecting theme of those who take a Straussian approach to the history of political ideas, even though particular interpretations will vary in important particulars. A good example is the collection of essays by Martin Daimond, especially his "The Declaration and the Constitution: Liberty, Democracy, and the Founders," in *As Far as Republican Principles Will Admit* (Washington D.C.: The AEI Press, 1992). Though both Jaffa and Daimond disagree in certain important details that go beyond the scope of this review, they are united in their understanding of the centrality of the natural rights philosophy of the Declaration for interpreting the Constitution and the American political tradition.

One crucial difference between the Straussian approach and the perspective presented here, however, is the persistent emphasis of the former on the importance of statesmanship, which tends to privilege the political conception of how rights are to be realized. That focus tends to obscure the very limited role that the national government was granted in the founding era even in protecting individual rights, as evidenced by the founders consciously organizing the general or national government into a federal structure. Considerable emphasis is placed by Straussians on the energy with which the Federalists sought to infuse government, as opposed to the limits that they insisted upon. Consequently, the massive concentration of power that became possible in the federal government after the Civil War rarely receives its due. Rather, Lincoln is usually seen to fulfill the revolutionary promise through wise leadership, and the more problematic aspects of the conflict are not fully developed. See, for example, Thomas G. West's section on the Civil War in *Vindicating the Founders: Race, Sex, Class, and Justice in the Origins of America* (New York: Rowman and Littlefield Publishers, 1977), 32–36. While natural rights thinking was a key element in the founders' understanding, they were not willing to admit that a single conception of those rights could be perfectly articulated and handed down by a supreme lawgiver or institution of government. Government was limited by the imperfections of man and the law of nature as ordained by God—ideas that were fundamentally the product of American religious sensibilities. Consequently, we need a closer examination of the role of Christian thought with regard to the way it shaped the early American perception of human nature, government, and society.

For most of the past century, historians have followed the lead of Max Weber and recognized the compatibility of capitalism and Protestantism, focusing on the importance of the work ethic, thrift, and diligence. Recently, however, these traditions have been set against each other in an interesting way in a book by yet another political scientist, Barry Alan Shain, in his *Myth of American Individualism: The Protestant Origins of American Political Thought* (Princeton, New Jersey: Princeton University Press, 1994). Shain rejects the liberal Lockean interpretation of the Revolution to assert that Americans were entirely of a Christian communitarian or corporatist understanding, and the purpose of the Declaration was simply to express their collective right to secede "from an oppressive and increasingly separate people." (See Shain, 246–247.) The importance of his study is in the volume of evidence demonstrating the vibrancy of Protestantism during the Revolution for the majority of Americans. He is especially good at discussing the important role that the idea of sin continued to play in shaping attitudes towards the individual and pessimism about his earthly existence. Shain's perception of liberalism, however, is limited to its secularism and supposed equation of the good with unfettered individual autonomy. If he is correct, one wonders how an enterprising capitalist society with a commitment to individual liberty was ever possible in the nineteenth century. His account suffers from the same difficulty as the republican thesis. For Shain, it is an enterprising and secularized elite who bring on a liberal corruption via the Revolution. Thus, like the republican thesis, there is a Revolutionary world that ill fits with the world that comes after. An alternative interpretation is offered in Michael Zuckert's penetrating analysis, *The Natural Rights Republic: Studies in the Foundation of the American Political Tradition* (Notre Dame, Indiana: University of Notre Dame Press, 1996). Like others of a Straussian perspective, Zuckert is especially concerned with revealing the centrality of natural rights to properly understand the Declaration and American political institutions, but he goes further than most by taking a serious look at the compatibility of Protestant Christianity, at least in its late eighteenth-century form, with Locke's political theory. What he finds is that many New England clergymen were deeply influenced by Locke. Most interestingly, he shows that the classic Protestant distinction between the kingdom of God and the earthly kingdom of man was reworked into a liberal justification for religious freedom. With special attention paid to Elisha Williams, Zuckert argues that contrary to the early puritan tendency to enlist government in the defense of orthodoxy, for both Williams (as with Locke), the only feasible understanding of the relationship of politics to religion was "to leave religious opinion and practice per se entirely in the sphere of the private and voluntary and to base public coerced life on rational principles presumably more open to agreement, or at least less explosive." (See Zuckert, 192.) Yet how does this picture square with the starkly sinful perception of man that Shain finds to be the basis for a most illiberal localist theocratic communitarianism, operative from earliest Puritan days to the late eighteenth century? The answer, as I have tried to suggest, picks up exactly where Zuckert concludes his study: the voluntary realm of society.

Shain's argument rests on a distinction between the sinful private self and the morally constraining community, but he makes no allowance for the more fundamental distinction between the community and political governance that was part of the lived experience of most Americans. (See Shain, 117–121.) As his own evidence indicates, Americans could not effectively sustain authoritarian regimes even at the local level because of the ability of individuals to escape to numerous other jurisdictions beyond the borders of their own particular communities. The very common law Americans brought with them and the "paucity of powerful coercive mechanisms" at their disposal laid the basis for the distinction between social forms of moral suasion (such as guilt and ostracism) that could be exercised against an errant individual and the more cumbersome and rarely used mechanisms of government power. (See Shain, 111–112.) Consequently, while it could be argued that the state/society distinction was consciously held only by an enlightened few, it was fundamentally part of the social experience of most Americans. This is why Whig theory had such resonance in the colonies when people set themselves to thinking about the relationship of power to liberty. It was a natural synthesis of views that readily described the American experience. In this environment, Christianity worked directly on the hearts of believers through the moral suasion of the particular group. It was communitarian, in a very direct and practical way, but not essentially political. The shared beliefs of all Christians in the imperfection of man, underscored for most denominations the problematic nature of power and the need to limit government through divided powers and federalism. The concept of sin served as both an explanation for the origins of government as well as the reason for restraining it. A further elucidation of the compatibility of Christianity and early American political thought as it relates to the Declaration of Independence can be found in chapter thirteen of M. Stanton Evans' *The Theme Is Freedom: Religion, Politics, and the American Tradition* (Washington, D.C.; Regnery Publishing, Inc., 1994). Rather than the "failure of Western communal ideals" to arrest the "unsought individualistic and materialistic consequences" unleashed by the war, America's Protestant and Lockean heritages worked in unison to preserve American liberty. (For quotations see Shain, 322.) For Evans, in fact, the Lockean perspective is itself derived from the medieval Christian concern to limit the power of earthly kings. Here the reader might consider taking a look at the interesting, if more speculative, approach taken by John Alvis where he considers the possible influence of Milton's Christian theological political ideas in his essay, "Milton and the Declaration of Independence," *Interpretations*, vol. 25, no. 3 (Spring 1998): 367–405. At this point we should turn to yet another important intellectual component of Whig thought, namely political economy. As God's creation, man exhibited in his social affairs, when conducted without violence or fraud, the same orderliness evident in the other realms of creation.

Joyce Appleby's earlier study of the formation of economic thought revealed the degree to which the scientific discovery of natural laws was translated into a search for natural forces governing the market order, and this insight shaped her interpretation of the Revolution. Her many essays on this subject are gathered in *Liberalism and Republicanism in the Historical Imagination* (Cambridge, Massachusetts: Harvard University Press, 1992). These studies fit nicely with another perspective on Locke presented by the economist Karen Vaughn in her book, *John Locke: Economist and Social Scientist* (Chicago: University of Chicago Press, 1980). Each of these scholars has elucidated the powerful influence which economic thought had on the early modern understanding of natural rights and a self-regulating social order. Both economics and the philosophy of natural rights derived from the scientific worldview that saw a natural self-ordering tendency in the physical universe. That insight explains much of the reason why the state of nature for Locke could not be as bad as that portrayed by Hobbes. The aim of economics was to discover the equivalent of natural forces operating in the social realm. This "scientific" understanding is insightfully related to the Declaration in the work by I. Bernard Cohen, *Science and the Founding Fathers*, where Cohen observes that

"Whatever was in Jefferson's conscious mind when he wrote about 'the laws of nature,' these words had necessarily the sense of laws or principles of science"(New York: W. W. Norton and Co., 1995; 132).

An offshoot of the interest in the scientific project of the Enlightenment has been the investigation of the influence of the Scottish Enlightenment. This was set in motion most dramatically by Gary Wills' *Inventing America: Jefferson's Declaration of Independence* (New York: Vintage Books, 1979). Like the republican synthesizers, Wills set out to dethrone Locke, and like them he discovered another line of thought that seemed more communitarian than individualistic. Jefferson, he argued, derived his understanding of rights and morality not from Locke but from Francis Hutcheson, and it was not man's capacity for rationality but his moral sense that drove him into community. Consequently, Wills argued, the Declaration embraced not a private but a public morality, in which political governance played a leading role. A good portion of Wills' evidence consists of comparisons of phraseology between the Declaration and Hutcheson. However, in a devastating review article Ronald Hamowy showed conclusively that the choice of words in the Declaration was far more similar to Locke, and the similarity between Hutcheson and Jefferson was owed to Locke's influence on Hutcheson. (See Ronald Hamowy, "Jefferson and the Scottish Enlightenment: A Critique of Gary Wills' *Inventing America: Jefferson's Declaration of Independence*," *William and Mary Quarterly*, 3rd Series [October 1979]: 503–523). Another problem with Wills' understanding is the extent to which he makes the modern confusion of the state with the public and the social. The moral sense becomes public in the current political sense, thus obscuring the way both Locke and Hutcheson viewed society. They saw a capacity for order that was rooted in man's nature; government's role was limited to protecting that order by keeping the peace. Such an understanding of limited government and an expansive view of society firmly grounded both men in the Whig tradition. Indeed, Hutcheson was deeply critical of government when it attempted to regulate men's private and economic affairs. If Wills had recognized the Whig distinction between society and the state, between the larger order of voluntary commitments contained in the notion of civil society and the smaller subset of coercive relations embraced by government, he would have recognized that human action could be simultaneously public and private in nature—privately organized for public ends. A far more balanced view of the influence of the Scots on Jefferson and the Declaration, with none of the overstatement of Wills' study, is a recent book by Allen Jayne, *Jefferson's Declaration of Inde-*

pendence: Origins, Philosophy, and Theology (Lexington: University of Kentucky Press, 1998). Here, the emphasis is on the influence of Henry Home, Lord Kames, rather than Hutcheson. Jayne goes a long way toward showing how Kames' theory of the moral sense reinforced the Whig conception of social order, rather than overturning it.

At this point we have five distinctive voices in the American cause: the Lockean discourse on natural rights, the classical republican voice on power and political virtue, the Protestant understanding of sin and the divine order, the scientific understanding of natural law and political economy, and the Scottish philosophy of the moral sense. Far from being incompatible, each was a reinforcing part of what had been a robust Whig conception of civil society that resonated with the lived experience of Americans. Four of these voices refer to sources of authority and order that come from outside of political government, and one, republicanism, speaks directly to the issue of controlling for the abuse of power. There is yet another tradition, and that is the customary understanding of the common law and the ancient constitution. Both of these ideas looked to the past and to the community for justification. The common law and the ancient constitution were part of the British idea that precedent, custom, and history could reveal justice through what has been generally practiced and accepted by the people as opposed to what was handed down by a king. Their reliance on the past did not mean that they were unsuitable for radical applications. Quite the contrary. Where political power has caused a deviation in course, revolutionaries have called for a restoration of the true tradition. Thus Jefferson could call for the restoration of the ancient Saxon understanding of property ownership as among the most ancient of English rights, and consider it a natural right as well. This was a part of the legendary ancient constitution overturned by the Norman conquest, but which was legitimately reclaimed by Americans. One of the best discussions of this is to be found in the work of Trevor Colbourn, *The Lamp of Experience: Whig History and the Intellectual Origins of the American Revolution* (Indianapolis: Liberty Fund, 1998), originally published in 1965. Colbourn's work directed attention to the charges in both the *Summary View* and the Declaration, and revealed the crucial role that Whig history played in the substantiation of natural rights claims and legal argument. But these important insights into the relationship of history and law were only much later developed by the monumental efforts of John Phillip Reid in his four-volume study, *The Constitutional History of the American Revolution* (Madison: University of Wisconsin Press, 1993). Like the republican interpreters, or Shain on Protestant communitarianism, however, Reid makes what this author considers to be an unnecessary rejection of natural rights and of Locke. After marshalling a massive amount of evidence in support of the important role of the customary understanding of common law and the argument for the ancient constitution, Reid dismisses Locke; he insists that the heart of the Declaration is in the charges against the King, and proceeds to write off the rest of the document as so much rhetorical flourish. A good way to address that imbalance is to consider Ross Lence's "Jefferson and the Declaration of Independence: The Power and Natural Rights of A Free People" (*The Political Science Reviewer* 6 [Fall, 1976], 1–31). Lence looks at the Declaration in its entirety and relates the theory of natural rights expressed in the opening paragraphs to the charges against the King, taking seriously the Declaration's division of grievances into abuses and usurpations.

From this brief survey, it is fairly evident that there exists an embarrassment of riches with regard to interpretations of American revolutionary ideology. What has been lacking, however, is the attempt to bring all of the various strands together. The main obstacle has been the confusion about the distinction between government and society that rests at the heart of the American idea of self-government. Yehoshua Arieli pointed this out in *Individualism and Nationalism in American Ideology* in the early 1960s when he wrote, "Because most historians have interpreted the term 'society' in purely political terms, they have been puzzled by the apparent contradictions in the American concept of democracy, its insistence on the rights of man and on the constitutionally limited powers of democracy" (Cambridge, Massachusetts: Harvard University Press, 1964), 98. As we have seen, this warning has been largely ignored by both the communitarian and republican schools of interpretation. Even more remarkable is the lack of attention paid to this distinction by those who continue to defend Locke's influence on America. With its roots thus obscured, the Declaration's real significance in American political life is overlooked.

This now brings us to the most recent, and most sustained historical treatment of the Declaration to be done in recent time, Pauline Maier's *American Scripture: Making the Declaration of Independence* (New York: Alfred A. Knopf, 1997). Like both Colbourn and Reid, Maier sees the heart of the Declaration to be in the charges against the King, and attempts to place it in its proper historical context. Indeed, the whole purpose of the book is to situate the document among all of the other declarations in favor of independence that were issued before and after the congressional issue of the Declaration of Independence. In the course of her work she finds not an original document, but one very much in the spirit of its time. In fact, she goes even further to assert that it was not greatly admired for its wording, as seen in the fact that most states preferred the Virginia Bill of Rights written by George Mason to Jefferson's prose. In writing her book, Maier has performed an invaluable service, and collected an impressive list of sources which others may draw upon to great benefit, but she leaves a number of important elements unexplained.

Early on she makes it clear that she has no interest in analyzing yet again the seventeenth- and eighteenth-century European intellectual world to explicate the ideological origins of the Declaration. This has been done, she notes, innumerable times before. Rather, she seeks to emphasize that the Declaration was the collective expression of the American people, and not simply the product of Thomas Jefferson. All of this is unexceptionable, but Maier then goes on to argue that the Declaration was at best ancillary to the later debates over the founding, and was only made into the symbol it now is by the politics of the early republic—by the skillful manipulation of Jeffersonians who wished to elevate the status of their leader. I would suggest a different construction.

Initially, during the debates over the Constitution, the essential principles of the Declaration did not take center stage because few questioned them. They were a part of nearly every state's own revolutionary heritage as Maier makes clear. But when the subject of the Declaration was raised, such as in the debates in Pennsylvania between James Wilson and his Antifederalist opponents, the argument was spiritedly joined. And it is telling that the subject of the Declaration was first raised, not over a dispute of its basic argument and principles (which would have been odd since it was the justification for their erecting new governments in the first place), but over whether or not America had entered the Revolution as a union of one people or a confederation of many. Secondly, the spirit or principles of 1776 or of the Revolution were often invoked, and it would be strange to think that these were meant to refer only to the declarations of the states and not the Declaration of Independence. Finally, the debates of the 1790s were not mere political games. They were a healthy return to a discussion of first principles in a new republic struggling to find its way. With Federalist legislation to squelch debate and deport alien troublemakers, Jeffersonian Republicans legitimately questioned whether or not Federalist policies were an affront to the meaning of independence.

The Jeffersonian Republicans in the 1790s were reacting to the same development American Whigs had responded to when Parliament sought to extend its power throughout the empire. In England, the Whigs had forgotten their origins, and had given themselves over to the supremacy of Parliament. Likewise, American Federalists were becoming far too comfortable with political power, reading too much into a document that was created to establish a government of limited authority, where all powers not given in the Constitution were reserved to the people or to the states. One need only look to the statements of some Federalists to see a growing Tory disposition. The Jeffersonian reaction was a perfectly natural and legitimate assertion of the Whig tradition of self-government against the perception of the abuse of power. Inconsistencies abound, but the general assertion of the principles and the symbolism of the Declaration in the first decades of the republic was wholly in keeping with the tradition and spirit of the document. That fact is more easily brought out when the document is placed in its proper context as an encapsulation of the early American understanding of self-government with its roots in the Whig notion of a natural social order. Far from there being too much explication of the Declaration's intellectual origins, there is not enough. There are, however, some notable exceptions.

Two have already been mentioned: Michael Zuckert's *The Natural Rights Republic* and M. Stanton Evans, *The Theme Is Freedom*. Two other works to consider are David N. Mayer's *The Constitutional Thought of Thomas Jefferson* (Charlottesville: University Press of Virginia, 1995), and Jean M. Yarbrough's *American Virtues: Thomas Jefferson on the Character of a Free People* (Lawrence, Kansas: University Press of Kansas, 1998). The virtue of both these works is their well-developed understanding of the distinction between government and society in the Whig or liberal tradition of the Revolution.

Mayer's interpretation is close to my own, but his focus is on Jefferson's constitutional thought in general rather than on the Declaration in particular. Taken as a whole, his book is a powerful illustration of the reasons why Jefferson was such a good choice for authoring the Declaration, reflecting, as Jefferson did, the breadth and depth of the American understanding of civil society. Jean Yarbrough has taken a similar approach with regard to Jefferson's moral philosophy and his ideas about the virtues necessary for self-government in a republic. Like Mayer, she is careful to note the distinction between government and society that is at the heart of early liberalism and observes that "It is the glory of modern *liberal* republicanism (as opposed to the ancient republics of Greece and Rome) that the perfection of the individual is not exclusively or even primarily bound up with political activity."(See Yarbrough, xvi.) At the core of her argument is the contention that the happiness referred to in the Declaration embraces those moral virtues of benevolence and association that flourish beyond the realm of politics. It would be good, at this point, for the reader to consider some earlier studies of the meaning of happiness such as Herbert Lawrence Ganter's "Jefferson's 'Pursuit of Happiness' and Some Forgotten Men," *William and Mary Quarterly*, 2d series 16 (July 1936): 422–585; and Caroline Robbins' "The Pursuit of Happiness," in Stephen J. Tonsor, ed., *America's Continuing Revolution: An Act of Conservation* (Washington, D.C.: American Enterprise Institute, 1975), 119–139. Yarbrough goes beyond historical considerations, however, and argues that government does have an important role to play in the fostering of virtuous behavior. She finds troubling the more radical aspect of Jeffersonianism that "may encourage a libertarian disdain for all government action even at the local level, as individuals, taking undue pride in their self-sufficiency, come to question any sense of collective purpose." (See Yarbrough, 152.) Yarbrough thus brings the conversation about our civil institutions into the present by asking us first to rediscover Jefferson's understanding of character formation in society and government, and then to reconsider what is best for our own time. The importance of this question is magnified when we turn our consideration to the Founding period.

The argument in favor of the view that the Revolution and the Declaration were informed by a coherent philosophical tradition does not mean that disagreements and political conflicts were not possible or did not take place. Different individuals and parties emphasized different strands of this rich tradition. They disagreed, as we have seen, about whether the most dangerous sources of power resided in the state governments or the general government. They argued over how much the principles of democracy or republican representation should be operative. They gave emphasis to either common law, religion, or economics in their descriptions of society, but there was no deep discord, until perhaps the early republican period, over fundamental commitments. Adams felt more at home in law and history, but he still agreed with Jefferson over the value of Destutt de Tracy's political economy. This was because they both maintained a fairly clear understanding that government and society were not the same. Society possessed a natural capacity for order. The purpose of government was to extend and protect the fruits of that order by limiting violence and injustice, not to presume to establish that order by virtue of its monopoly over coercive force. If government could be contained within its proper bounds, social life would develop of its own accord through all the natural channels of custom, faith, trade, and fellow feeling, establishing a flourishing state of civil society, of which government was but a very small part. How to attain this healthy state of civil society, however, was not an easy thing to figure out, and this raises the whole question of the relationship of the Declaration, and the independence it announced, to the Constitution.

The number of studies done along this line is immense. Certainly it is a major concern of the Straussian school of political theory discussed earlier. Another important source to consider is the work by Donald S. Lutz, *The Origins of American Constitutionalism* (Baton Rouge: Louisiana State University Press, 1988). Before Pauline Maier had situated the Declaration among the various state resolutions in favor of independence, Lutz had placed it in the context of the colonial charters and the Protestant covenanting tradition, all of which preceded the theories of Locke and Sidney, but made fertile ground for their reception into American thought. Lutz presents a strong case for why the Declaration should be seen as containing "the grounding for the Constitution, as well as the values underlying the American system of government." (See Lutz, 121.) His understanding of the covenanting tradition would be good to place alongside Zuckert's interpretation of the same in his book discussed above. Another source for consideration is the essay by Daniel L. Dreisbach, "In Search of a Christian Commonwealth: An Examination of Selected Nineteenth-Century Commentaries on References to God and the Christian Religion in the United States Constitution," in volume 48 of the *Baylor Law Review* (1996). Dreisbach's interest in the Declaration stems from the uses that have been made of the Declaration's reference to "Nature and Nature's God" in the interpretive history of the Constitution. It is an article packed with useful references.

A recent full-length treatment of the Declaration's relationship to the Constitution, however, can be found in Scott Douglas Gerber's *To Secure These Rights: The Declaration of Independence and Constitutional Interpretation* (New York: New York University Press, 1995). Gerber's review of the literature is superb, as is his defense of the Lockean basis for both the Declaration and the Constitution. Again, however, the state/society distinction is not clear, and government becomes the vehicle for securing the right to happiness, essentially leaving the domain of government limitless, so long as its actions are in the public interest. Thus Gerber concludes that "the Constitution should be interpreted in light of the natural-rights political philosophy of the Declaration of Independence and that the Supreme Court is the institution of American government that should be primarily responsible for identifying and applying that philosophy in American life." Nothing could be further from the intentions of the founders. Save perhaps for the most basic natural rights, they were well aware that rational men could come to different conclusions about the contents of rights and left these to the people in their states to determine. The Constitution insisted only that those rights be equally applied to all within a state. This was the original understanding of privileges and immunities, for example, and the basis of the ninth and tenth amendments. An excellent source for understanding this notion is the recent study by James E. Bond, *No Easy Walk to Freedom: Reconstruction and the Ratification of the Fourteenth Amendment* (Westport, Connecticut: Praeger, 1997; see esp. 262–263). Bond explicitly relates the original idea of rights found in the Declaration to the earliest understanding of privileges and immunities and its manifestation in the debates over the fourteenth amendment. But Bond's is an exceptional study. Present political concern with national politics permeates most historical treatments.

Because we find it hard to imagine life without the close involvement of political regulation in our daily lives, we find it difficult to conceive of self-government in the way our forebears did. One essential primary source for recapturing this idea would be any edition of Alexis de Tocqueville's *Democracy in America* (1835–40). The best current examination of the social experience of colonial and revolutionary Americans, however, is Jack P. Greene's *Pursuits of Happiness: The Social Development of Early Modern British Colonies and the Formation of American Culture* (Chapel Hill: University of North Carolina Press, 1988). Greene's book shows just how small and limited the sphere of politics actually was and provides a useful corrective to interpretations that place too much faith in the claims to power made by some colonial governments. Reading the two works together will give the reader an excellent idea of how American society, by virtue of the fact that it was not essentially political, could be both communal *and* individualistic—both concerned with the enduring values of community *and* engaged in the material production of wealth in a dynamic economy.

To conclude, it was the purpose of this study to recapture a sense of the meaning of the Declaration of Independence by drawing together the various strands of interpretation presented above. The Whig conception and its American expression in the Jeffersonian tradition is principally one of social, rather than political, self-regulation. The individual was expected to govern himself or herself in the context of a society composed primarily of voluntary commitments. Those commitments formed the basis for a rich variety of associations and communities for reasons of religious fellowship, self-interest, and philanthropy. Such communities and associations could and did exact high costs from individuals as a condition of membership, and those who chose not to comply with the rules risked social stigma and losing the benefits of a particular group, but government was not the primary means for regulating individual behavior. Political institutions were intended ideally only to limit violence by discouraging and punishing criminal acts, protecting against foreign aggression, and undertaking those few projects such as roads and harbors that were not easily done by voluntary means (though even here the historical experience was mixed and most projects for internal improvements, as they were called, were often hotly contested). Happiness, on the other hand, was to be found in society through the flourishing and prospering of the rich variety of associations and communities. This was what the American Whig or Jeffersonian had in mind when he conceived of civil society. Government in that tradition was not primary, and to give it such a place in the Declaration is a misreading and a source of confusion. This is not to say that we should embrace that conception today, but it is important to keep the message of the past clear by translating its textual remnants into language that can be understood in the present. Only then can we make a clear choice whether to accept or reject the message in our own time. Each of the works discussed above has done that to a degree. It is my hope that this study has provided some useful linkages among them by focusing on the concept of self-government and the distinction between political government and society. It is, of course, up to the student to reevaluate those texts and to participate in the ongoing conversation about the meaning of American political and social life.

Appendix A

Declaration of Independence

In CONGRESS, *July 4, 1776*

The unanimous Declaration of the thirteen united States of America[1]

WHEN in the Course of human Events, it becomes necessary for one People to dissolve the Political Bands which have connected them with another, and to assume among the Powers of the Earth, the separate and equal Station to which the Laws of Nature and of Nature's God entitle them, a decent respect to the opinions of Mankind requires that they should declare the causes which impel them to the Separation.

WE hold these Truths to be self-evident, that all Men are created equal, that they are endowed by their Creator with certain unalienable Rights, that among these are Life, Liberty, and the Pursuit of Happiness—That to secure these Rights, Governments are instituted among Men, deriving their just Powers from the Consent of the Governed, that whenever any Form of Government becomes destructive of these Ends, it is the Right of the People to alter or to abolish it, and to institute new Government, laying its Foundation on such Principles, and organizing its Powers in such Form, as to them shall seem most likely to effect their Safety and Happiness. Prudence, indeed, will dictate that Governments long established should not be changed for light and transient Causes; and accordingly all Experience hath shewn, that Mankind are more disposed to suffer, while Evils are sufferable, than to right themselves by abolishing the Forms to which they are accustomed. But when a long Train of Abuses and Usurpations, pursuing invariably the same Object, evinces a Design to reduce them under absolute Despotism, it is their Right, it is their Duty, to throw off such Government, and to provide new Guards for their future

Security. Such has been the patient Sufferance of these Colonies; and such is now the Necessity which constrains them to alter their former Systems of Government. The History of the present King of Great-Britain is a History of repeated Injuries and Usurpations, all having in direct Object the Establishment of an absolute Tyranny over these States. To prove this, let Facts be submitted to a candid World.

[1] HE has refused his Assent to Laws, the most wholesome and necessary for the public Good.

[2] HE has forbidden his Governors to pass Laws of immediate and pressing Importance, unless suspended in their Operation till his Assent should be obtained; and when so suspended, he has utterly neglected to attend to them.

[3] HE has refused to pass other Laws for the Accommodation of large Districts of People, unless those People would relinquish the Right of Representation in the Legislature, a right inestimable to them, and formidable to Tyrants only.

[4] HE has called together Legislative Bodies at Places unusual, uncomfortable, and distant from the Depository of their public Records, for the sole Purpose of fatiguing them into Compliance with his Measures.

[5] HE has dissolved Representative Houses repeatedly, for opposing with manly Firmness his Invasions on the Rights of the People.

[6] HE has refused for a long Time, after such Dissolutions, to cause others to be elected; whereby the Legislative Powers, incapable of Annihilation, have returned to the People at large for their exercise; the State remaining in the mean time exposed to all the Dangers of Invasion from without, and Convulsions within.

[7] HE has endeavoured to prevent the Population of these States; for that Purpose obstructing the Laws for Naturalization of Foreigners; refusing to pass others to encourage their Migrations hither, and raising the Conditions of new Appropriations of Lands.

[8] HE has obstructed the Administration of Justice, by refusing his Assent to Laws for establishing Judiciary Powers.

[9] HE has made Judges dependent on his Will alone, for the Tenure of their Offices, and the Amount and Payment of their Salaries.

[10] HE has erected a Multitude of new Offices, and sent hither Swarms of Officers to harass our People, and eat out their Substance.

[11] HE has kept among us, in Times of Peace, Standing Armies, without the consent of our Legislatures.

[12] HE has affected to render the Military independent of and superior to the Civil Power.

[13] HE has combined with others to subject us to a Jurisdiction foreign to our Constitution, and unacknowledged by our laws; giving his Assent to their Acts of pretended Legislation:

[13.1] FOR quartering large Bodies of Armed Troops among us:

[13.2] FOR protecting them, by a mock Trial, from Punishment for any Murders which they should commit on the Inhabitants of these States:

[13.3] FOR cutting off our Trade with all parts of the World:

[13.4] FOR imposing Taxes on us without our Consent:

[13.5] FOR depriving us, in many Cases, of the Benefits of Trial by Jury:

[13.6] FOR transporting us beyond Seas to be tried for pretended Offences:

[13.7] FOR abolishing the free System of English laws in a neighbouring Province, establishing therein an arbitrary Government, and enlarging its Boundaries, so as to render it at once an Example and fit Instrument for introducing the same absolute Rule into these Colonies:

[13.8] FOR taking away our Charters, abolishing our most valuable laws, and altering fundamentally the Forms of our Governments:

[13.9] FOR suspending our own Legislatures, and declaring themselves invested with Power to legislate for us in all Cases whatsoever.

[14] HE has abdicated Government here, by declaring us out of his Protection and waging War against us.

[15] HE has plundered our Seas, ravaged our Coasts, burnt our Towns, and destroyed the Lives of our People.

[16] HE is, at this Time, transporting large Armies of foreign Mercenaries to compleat the Works of Death, Desolation, and Tyranny, already begun with circumstances of Cruelty and Perfidy, scarcely paralleled in the most barbarous Ages, and totally unworthy the Head of a civilized Nation.

[17] HE has constrained our fellow Citizens taken Captive on the high Seas to bear Arms against their Country, to become the Executioners of their Friends and Brethren, or to fall themselves by their Hands.

[18] HE has excited domestic Insurrections amongst us, and has endeavoured to bring on the Inhabitants of our Frontiers, the merciless Indian Savages, whose known Rule of Warfare, is an undistinguished Destruction, of all Ages, Sexes and Conditions.

[19] IN every stage of these Oppressions we have Petitioned for Redress in the most humble Terms: Our repeated Petitions have been answered only by repeated Injury. A Prince, whose Character is thus marked by every act which may define a Tyrant, is unfit to be the Ruler of a free People.

NOR have we been wanting in Attentions to our British Brethren. We have warned them from Time to Time of Attempts by their Legislature to extend an unwarrantable Jurisdiction over us. We have reminded them of the Circumstances of our Emigration and Settlement here. We have appealed to their native Justice and Magnanimity, and we have conjured them by the Ties of our common Kindred to disavow these Usurpations, which, would inevitably interrupt our Connections and Correspondence. They too have been deaf to the Voice of Justice and of Consanguinity. We must, therefore, acquiesce in the Necessity, which denounces our Separation, and hold them, as we hold the rest of Mankind, Enemies in War, in Peace, Friends.

We, therefore, the Representatives of the united States of America, in General Congress, Assembled, appealing to the Supreme Judge of the World for the Rectitude of our Intentions, do, in the Name, and by Authority of the good People of these Colonies, solemnly Publish and Declare, That these United Colonies are, and of right ought to be, Free and

Independent States; that they are absolved from all Allegiance to the British Crown, and that all political Connection between them and the State of Great-Britain, is and ought to be totally dissolved; and that as Free and Independent States, they have full Power to levy War conclude Peace, contract Alliances, establish Commerce, and to do all other Acts and Things which Independent States may of right do. --And for the support of this Declaration, with a firm Reliance on the Protection of divine Providence, we mutually pledge to each other our Lives, our Fortunes, and our sacred Honor.

Signed by Order *and in* Behalf *of the* Congress,

JOHN HANCOCK, President

[The following names were signed to the final engrossed copy of the Declaration hanging in the Department of state. They appear here under their state affiliations and in the approximate style in which they were signed.]

Georgia:
Button Gwinnett
Lyman Hall
Geo. Walton

North Carolina:
Wm. Hooper
Joseph Hewes
John Penn

Virginia:
George Wythe
Richard Henry Lee
Th Jefferson
Benja. Harrison
Thos. Nelson, jr.
Francis Lightfoot Lee
Carter Braxton

South Carolina:
Edward Rutledge
Thos. Heyward, Junr.
Thomas Lynch, Junr.
Arthur Middleton

New Jersey:
Richd. Stockton
Jno. Witherspoon
Fras. Hopkinson
John Hart
Abra. Clark

New York:
Wm. Floyd
Phil. Livingston
Frans. Lewis
Lewis Morris

Maryland:
Samuel Chase
Wm. Paca
Thos. Stone
Charles Carrol of Carrollton

Delaware:
Caesar Rodney
Geo. Read
Tho. M'Kean

Pennsylvania:
Robt. Morris
Benjamin Rush
Benja. Franklin
John Morton
Geo. Clymer
Jas. Smith
Geo. Taylor
James Wilson
Geo. Bass

Connecticut:
Roger Sherman
Sam'el Huntington
Wm. Williams
Oliver Wolcott

Rhode Island:
Step. Hopkins
William Ellery

Massachusetts Bay:
Saml. Adams
John Adams
Robt. Treat Paine
Elbridge Gerry

New Hampshire:
Josiah Bartlett
Wm. Whipple
Mathew Thornton

Appendix B

Strictures upon the Declaration of the Congress at Philadelphia in a Letter to a Noble Lord, &c.

by Thomas Hutchinson, former Governor of Massachusetts

(London, 1776)

MY LORD,

[3][1] The Last time I had the honour of being in your Lordships company, you observed that you was utterly at a loss to what facts many parts of the Declaration of Independence published by the Philadelphia Congress referred, and that you wished they had been more particularly mentioned, that you might better judge of the grievances, alleged as special causes of the separation of the Colonies from the other parts of the Empire. This hint from your Lordship induced me to attempt a few Strictures upon the Declaration. Upon my first reading it, I thought there would have been more policy in leaving the World altogether ignorant of the motives of the Rebellion, than in offering such false and frivolous reasons in support of it; and I flatter myself, that before I have finished this letter, your Lordship will be of the same mind. But I beg leave, first to make a few remarks upon its rise and progress.

I have often heard men, (who I believe were free from party influence) express their wishes, that the claims of the Colonies to an exemption from the authority of Parliament in imposing taxes had been conceded; because they had no doubts that America would have submitted in all other cases; and so this unhappy Rebellion, which has already proved fatal to many hundreds of the Subjects of the Empire, and probably will to many thousands more, might have been prevented.

The Acts for imposing Duties and Taxes may have accelerated the Rebellion, and if this could have been foreseen, perhaps, it might have been good policy to have omitted or deferred them; but I am of opinion, that if no Taxes or Duties had been laid upon the Colonies, other pretences would have been found for [4] exception to the authority of Parliament. The body of the people in the Colonies, I know, were easy and quiet. They felt no burdens. They were attached, indeed, in every Colony to their own particular Constitutions, but the Supremacy of Parliament over the whole gave them no concern. They had been happy under it for an hundred years past: They feared no imaginary evils for an hundred years to come. But there were men in each of the principal Colonies, who had independence in view, before any of those Taxes were laid, or proposed, which have since been the ostensible cause of resisting the execution of Acts of Parliament. Those men have conducted the Rebellion in the several stages of it, until they have removed the constitutional powers of Government in each Colony, and have assumed to themselves, with others, a supreme authority over the whole.

Their designs of Independence began soon after the reduction of Canada, relying upon the future cession of it by treaty. They could have no other pretence to a claim of independence, and they made no other at first, than what they called the natural rights of mankind, to chuse their own forms of Government, and change them when they please. This, they were soon convinced, would not be sufficient to draw the people from their attachment to constitutions under which they had so long been easy and happy: Some grievances, real or imaginary, were therefore necessary. They were so far from holding Acts for laying Duties to be unconstitutional, and, as has been since alledged, meer nullities, that in Massachusetts Bay the General Assembly, about the year 1762, ordered an Action to be brought against the Officers of the Customs, for charges made in the Court of Admiralty, which had caused a diminution of the part of forfeitures to the Province, by virtue of what is called the Sugar Act, passed in the sixth year of George the Second. Surely they would not deny the authority of Parliament to lay the Duty, while they were suing for their part of the penalty for the non-payment of it.

[5] Their first attempt was against the Courts of Admiralty, which they pronounced unconstitutional, whose judgements, as well as jurisdiction, they endeavored to bring into examen before the Courts of Common Law, and a Jury chosen from among the people: About the same time, a strong opposition was formed against Writs of Assistants, granted to the Officers of the Customs by the Supreme Courts, and this opposition

finally prevailed in all the Colonies, except two or three, against, and in defiance of, an Act of Parliament which required the Supreme Courts to grant these writs.

It does not, however, appear that there was any regular plan formed for attaining to Independence, any further than that every fresh incident which could be made to serve the purpose, by alienating the affections of the Colonies from the Kingdom, should be improved accordingly. One of these incidents happened in the year 1764. This was the Act of Parliament granting certain duties on goods in the British Colonies, for the support of Government, etc. At the same time a proposal was made in Parliament, to lay a stamp duty upon certain writings in the Colonies; but this was deferred until the next Session, that the Agents of the Colonies might notify the several Assemblies in order to their proposing any way, to them more eligible, for raising a sum for the same purpose with that intended by a stamp duty. The Colony of Massachusetts Bay was more affected by the Act for granting duties, than any other Colony. More molasses, the principal article from which any duty could arise, was distilled into spirits in that Colony than in all the rest. The Assembly of Massachusetts Bay, therefore, was the first that took any publick of the Act, and the first which ever took exception to the right of Parliament to impose Duties or Taxes on the Colonies, whilst they had no representatives in the House of Commons. This they did in a letter to their Agent in the summer of 1764, which they took care to print and publish before it was possible for him to receive it. And in this letter they recommend to him a pamphlet, wrote by one of their [6] members, in which there are proposals for admitting representatives from the Colonies to fit in the House of Commons.

I have this special reason, my Lord, for taking notice of this Act of the Massachusetts Assembly; that though an American representation is thrown out as an expedient which might obviate the objections to Taxes upon the Colonies, yet it was only intended to amuse the authority in England; and as soon as it was known to have its advocates here, it was renounced by the colonies, and even by the Assembly of the Colony which first proposed it, as utterly impracticable. In every stage of the Revolt, the same disposition has always appeared. No precise, unequivocal terms of submission to the authority of Parliament in any case, have ever been offered by any Assembly. A concession has only produced a further demand, and I verily believe if every thing had been granted short of absolute Independence, they would not have been contented; for this was not the object from the beginning. One of the most noted among the

American clergy, prophesied eight years ago, that within eight years from that time, the Colonies would be formed into three distinct independent Republics, Northern, Middle, and Southern. I could give your Lordship many irrefragable proofs of this determined design, but I reserve them for a future letter, the subject of which shall be the rise and progress of the Rebellion in each of the Colonies.

Soon after the intention of raising monies in America for the purpose of a revenue was known, the promoters of Independence, and Revolt, settled certain principles of polity, such as they thought would be best adapted to their purpose.

"The authority of Parliament over the Colonists ceased upon their leaving the Kingdom. Every degree of subjection is therefore voluntary, and ought to continue no longer than the authority shall be for the public good.

"If there had been no express *compact* by charters, or implied by submitting to be governed under Royal Commissions, the Colonists would be under no obligations to acknowledge the King of Great Britain as their Sovereign, [7] and this obligation must cease when he shall cease to perform his part of the conditions of the compact.

"As every Colony, by charters or by Royal Commissions, was constituted with special legislative powers to raise monies by Taxes, Duties, &c. no monies ought to be raised from the inhabitants, by any other powers than the several legislatures.

"As the Colonies were settled by encouragement from, and some at great expense of, the Kingdom, and principally for commercial purposes, subjection to *necessary* and *reasonable* Acts for regulating commerce ought to be specially acknowledged.

"Other Acts to be submitted to, or not, as they may, or may not, be for the benefit of the Colonies."

These principles of Government in Colonies must soon work an Independence.

To carry them to effect, Confederacies were formed by the chiefs of the revolters in each Colony; and Conventions were held by Delegates when judged necessary. Subjects for controversy in opposition to Government were fought for in each of the Colonies, to irritate and inflame the minds of the people, and dispose them to revolt: Dissentions and commotions in any Colony, were cherished and increased, as furnishing proper matter to work upon: For the same purpose, fictitious letters were published, as having been received from England, informing of the designs of ministry, and even of Bills being before the Parliament for introducing into the Colonies arbitrary Government, heavy Taxes, and other cruel oppressions: Every legal measure for suppressing illicit trade was represented as illegal and grievous; and the people were called upon to resist it: A correspondence was carried on with persons in England, promoters of the revolt, whose intelligence and advice from time to time were of great use: Persons in England of superior rank and characters, but in opposition to the measures of administration, were courted and deceived, by false professions; and the real intentions of the revolters were concealed: The tumults, riots, contempt, [8] and defiance of law in England, were urged to encourage and justify the like disorders in the Colonies, and to annihilate the powers of Government there.

Many thousands of people who were before good and loyal subjects, have been deluded, and by degrees induced to rebel against the best of Princes, and the mildest of Governments.

Governors and other servants of the Crown, and Officers of Government, with such as adhered to them, have been removed and banished under pretence of their being the instruments of promoting ministerial tyranny and arbitrary power; and finally the people have subjected themselves to the most cruel oppressions of fifty or sixty Despots.

It will cause greater prolixity to analize the various parts of this Declaration, than to recite the whole. I will therefore present it to your Lordship's view in distinct paragraphs, with my remarks, in order as the paragraphs are published.

In Congress, July 4, 1776

A Declaration by the Representatives of the United States of America in General Congress assembled.

When in the course of human Events, it becomes necessary for one People to dissolve the political bands which have connected them with another, and to assume among the Powers of the earth, the separate and equal Station to which the Laws of nature and of nature's God entitle them, a decent respect to the opinions of mankind requires that they should declare the causes which impel them to the separation.

WE hold these truths to be self-evident—That all Men are created equal, that they are endowed by their Creator with certain unalienable rights, that among these are life, liberty, and the pursuit of happiness, that to secure these rights, governments are instituted among men, deriving their just powers from the consent of the governed; and whenever [, that whenever] any form of government becomes destructive of these ends, it is the right of the people to alter or to abolish it, and to institute new government, laying its foundation on such

principles, and organizing its powers in such form as to them shall
seem most likely to effect their safety and happiness. Prudence, [9]
indeed, will dictate that governments long established should not be
changed for light and transient causes; and accordingly all experi-
ence hath shewn, that Mankind are more disposed to suffer, while
evils are sufferable, than to right themselves by abolishing the forms
to which they are accustomed. But when a long train of abuses and
usurpations, pursuing invariably the same object, evinces a design to
reduce them under absolute despotism, it is their right, it is their
duty, to throw off such government, and to provide new guards for
their future security. Such has been the patient sufferance of these
Colonies, and such is now the necessity which constrains them to
alter their former systems of Government. The History of the present
King of Great Britain is a history of repeated injuries and usurpa-
tions, all having in direct object the establishment of an absolute tyr-
anny over these States. To prove this, let facts be submitted to a
candid world.

They begin my Lord, with a false hypothesis, that the colonies are one
distinct people, and the kingdom another, connected by *political* bands.
The Colonies, *politically* considered, never were a *distinct* people from
the kingdom. There never has been but one *political* band, and that was
just the same before the first Colonists emigrated as it has been ever
since, the Supreme Legislative Authority, which hath essential right, and
is indispensably bound to keep all parts of the Empire entire, until there
may be a separation consistent with the general good of the Empire, of
which good, from the nature of government, this authority must be the
sole judge. I should therefore be impertinent, if I attempted to shew in
what case a *whole people* may be justified in rising up in oppugnation to
the powers of government, altering or abolishing them, and substituting,
in whole or in part, new powers in their stead; or in what sense all men
are created equal; or how far life, liberty, and the *pursuit of happiness*
may be said to be unalienable; only I could wish to ask the Delegates of
Maryland, Virginia, and the Carolinas, how their Constituents justify the
depriving more than an hundred thousand Africans of their rights to liberty, and [10] *the pursuit of happiness*, and in some degree to their
lives, if these rights are so absolutely unalienable; nor shall I attempt to
confute the absurd notions of government, or to expose the equivocal or
inconclusive expressions contained in this Declaration; but rather to shew
the false representation made of the facts which are alledged to be the
evidence of injuries and usurpations, and the special motives to Rebel-

lion. There are many of them, with designs, left obscure; for as soon as they are developed, instead of justifying, they rather aggravate the criminality of this Revolt.

The first in order, *He has refused his assent to laws the most wholesome and necessary for the public good*; is of so general a nature, that it is not possible to conjecture to what laws or to what Colonies it refers. I remember no laws which any Colony has been restrained from passing, so as to cause any complaint of grievance, except those for issuing a fraudulent paper currency, and making it a legal tender; but this is a restraint which for many years past has been laid on Assemblies by an act of Parliament, since which such laws cannot have been offered to the King for his allowance. I therefore believe this to be a general charge, without any particulars to support it; fit enough to be placed at the head of a list of imaginary grievances.

The laws of England are or ought to be the laws of its Colonies. To prevent a deviation further than the local circumstances of any Colony may make necessary, all Colony laws are to be laid before the King; and if disallowed, they then become of no force. Rhode-Island, and Connecticut, claim by Charters, an exemption from this rule, and as their laws are never presented to the King, they are out of the question. Now if the King is to approve of all laws, or which is the same thing, of all which the people judge for the public good, for we are to presume they pass no other, this reserve in all Charters and Commissions is futile. This Charge is still more inexcusable, because I am well informed, the disallowance of Colony laws has been much more frequent in preceding reigns, than in the present.

[11] *He has forbidden his Governors to pass Laws of immediate and pressing Importance, unless suspended in their Operation till his Assent should be obtained; and when so suspended, he has utterly neglected to attend [to] them.*

Laws, my Lord, are in force in the Colonies, as soon as a Governor has given his assent, and remain in force until the King's disallowance is signed. Some laws may have their full effect before the King's pleasure can be known. Some may injuriously affect the property of the subject; and some may be prejudicial to the prerogative of the Crown, and to the trade, manufactures and shipping of the kingdom. Governors have been instructed, long before the present or the last reign, not to consent to such laws, unless with a clause suspending their operations until the pleasure of the King shall be known. I am sure your Lordship will think that nothing is more reasonable. In Massachusetts Bay, the Assembly would never pass a law with a suspending clause. To pass laws which must have their whole operation, or which must cause some irreparable mischief before the King's pleasure can be known, would be an usurpation of the People upon the Royal Prerogative: To cause the operation of such laws to be suspended until the King can signify his pleasure by force of instructions, similar to what has been given in all former Reigns, can never be charged as an usurpation upon the rights of the People.

I dare say, my Lord, that if there has ever been an instance of any laws lying longer than necessary before the King's pleasure has been signified, it has been owing to the inattention in some of the servants of the Crown, and that upon proper application any grievance would have been immediately redressed.

He has refused to pass other laws for [the] *accommodation of large districts of People, unless those People would relinquish the rights* [right] *of Representation in the legislature, a right* inestimable *to them, and formidable to tyrants only.*

[12] We shall find, my Lord, that Massachusetts Bay is more concerned in this Declaration than any other Colony. This article respects that Colony alone. By its charter, a legislature is constituted: The Governor is appointed by the King—The Council, consisting of twenty-eight members, were appointed, in the first instance by the King, but afterwards are to be elected annually by the two Houses—The House of Representatives is to consist of two members elected annually by each town, but the number of the House is nevertheless made subject to future regulations by acts of the General Assembly. Besides the Council, the Civil Officers of the Government are also to be annually elected by the two Houses. It appeared in a course of years, that by multiplying towns, the House of Representatives had increased to double the number of which it consisted at first. Their importance in all elections was increased in proportion; for the number of the Council continued the same as at first. To prevent further deviation from the spirit of the Charter, an instruction was then first given to the Governors, not to consent to laws for making new towns so as to increase the number of the House; unless there should be a clause in the law to suspend its operation, until the King signifies his pleasure upon it. But here, my Lord, lies the most shameful falsity of this article. No Governor ever refused to consent to a law for making a new town, even without a suspending clause, if provision was made that the inhabitants of the new town should continue to join with the old, or with any other town contiguous or near to it, in the choice of Representatives; so that there never was the least intention to deprive a single inhabitant of the right of being represented; and, in fact, such provision has ever been

made, except where the inhabitants of the new town chose to forego the right, which we must suppose they did not think *inestimable*, rather than pay the wages of their Representatives. This has been the case in several instances, and it is notorious that the Assembly of that Province have [13] made it their practice, from year to year, to lay fines on their towns for not chusing Representatives. This is a wilful misrepresentation made for the sake of the brutal insult at the close of the article.

He has called together legislative bodies at places unusual, uncomfortable, and distant from the depository of their public records, for the sole purpose of fatiguing them into compliance with his measures.

To the same Colony this article also has respect. Your Lordship must remember the riotous, violent opposition to Government in the Town of Boston, which alarmed the whole Kingdom, in the year 1768. Four Regiments of the King's forces were ordered to that Town, to be aiding to the Civil Magistrate in restoring and preserving peace and order. The House of Representatives, which was then sitting in the Town, remonstrated to the Governor against posting Troops there, as being an invasion of their rights. He thought proper to adjourn them to Cambridge, where the House had frequently sat at their own desire, when they had been alarmed with fear of small pox in Boston; the place therefor was not unusual. The public rooms of the College, were convenient for the Assembly to sit in, and the private houses of the Inhabitants for the Members to lodge in; it therefore was not *uncomfortable*. It was within four miles of the Town of Boston, and less *distant* than any other Town fit for the purpose.

When this step, taken by the Governor, was known in England, it was approved, and conditional instructions were given to continue the Assembly at Cambridge. The House of Representatives raised the most frivolous of objections against the authority of the Governor to remove the Assembly from Boston, but proceeded, nevertheless, to the business of the Session as they used to do. In the next Session, without any new cause, the Assembly refused to do any business unless removed to Boston. This was making themselves judges of the place, and by the same reason, of the time of holding the Assembly, instead of the Governor, [14] who thereupon was instructed not to remove them to Boston, so long as they continued to deny his authority to carry them to any other place.

They *fatigued* the Governor by adjourning from day to day, and refusing to do business one session after another, while he gave his constant attendance to no purpose; and this they make the King's *fatiguing* them to compel them to comply with his measures.

A brief narrative of this unimportant dispute between an American Governor and his Assembly, needs an apology to your Lordship; how

ridiculous then do those men make themselves, who offer it to the world
as a ground to justify rebellion?

He has dissolved Representative Houses repeatedly for opposing
with manly firmness his Invasions of [on] *the Rights of the People.*

Contention between Governors and their Assemblies have caused dissolutions of such Assemblies, I suppose, in all the Colonies, in former as
well as later times. I recollect but one instance of the dissolution of an
Assembly by special order from the King, and that was in Massachusetts
Bay. In 1768, the House of Representatives passed a vote or resolve, in
prosecution of the plan of Independence, incompatible with the subordination of the Colonies to the supreme authority of the Empire; and directed their Speaker to send a copy of it in circular letters to the Assemblies of the other Colonies, inviting them to avow the principles of the
resolve, and to join in supporting them. No Government can long subsist,
which admits of combinations of the subordinate powers against the supreme. This proceeding was therefore, justly deemed highly unwarrantable; and indeed it was the beginning of that unlawful confederacy, which
has gone on until it has caused at least temporary Revolt of all the Colonies which joined in it.

The Governor was instructed to require the House of Representatives,
in their next Session to rescind or disavow this resolve, and if they refused, to dissolve them, as the only way to prevent their prosecuting the
plan of [15] Rebellion. They delayed a definitive answer, and he indulged
them, until they had finished all the business of the Province, and then
appeared his *manly firmness* in a rude answer and a peremptory refusal
to comply with the King's demand. Thus my Lord, the regular use of the
prerogative in suppressing a begun Revolt, is urged as a grievance to
justify the Revolt.

HE has refused for a long time, after such dissolutions to cause
others to be erected [elected] *whereby the legislative powers, incapable*
of annihilation, have returned to the people at large for their exer-
cise; the state remaining in the mean time exposed to all the dangers
of invasions [invasion] *from without, and Convulsions within.*

This is connected with the last preceding article, and must relate to the
same Colony only; for no other ever presumed, until the year 1774,
when the general dissolution of the established government in all the
Colonies was taking place, to convene an Assembly, without the Governor, by the meer act of the People.

In less than three months after the Governor had dissolved the Assembly of Massachusetts Bay, the town of Boston, the first mover in all affairs
of this nature, applied to him to call another Assembly. The Governor

thought he was the judge of the proper time for calling an Assembly, and refused. The Town, without delay, chose their former members, whom they called a *Committee*, instead of Representatives; and they sent circular letters to all the other towns in the Province inviting them to chuse *Committees* also; and all these *Committees* met in what they called a *Convention*, and chose the Speaker of the last house their *Chairman*. Here was a House of Representatives in everything but name; and they were proceeding upon business in the town of Boston, but were interrupted by the arrival of two or three regiments, and a spirited message from the Governor, and in two or three days returned to their homes.

This vacation of three months was the *long time* the people waited before they exercised their unalienable powers; the *Invasions from without* were the arrival or expectation of three or four regiments sent by the [16] King to aid the Civil Magistrate in preserving the peace; and the *Convulsions within* were the tumults, riots and acts of violence which this Convention was called, not to suppress but to encourage.

He has endeavoured to prevent the population of these States; for that purpose obstructing the laws for naturalization of foreigners; refusing to pass others to encourage their migration[s] hither, and raising the conditions of new appropriations of lands.

By this and the next article, we have a short relief from the Province of Massachusetts Bay. I cannot conceive that the subjects in the Colonies would have had any cause of complaint if there never had been any encouragement given to foreigners to settle among them; and it was an act of meer favour to the Colonies which admitted foreigners to a claim of naturalization after a residence of seven years. How has the King obstructed the operation of this act? In no other way than by refusing his assent to colony acts for further encouragement. Nothing can be more regular and constitutional. Shall any other than the supreme authority of the Empire judge upon what terms foreigners may be admitted to the privilege of natural born subjects? Parliament alone may pass acts for this purpose. If there had been further conditions annexed to the grants of unappropriated lands, than have ever yet been, or even a total restriction of such grants when the danger of Revolt was foreseen, it might have been a prudent measure; it certainly was justifiable, and nobody has any right to complain.

He has obstructed the administration of justice, by refusing his assent to laws for establishing judiciary powers.

I was, My Lord, somewhat at a loss, upon first reading this article, to what transaction or to what Colony it could refer. I soon found, that the Colony must be North Carolina; and that the transaction, referred to, is a reproach upon the Colony, which the Congress have most wickedly perverted to cast reproach upon the King.

[17] In most, if not all, of the Colonies, laws have passed to enable creditors to attach the effects of absent or absconding debtors; and to oblige the trustees of such debtors to disclose upon oath the effects in their hands; and also all persons indebted to them to disclose their debts. Whatever these laws may have been in their original intention, they have proved most iniquitous in their operation. The creditors, who first come to the knowledge of any effects, seize them to the exclusion even of the other creditors in the Colony; and the creditors in England, or at the greatest distance, stand still a worse chance. I have known in some Colonies, instances of attachments of the effects of bankrupts in England, which by force of these laws have been made, by the American creditors, to the full satisfaction of their debts, when the creditors in England have received a few shillings only on the pound. This frustrates our own bankrupt laws. I believe they have never had any equitable bankrupt laws in any Colony, of any duration: In New York, they have done more towards them than any other Colony.

These laws for attachments in most of the Colonies were temporary. The Governors were very properly instructed not to consent to the revival of them, or not without a suspending clause. In North Carolina, the law for attachments was tacked to, or was part of, the same law which established their Courts of Justice. The Governor, as he ought to have done if he had received no instruction, refused a bill for reviving the law, because the provision for attachments was part of it: The Assembly refused to pass the bill without the provision, and in this way determined they would have no Courts of Justice, unless they were such as should be bound to support these iniquitous attachments, peculiarly injurious to British and other distant creditors, and very unequal to the creditors within the Colony.

All this was fully known to the Congress, who, notwithstanding, have most falsely represented the re–[18]gular use of the prerogative to prevent injustice, as an obstruction of justice.

He has made Judges dependent on his will alone, for the tenure of their offices, and the amount and payment of their salaries.

The Americans claim a right to the English constitution and laws, as they stood when the Colonies were planted. The Judges of England were then dependent on the Crown for their continuance in office, as well as for their salaries. The Judges in America, except the Charter–Colonies, have always been dependent on the Crown for their continuance in office; and in some Colonies, the salaries of the Chief Justice, and sometimes the other Judges, have been paid by the Crown, and the Colonies have considered it as an act of favour shewn to them.

There has been a change in the constitution of England in respect of the tenure of the office of the Judges. How does this give a claim to America? It will be said, the reason in both cases is the same. This will not be allowed, and until the King shall judge it so, there can be no room for exception to his retaining his prerogative.

And for the salaries, they are *fixed* and do not depend upon the behaviour of the Judges, nor have there ever been any instances of salaries being with-held. If the Assemblies in the Colonies would have *fixed* the like salaries on their Judges, no provision would ever have been made by the Crown; it being immaterial by whom the salary is paid, provided the payment be made sure and certain.

This is a complaint against the King, for not making a change in the constitution of the Colonies, though there is not so much as a pretence that there has been the least grievance felt in any Colony for want of this change; nor has there been any complaint even of danger, in any Colony, except Massachusetts Bay.

[19] *He has erected a Multitude of new offices, and sent hither Swarms of officers to harass our people, and eat out their substance.*

I know of no new offices erected in America in the present reign, except those of the Commissioners of the Customs and their dependents. Five Commissioners were appointed, and four Surveyors General dismissed; perhaps fifteen to twenty clerks and under officers were necessary for this board more than the Surveyors had occasion for before: Land and tide waiters, weighers, &c. were known officers before; the Surveyors used to encrease or lessen the number as the King's service required, and the Commissioners have done no more. Thirty or forty additional officers in the whole Continent, are the *Swarms* which eat out the substance of the boasted number of three millions of people.

Cases had often happened in America, which Surveyors General had not authority to decide. The American merchants complained of being obliged to apply to the Commissioners of the Customs in London. The distance caused long delay, as well as extraordinary charge. A Board in America, was intended to remove the cause of these complaints, as well as to keep the inferior officers of the Customs to their duty. But no powers were given to this Board more than the Commissioners in London had before; and none but illicit traders ever had any reason to complain of grievances; and they of no other than of being better watched than they had ever been before. At this time the authority of Parliament to pass

Acts for regulating commerce was acknowledged, but every measure for carrying such Acts into execution was pronounced an injury, and usurpation, and all the effects prevented.

He has kept among us, in times of peace, standing armies, without the consent of our legislatures.

This is too nugatory to deserve any remark. He has kept no armies among them without the consent of the Supreme Legislature. It is begging the question, [20] to suppose that this authority was not sufficient without the aid of their own Legislatures.

He has affected to render the Military independent of and superior to the Civil Power.

When the Subordinate Civil Powers of the Empire became Aiders of the people in acts of Rebellion, the King, as well he might, has employed the Military Power to reduce those rebellious Civil Powers to their constitutional subjection to the Supreme Civil Power. In no other sense has he ever *affected* to render the Military independent of, and superior to, the Civil Power.

He has combined with others to subject us to a jurisdiction foreign to our Constitution and unacknowledged by our laws; giving his assent to their pretended Acts of [Acts of pretended] *Legislation.*

This is a strange way of defining the part which the Kings of England take in conjunction with the Lords and Commons in passing Acts of Parliament. But why is our present Sovereign to be distinguished from all his predecessors since Charles the Second? Even the Republic which they affected to copy after, and Oliver, their favourite, because an Usurper, *combined* against them also. And then, how can a jurisdiction submitted to for more than a century be *foreign* to their constitution? And is it not the grossest prevarication to say this jurisdiction is *unacknowledged* by their laws, when all Acts of Parliament which respect them, have at all times been their rule of law in all their judicial proceedings? If this is not enough; their own subordinate legislatures have repeatedly in addresses, and resolves, in the most express terms *acknowledged* the supremacy of Parliament; and so late as 1764, before the conductors of this Rebellion had settled their plan, the House of Representatives of the leading Colony made a public declaration in an address to their Governor, that, although they humbly apprehended they might propose their objections, to the late Act of Parliament for granting certain duties in the British Colonies and Plantations in America, yet [21] they at the same time, *acknowledged* that it was their duty to yield obedience to it while it continued unrepealed.

If the jurisdiction of Parliament is foreign to their Constitution, what need of specifying instances, in which they have been subjected to it?

Every Act must be an usurpation and injury. They must then be mentioned, my Lord, to shew, hypothetically, that even if Parliament had jurisdiction, such Acts would be a partial and injurious use of it. I will consider them to know whether they are so or not.

For quartering large bodies of armed troops among us.

When troops were employed in America, in the last reign, to protect the Colonies against the French invasion, it was necessary to provide against mutiny and desertion, and to secure proper quarters. Temporary Acts of Parliament were passed for that purpose, and submitted to in the Colonies. Upon the peace, raised ideas took place in the Colonies, of their own importance, and caused a reluctance against Parliamentary authority, and an opposition to the Acts for quartering troops, not because the provision made was in itself unjust or unequal, but because they were Acts of a Parliament whose authority was denied. The provision was as similar to that in England as the state of the Colonies would admit.

For protecting them by a mock trial from punishment, for any murder[s] which they should commit on the Inhabitants of these States.

It is beyond human wisdom to form a system of laws so perfect as to be adapted to all cases. It is happy for a state, that there can be an interposition of legislative power in those cases, where an adherence to established rules would cause injustice. To try men before a biassed and predetermined Jury would be *a mock trial*. To prevent this, the Act of Parliament, complained of, was passed. Surely, if in any case Parliament may interpose and alter the general rule of law, it may in this. America has not been distinguished from other parts of the Empire. Indeed, the removal of trials [22] for the sake of unprejudiced disinterested Juries, is altogether consistent with the spirit of our laws, and the practice of courts in changing the venue from one county to another.

For cutting off our trade with all parts of the world.

Certainly, my Lord, this could not be a *cause* of Revolt. The Colonies had revolted from the Supreme Authority, to which, by their constitutions, they were subject, before the Act was passed. A Congress had assumed an authority over the whole, and had rebelliously prohibited all commerce with the rest of the Empire. This act, therefore, will be considered by the *candid world*, as a proof of the reluctance in government against what is dernier* resort in every state, and as a milder measure to bring the Colonies to a re–union with the rest of the Empire.

---

* last

For imposing taxes on us without our consent.

How often has your Lordship heard it said, that the Americans are willing to submit to the authority of Parliament in all cases except that of taxes? Here we have a declaration made to the world of the causes which have impelled separation, and that if any one cause was distinguished from another, special notice would be taken of it. That of taxes seems to have been in danger of being forgot. It comes in late, and in as slight a manner as is possible. And I know, my Lord, that these men, in the early days of their opposition to Parliament, have acknowledged that they pitched upon this subject of taxes, because it was most alarming to the people, every man perceiving immediately that he is personally affected by it; and it has, therefore, in all communities, always been a subject more danger-ous to government than any other, to make innovation in; but as their friends in England had fell in with the idea that Parliament could have no right to tax them because not represented, they thought it best it should be believed they were willing to submit to other acts of legislation [23] until this point of taxes could be gained; owing at the same time, that they could find no fundamentals in the English Constitution, which made representation more necessary in acts for taxes, than acts for any other purpose; and that the world must have a mean opinion of their under-standing, if they should rebel rather than pay a duty of three–pence *per* pound on tea, and yet be content to submit to an act which restrained them from making a nail to shoe their own horses. Some of them, my Lord, imagine they are as well acquainted with the nature of government, and with the constitution and history of England, as many of their parti-sans in the kingdom; and they will sometimes laugh at the doctrine of fundamentals from which even Parliament itself can never deviate; and they say it has been often held and denied merely to serve the cause of party, and that it must be so until these unalterable fundamentals shall be ascertained; that the great Patriots in the reign of King Charles the Sec-ond, Lord Russell, Hampden, Maynard, &c. whose memories they rever-ence, declared their opinions, that there were no bounds to the power of Parliament by any fundamentals whatever, and that even the hereditary succession to the Crown might be, as it since has been, altered by Act of Parliament; whereas they who call themselves Patriots in the present day have held it to be a fundamental, that there can be no taxation without representation, and that Parliament cannot alter it.

But as this doctrine was held by their friends, and was of service to their cause until they were prepared for total independence, they ap-peared to approve it: As they have now no further occasion for it, they take no more notice of an act for imposing taxes than of many other acts;

for a distinction in the authority of Parliament in any particular case, cannot serve their claim to a general exemption, which they are now preparing to assert.

For depriving us, in many cases, of the benefit[s] *of a trial* [of trial] *by jury.*

[24] Offences against the Excise Laws, and against one or more of late Acts of Trade, are determined without a Jury in England. It appears by the law books of some of the Colonies, that offences against their Laws of Excise, and some other Laws, are also determined without a Jury; and civil actions, under a sum limited, are determined by a Justice of the Peace. I recollect no cases in which trials by Juries are taken away in America, by Acts of Parliament, except such as are tried by the Courts of Admiralty, and these are either for breaches of the Acts of trade, or trespasses upon the King's woods. I take no notice of the Stamp Act, because it was repealed soon after it was designed to take place.

I am sorry, my Lord, that I am obliged to say, there could not be impartial trials by Juries in either of these cases. All regulation of commerce must cease, and the King must be deprived of all the trees reserved for the Royal Navy, if no trials can be had but by Jury. The necessity of the case justified the departure from the general rule; and in the reign of King William the Third, jurisdiction, in both these cases, was given to the Admiralty by Acts of Parliament; and it has ever since been part of the constitution of the Colonies; and it may be said, to the honour of those Courts, that there have been very few instances of complaint of injury from their decrees. Strange that in the reign of King George the Third, this jurisdiction should suddenly become an usurpation and ground of Revolt.

For Transporting us beyond seas to be tried for pretended offences.

I know of no Act, but that of the 12th of the present reign, to prevent the setting fire to his Majesty's Ships, Docks, Arsenals, &c. to which this article can refer—But are these *pretended* offences?

By an Act of Parliament made in the 35th year of King Henry the Eighth, all treasons committed in any parts without the realm, may be tried in any county of England; and in the reign of Queen Anne, persons were condemned in England for offences against [25] this Act in America; but the Act does not comprehend felonies.

The offences against the last Act are made felony; and as it is most likely they should be committed in times of faction and party–rage, the Act leaves it in the power of the Crown to order the trial of any offence committed without the realm, either in the Colony, Island, Fort, where it may be committed, or in any County within the Realm.

An opinion prevailed in America, that this Act was occasioned by the burning of the King's Schooner, Gaspee, by people in the Colony of Rhode Island; but the Act had passed before that fact was committed, though it was not generally known in America, until some months after. The neglect of effectual inquiry into that offence, by the authority in Rhode Island Colony, shews that the Act was necessary; but when it passed, there does not appear to have been any special view to America, more than to the forts and settlements in Europe, Asia, or Africa.

For abolishing the free system of English laws in a neighbouring province, establishing therein an arbitrary Government, and enlarging its boundaries, so as to render it at once an example and fit instrument for introducing it [the same absolute Rule into these Colonies] *into their colonies.*

It would be impertinent to make any remarks upon the general fitness of the Quebec Act for the purposes for which it passed, seeing your Lordship has so lately fully considered and given your voice to it.

But what, my Lord, have the American Colonies to do with it? There are four New England Colonies: In two of them, both Governor and Council are annually elected by the body of the people; in a third, the Council is annually elected by the Assembly; in the fourth, both Governor and Council are appointed by the Crown: The three Charter Governments, four near a century past, have never felt, nor had any reason to fear, any change in their constitutions, from the example of the Fourth. Just as much reason have the Colonies in general to fear a change in their [26] several constitutions, no two of which are alike, from the example of Quebec.

With as little reason may they complain of the enlargement of the boundaries of Quebec. It was time to include the ungranted territory of America in some jurisdiction or other, to prevent further encroachment upon it. What claim could any of the Colonies have to a territory beyond their own limits? No other security against an improper settlement of this country could have been made equally judicious and unexceptionable. This exception is therefore utterly impertinent, and seems to proceed from disappointment in a scheme for engrossing the greatest part of this ungranted territory.

For taking away our Charters, abolishing our most valuable laws, [and] *altering fundamentally the forms of our Governments.*

For suspending our own legislatures, and declaring themselves [in]*vested with power, to legislate for us in all cases whatsoever.*

These two articles are so much of the same nature, that I consider them together. There has been no Colony Charter altered except that of Massachusetts Bay, and that in no respect, that I recollect, except that the appointment and power of the Council are made to conform to that of the Council of the other Royal Governments, and the laws which relate to grand and petit juries are made to conform to the general laws of the Realm.

The only instance of the suspension of any legislative power is that of the province of New York, for refusing to comply with an Act of Parliament for quartering the King's troops posted there for its protection and defence against the French and Indian enemies.

The exceptions, heretofore, have rather been to the authority of Parliament to revoke, or alter Charters, or legislative powers once granted and established, than to the injurious or oppressive use of the authority upon these occasions.

When parties run high, the most absurd doctrines, if a little disguised, are easily received, and embraced. [27] Thus, because in the Reign of Charles the First, resistance to Taxes imposed by the authority of the *King alone* was justifiable, and the contrary doctrine of having taken the names *Passive Obedience and Non–Resistance*, those terms became odious; therefore in the Reign of George the Third, resistance to Taxes imposed, by the *King, Lords and Commons*, upon America while not represented in Parliament, is justifiable also; and the contrary doctrine is branded with the odious terms of *Passive Obedience and Non–Resistance*; as if the latter case were analogous to the former. And because in the Reign of Charles the Second and James the Second, Royal Charters were deemed *sacred* and not to be revoked or altered at the will and pleasure of the *King alone*; therefore in the Reign of George the Third, they are *sacred* also, and not to be revoked nor altered by the authority of *Parliament*.

The common people who, relying upon the authority of others, confound cases together which are so essentially different, may be excused; but what excuse, my Lord, can be made for those men, in England as well as in America, who, by such fallacies, have misguided the people and provoked them to rebellion?

He has abdicated Government here, by declaring us out of his protection and waging War against us.

He has plundered our Seas, ravaged our Coasts, burnt our Towns and destroyed the Lives of our People.

He is, at this Time, transporting large Armies of foreign mercenaries to compleat the works of death, desolation, and tyranny, already begun with circumstances of cruelty and perfidy scarcely paralleled in the most barbarous ages, and totally unworthy the head of a civilized Nation.

He has constrained our fellow Citizens, taken captive on the high Seas, to bear arms against their Country, to become the executioners of their Friends and Brethren, or to fall themselves by their hands.

He has excited domestick [domestic] *insurrections amongst us and has endeavoured to bring on the Inhabitants of our frontiers, the merciless Indian Savages, whose known rule of warfare, is an undistinguished destruction of all ages, sexes and conditions.*

[28] These, my Lord, would be weighty charges from a *loyal and dutiful* people against an *unprovoked* Sovereign: They are more than the people of England pretended to bring against King James the Second, in order to justify the Revolution. Never was there an instance of more consummate effrontery. The Acts of a *justly incensed* Sovereign for suppressing a most *unnatural, unprovoked* Rebellion, are here assigned as the *causes* of this Rebellion. It is immaterial whether they are true or false. They are all short of the penalty of the laws which had been violated. Before the date of any one of them, the Colonists had as effectually renounced their allegiance by their deeds as they have since done by their words. They had displaced the civil and military officers appointed by the King's authority and set up others in their stead. They had new modelled their civil governments, and appointed a general government, independent of the King, over the whole. They had taken up arms, and made a public declaration of their resolution to defend themselves, against the forces employed to support his legal authority over them. To subjects, who had forfeited their lives by acts of Rebellion, every act of the Sovereign against them, which falls short of the forfeiture, is an act of favour. A most ungrateful return has been made for this favour. It has been improved to strengthen and confirm the Rebellion against him.

In every stage of these oppressions, we have petitioned for redress in the most humble terms; our repeated petitions have been answered only by repeated injury.

What these oppressions were your Lordship has seen, for we may fairly conclude, that every thing appears in this Declaration, which can give colour to this horrid Rebellion, so that these men can never complain of being condemned without a full hearing.

But does your Lordship recollect any petitions in the several stages of these pretended oppressions? Has there ever been a petition to the King?

—To give his Assent to these wholesome and necessary Laws to which he had refused it?

[29]—To allow his Governors to pass laws without a suspending clause, or without the people's relinquishing the right of representation?

—To withdraw his instructions for calling legislative bodies at unusual, uncomfortable and distant places?

—To allow Assemblies, which had been dissolved, by his order, to meet again?

—To pass laws to encourage the migration of foreigners?

—To consent to the establishment of judiciary Powers?

—To suffer Judges to be independent for the continuance of their offices and salaries?

—To vacate or disannul new erected offices?

—To withdraw his troops *in times of peace*, until it appeared that the reason for it was to give a free course to Rebellion?

And yet these, my Lord, are all the oppressions pretended to have been received from the King, except those *in combination* with the two Houses of Parliament; and they are all either grossly misrepresented, or so trivial and insignificant as to have been of no general notoriety in the time of them, or mere contests between Governors and Assemblies, so light and transient, as to have been presently forgot. All the petitions we have heard of, have been against Acts of the Supreme Legislature; and in all of them something has been inserted, or something has been done previous to them, with design to prevent their being received.

They have petitioned for the repeal of a law, because Parliament had not right to pass it. The receiving and granting the prayer of such petition, would have been considered as a renunciation of right; and from a renunciation in one instance, would have been inferred a claim to renunciation in all other instances. The repealing, or refraining from enacting any particular laws, or relieving from any kind of service, while a due submission to the laws in general shall be continued, and suitable return be made of other services, seems to be all which the Supreme Authority may grant, or the [30] people or any part of them, require. If anything, my Lord, short of Independence was the redress sought for, all has been granted which has been prayed for, and could be granted.

A Prince, whose character is thus marked, by every act which defines the [may define a] *tyrant; is unfit to be the ruler of a free people.*

Indignant resentment must seize the breast of every loyal subject. A tyrant, in modern language, means, not merely an absolute and arbitrary, but a cruel, merciless Sovereign. Have these men given an instance of any one Act in which the King has exceeded the just Powers of the Crown as limited by the English Constitution? Has he ever departed from known established laws, and substituted his own will as the rule of his actions? Has there ever been a Prince by whom subjects in rebellion, have been treated with less severity, or with longer forbearance?

Nor have we been wanting in Attention[s] to our British Brethren. We have warned them from time to time of attempts by their legislature, to extend an unwarrantable jurisdiction over us. We have reminded them of the circumstances of our emigration and settlement here. We have appealed to their native justice and magnanimity, and we have conjured them by the ties of our common kindred to disavow these usurpations, which, would inevitably interrupt our connections and correspondence. They too have been deaf to the voice of justice and of consanguinity. We must, therefore, acquiesce in the necessity, which denounces our separation, and hold them, as we hold the rest of mankind, Enemies in War, in Peace, Friends.

We therefore, the Representatives of the United States of America, in General Congress assembled, appealing to the Supreme Judge of the World for the rectitude of our intentions, do in the name and by the authority [by Authority] of the good People of these Colonies, solemnly publish and declare, That these United Colonies, are, and [of right] ought to be, Free and Independent States, and [States;] that they are absolved from all allegiance to the British Crown, and that all political Connection between them and the State of Great Britain, is and ought [31] to be totally dissolved, and that as free and Independent States, they have full power to levy War, conclude Peace, contract Alliances, establish Commerce, and to do all other Acts and things which Independent States may of right do. And for the support of this Declaration, with a firm Reliance on the protection of Divine Providence, we mutually pledge to each other, our Lives, our Fortunes and our sacred Honor. Signed by order and in behalf of the Congress.

John Hancock, President

They have, my Lord, in their late address to the people of Great Britain, fully avowed these principles of Independence, by declaring they will pay no obedience to the laws of the Supreme Legislature; they have also pretended, that these laws were the mandates of edicts of the Ministers, not the acts of a constitutional legislative power, and have endeavoured to persuade such as they called their British Brethren, to justify the Rebellion begun in America; and from thence they expected a general convulsion in the Kingdom, and that measures to compel a submission would in this way be obstructed. These expectations failing, after they had gone too far in acts of Rebellion to hope for impunity, they were under *necessity* of a separation, and of involving themselves, and all over whom they had usurped authority, in the distresses and horrors of war against that power from which they revolted, and against all who continued in their subjection and fidelity to it.

Gratitude, I am sensible, is seldom to be found in a community, but so sudden a revolt from the rest of the Empire, which had incurred so immense a debt, and with which it remains burdened, for the protection and defence of the Colonies, and at their most importunate request, is an instance of ingratitude no where to be paralleled.

Suffer me, my Lord, before I close this Letter, to observe, that though the professed reason for publishing the Declaration was a decent respect to the opinions of mankind, yet the real design was to reconcile the people of America to that Independence, which always before, they had been made to believe was not [32] intended. This design has too well succeeded. The people have not observed the fallacy in reasoning from the *whole* to *part*; nor the absurdity of making the *governed* to be *governors*. From a disposition to receive willingly complaints against Rulers, facts misrepresented have passed without examining. Discerning men have concealed their sentiments, because under the present *free* government in America, no man may, by writing or speaking, contradict any part of this Declaration, without being deemed an enemy to his country, and exposed to the rage and fury of the populace.

I have the honour to be,
    My Lord,
        Your Lordship's most humble,
           And most obedient servant.

To the Right Honourable
   The E— of —

London, October 15th, 1776.

Notes

Introduction

1   William Findley, *History of the Insurrection in the Four Western Counties of Pennsylvania* (Philadelphia: Samuel Harrison Smith, 1796), vi.

2   The earliest entry in America is for "self-governed," meaning, "Governed by one's self," in Noah Webster, *An American Dictionary of the English* Language; *First Edition in Octavo 2* (New Haven, Connecticut: B. L. Hamlen for Noah Webster, 1841), 562. See also *An American Dictionary of the English Language by Noah Webster; Revised and Enlarged* (Springfield, Massachusetts: G. and C. Merriam Company, 1854), 1004; *Webster's New International Dictionary of the English Language,* 2d edition, unabridged (Springfield, Massachusetts: G. and C. Merriam Company, 1959), 767.

3   The most insightful and succinct discussion of this earlier understanding of self-government is to be found in Joyce Appleby's "The Radical *Double-Entendre* in the Right to Self-Government," in James and Margaret Jacobs, eds., *The Origins of Anglo-American Radicalism* (Boston: George Allen Unwin, 1984), 275–283. Her essay serves as a cautionary reminder about using terms like "earlier" and "older" to describe definitions of self-government. By "older" I mean simply the definition that was operative at the time of the founding of the American republic, but clearly the *earliest* ideas, as she notes, were those of the ancient writers of Greco-Roman times who tended to see self-government in mainly collective, corporate terms. As Appleby argues, it was the individual meaning of self-government that was a radical innovation in the seventeenth century, and it was this idea that took deep root in American thought. The great irony today is that we have returned to the ancient idea apparently unaware of what we have lost.

   One difficulty with Appleby's essay, however, concerns her use of the word "autonomous" to describe the early liberal conception of the individual. The earliest use of "autonomous" in the English language appears to go back to the mid seventeenth century, and at that time, its meaning was synonymous with self-government as given above. But the current definition of the word has moved even more profoundly away from its early modern designation than has "self-government." Autonomous can now mean "self-contained." To employ this word risks the false impression that early liberalism favored an atomized view of the individual. Appleby lends some credence to this charge by insisting that early liberals hoped to free individuals from all manner of institutional restraints, including religion and the family. More accurately, I would say, the goal was to liberate the individual from the intrusions of state power into the legitimate institutions of civil society, not to attack institutions in general. Such was the case of liberal opposition to the political institutions of primogeniture and official religious establishments. Far different was the early liberal's perception of the complex matrix of voluntary institutions in civil society. These associations were seen to be the manifestations of the natural social order (see Chapter 3) that grew out of the self-governing capacity of individuals. Far from wishing to overturn these institutions, liberals hoped to enhance their flourishing in society by limiting the abuse of power by governments. For the history and meaning of autonomous and autonomy see *The Oxford English Dictionary*, 2nd edition, vol. 1 (Oxford: Clarendon Press, 1989), 807. For its definition as "self-contained" see *Webster's Ninth New Collegiate Dictionary* (Springfield, Massachusetts: Merriam-Webster Inc., 1989), 118.

4   For examples of the varieties of Lockean liberal interpretation see: Carl Becker, *The Declaration of Independence: A Study in the History of Political Ideas* (New York: Harcourt Brace and Co., 1922; reprint New York: Alfred A. Knopf, 1945; New York, Vintage Books, 1970); Louis Hartz, *The Liberal Tradition in America* (New York: Harcourt Brace and Co., 1955); Harry V. Jaffa, *How to Think About the American Revolution* (Durham, North Carolina: Carolina Academic Press, 1976); Thomas L. Pangel, *The Spirit of Modern Republicanism: The Moral Vision of the American Founders and the Philosophy of John Locke* (Chicago: University of Chicago Press, 1988); Michael Zuckert, *The Natural Rights Republic: Studies in the Foundation of the American Political Tradition* (Notre Dame, Indiana: University of Notre Dame Press, 1996); Steven M. Dworetz, *The Unvarnished Doctrine: Locke, Liberalism, and the American Revolution* (Durham, Duke University Press; 1990). For a view that stresses the importance of liberal political economy, see the essays of Joyce Appleby, *Liberalism and Republicanism in the Historical Imagination* (Cambridge, Massachusetts: Harvard University Press, 1992). For a Christian communitarian reading see the recent work by Barry Alan Shain, *The Myth of American Individualism: The Protestant Origins of American Political Thought* (Princeton, New Jersey: Princeton University Press, 1994). For a Christian interpretation that stresses the "Miltonic" character of the Declaration, see John Alvis, "Milton and the Declaration of Independence," *Interpretations* 25 (Spring 1998): 367–405. For civic republicanism see Gordon S. Wood, *The Creation of the American Republic, 1776–1787* (New York: W. W. Norton and Co., 1969); J. G. A. Pocock, *The Machiavellian Moment: Florentine Political Thought and the Atlantic Republican Tradition* (Princeton, New Jersey: Princeton University Press, 1975); Lance Banning, *The Jeffersonian Persuasion: Evolution of a Party Ideology* (Ithaca, New York: Cornell University Press; 1978); Stanley Elkins and Eric McKitrick, *The Age of Federalism* (New York: Oxford University Press, 1993); and most recently Carl J. Richard, *The Founders and the Classics* (Cambridge, Massachusetts: Harvard University Press, 1994). For examples of the democratic egalitarian thesis, see

Charles A. Beard, *Economic Origins of Jeffersonian Democracy* (New York: Macmillan and Co., 1915); Merrill Jensen, *The Articles of Confederation* (Madison: The University of Wisconsin Press, 1962); and Richard K. Matthews, *The Radical Politics of Thomas Jefferson: A Revisionist View* (Lawrence: University Press of Kansas; 1986). For examples of those accepting a plethora of views among the Revolutionaries see Isaac Kramnick, "The Great National Discussion," *William and Mary Quarterly*, 3d series 45 (January 1988): 3–32; Michael Kammen, *A People of Paradox* (New York: Cornell University Press, 1990), 233; Good general reviews of the topic can be found in Robert Shalhope, "Republicanism and Early American Historiography," *William and Mary Quarterly*, 3d series 39 (April 1982): 334–356; and James T. Kloppenberg, "The Virtues of Liberalism," *Journal of American History* 74 (June 1987), 1–33.

5   Thomas Jefferson to Henry Lee, Monticello, May 8, 1825, in *Thomas Jefferson Writings*, ed. Merrill D. Petersen (New York: The Library of America, 1984), 1501.

6   See for example Mary Beth Norton, "The Loyalist Critique of the Revolution," in *The Development of a Revolutionary Mentality* (Washington D.C.: Library of Congress, 1972), 127–148.

7   The most notable treatments of the process of composition are John H. Hazelton, *The Declaration of Independence, It's History* (New York: Dodd, Mead and Company, 1906; reprint New York: Da Capo Press, 1970),141–180, see also Appendix, "Various Drafts, ETC., of the Declaration," 306–342; Becker, *The Declaration of Independence*, 138–193 (see note 4); Julian P. Boyd, *The Declaration of Independence: The Evolution of the Text as Shown in Facsimiles of Various Drafts by its Author, Thomas Jefferson* (Princeton, New Jersey: Princeton University Press, 1945); Wilfred J. Ritz, "*From the Here of Jefferson's Handwritten Rough Draft of the Declaration of Independence to the There of the Printed Dunlap Broadside*," *The Pennsylvania Magazine of History and Biography* 116 (October 1992): 499–512; Pauline Maier, *American Scripture: Making the Declaration of Independence* (New York: Alfred A. Knopf, 1997), 97–153.

8   George Burton Adams, *An Outline Sketch of English Constitutional History* (New Haven, Connecticut: Yale University Press, 1918), 30–31. See also the collection of primary sources, including the Magna Carta, the Petition of Right, and the English Bill of Rights of 1689 in Richard C. Perry and John C. Cooper, eds., *The Sources of Our Liberties* (New York: American Bar Foundation, 1960).

9   Maier, *American Scripture*, 51–55 (see note 7).

10 On Jefferson's possible use, see Maier, *American Scripture* 55 (see note 7).

11 Jack P. Greene, *Understanding the American Revolution* (Charlottesville: University Press of Virginia, 1995), 52–54, 72–80. Among the leading histories produced shortly after the Revolution and founding are David Ramsay, *History of the American Revolution* (1789; reprint vol. 1, ed. Lester H. Cohen, Indianapolis: Liberty Fund, 1990), 53–68; and Mercy Otis Warren, *History of the Rise,*

Progress, and Termination of the American Revolution (1805; reprint vol. 1, ed. Lester H. Cohen, Indianapolis: Liberty Fund, 1988), 17–30.

Chapter 1

1   See Ramsay, *American Revolution*, 60 (see Intro. note 11); Warren, *Rise Progress and Termination*, 16 (see Intro. note 11); A Londoner (Benjamin Franklin) to the Printer of the Publick Ledger, 'A War It Will Be,' London, 9 March 1774, in *Franklin Writings*, ed. J. A. Leo Lemay (New York: The Library of America, 1987), 712–713; Edward Countryman, *The American Revolution* (New York: Hill and Wang, 1985), 43—46; and Greene, *Understanding the American Revolution*, 73 (see Intro. note 11).

2   Greene, *Understanding the American Revolution*, 52-53 (see Intro. note 11); Jack P. Greene, "The origins of the new colonial policy, 1748–1763," in *The Blackwell Encyclopedia of the American Revolution*, eds. Jack P. Greene and J. R. Pole (Cambridge, Massachusetts: Basil Blackwell, 1991), 95–106.

3   Greene, *Understanding the American Revolution*, 53 (see Intro. note 11). This interpretation was recognized by contemporaries as well. David Ramsay noted in his *American Revolution* that British politicians "saw, or thought they saw, the seeds of disunion, planted in the too widely extended empire" (page 39 [see Intro. note 11]).

4   Ramsay, *American Revolution*, 55 (see Intro. note 11); Greene, "New colonial policy," 100–101, 105 (see note 2); Ian K. Steele, "Metropolitan administration of the colonies, 1696–1775," in *Blackwell Encyclopedia*, 15 (see note 2).

5   For primary samples of the offending acts, see Jack P. Greene, ed., *Colonies to Nation 1763–1789: A Documentary History of the American Revolution* (New York: W. W. Norton and Co., 1975), 12—26. For an excellent general overview see Peter D. G. Thomas, "The Grenville program, 1763–1765," in *Blackwell Encyclopedia*, 107–112 (see note 2).

6   Thomas, "The Grenville program," 107, 111 (see note 5); Bernhard Knollenberg, *Origin of the American Revolution: 1759–1766* (New York: The Macmillan Company, 1960), 23–43. See also, Edmund S. Morgan, *The Birth of the Republic, 1763–1789* (Chicago: The University of Chicago Press, 1992), 33–36.

7   Thomas, "The Grenville Program," 108 (see note 5); Knollenberg, *Origin*, 138–149 (see note 6); Morgan, *The Birth*, 37 (see note 6); Ramsay, *American Revolution*, 42–45 (see intro. note 11).

8   See extracts of James Otis' essay in Max Beloff, ed., *The Debate on the American Revolution* (Dobbs Ferry, New York: Sheridan House Inc., 1989), 47–69; See also Greene, *Colonies to Nation*, 26–33 (see note 5) and Knollenberg, *Origin*, 198 (see note 6).

9   For quotations see Ramsay, *American Revolution*, 46–47 (see Intro. note 11). On the Stamp Act generally see Knollenberg, *Origin*, 215–237 (see note 6).

10 On the nature of the "real Whigs" (or what is also called "Old Whig opposition" in this work) and their American counterparts, see David N. Mayer, *The Constitutional Thought of Thomas Jefferson* (Charlottesville: University Press of Virginia, 1995), 25–37. See also Merrill D. Peterson, *Thomas Jefferson and the New Nation* (New York: Oxford University Press, 1970), 56–63. On Jefferson and Bland see Peterson, 72. For Bland's essay see Charles S. Hyneman and Donald S. Lutz, eds., *American Political Writing During the Founding Era: 1760–1805,* vol. 1 (Indianapolis: Liberty Fund, 1983), 67–87. For Thomas Whately's essay see Greene, "New Colonial Policy," 46–51 (see note 2).

11 Greene, *Colonies to Nation,* 49 (see note 5); Hyneman and Lutz, *American Political Writings,* 72 (see note 10).

12 Hyneman and Lutz, *American Political Writing,* 70–72, 75–76, 81 (see note 10).

13 Ibid., 82.

14 Max Beloff, *Debate,* 73–76; quotation on page 75 (see note 8).

15 For a masterful discussion of the importance of custom and precedent in English legal understanding see John Phillip Reid, *Constitutional History of the American Revolution: The Authority to Legislate* (Madison: University of Wisconsin Press, 1991), 151–158; 159–171. See also John Phillip Reid, *Constitutional History of the American Revolution: The Authority to Tax* (Madison: University of Wisconsin Press, 1987), 130. Blackstone remarked just prior to citing Coke that the "mischiefs that have arisen to the public from inconsiderate alterations in our laws, are too obvious to be called in question; and how far they have been owing to the defective education of our senators, is a point well worthy the public attention." William Blackstone, *Commentaries on the Laws of England,* vol. 1 (1765; reprint Chicago: University of Chicago Press, 1979), 10.

16 On the supremacy of Parliament see Ibid., 157. On the doctrine of legislative supremacy generally, see John Phillip Reid, *Constitutional History of the American Revolution: The Authority of Law* (Madison: University of Wisconsin Press, 1993), 43–68; On the alarm with which American arguments were received in England, 163–166. Reid offers one of the most authoritative discussions of the Old Whigs and their understanding of the need to constrain even legislative power. His discussion is marred only by his perplexing insistence that John Locke be excluded from the ranks of Sir Edward Coke, John Selden, and Algernon Sidney. As Blackstone's reference makes clear, that exclusion is inaccurate, and as this work attempts to show, natural rights and custom were reinforcing and consistent parts of Whig social and political theory. Thus Locke could write in the same spirit as Coke and Sidney that a man "cannot subject himself to the Arbitrary Power over the Life, Liberty, or Possession of another . . . but only so much as the Law of Nature gave him for the preservation of himself, and the rest of Mankind; this is all he doth, or can give up to the Common-wealth, and by it to the *Legislative Power,* so that the Legislative can have no more than this." John Locke, *Two Treatises of Government,* ed. Peter Laslett (1698; reprint New York:

Cambridge University Press, 1992) 357. On British perceptions of Parliament's right to tax see Reid, *The Authority to Tax*, 26, 118–121 (see note 15).

17   Hyneman and Lutz, *American Political Writings*, 102, 162 (see note 10). John Tucker encapsulated nicely the conception of law as emanating from society and rooted in the very nature of man. The human being was thus fitted by the divine author for social interaction, and order stemmed from the nature of his creation, not from the arbitrary will of the powerful. A government fashioned to be in accord with that divine nature was properly called a civil government, and all others were tyranny. Thus Tucker could argue in his 1771 sermon, "civil government is founded in the very nature of man, as a social being, and in the nature and constitution of things. It is manifestly for the good of society:—It is the dictate of nature—It is the voice of reason, which may be said to be the voice of God." He could then conclude that "Hence all civil government, consistent with that natural freedom, to which all have equal claim, is founded in compact, or agreement between the two parties;—between Rulers and their Subjects, and can be no otherwise." Ibid., 161–162.

18   Perry and Cooper, *Sources of Our Liberties*, 264, 266, 270–271 (see Intro. note 8).

19   John Almon, ed., *A Collection of Interesting, Authentic Papers Relative to the Dispute Between Great Britain and America* (1777; reprint New York: Da Capo Press, 1971), 73.

20   Knollenberg, *Origin*, 239 (see note 6).

21   For the Declaratory Act see Greene, *Colonies to Nation*, 84–85 (see note 5). See also Knollenberg on William Pitt and Charles Townshend in *Origin*, 240–241 (see note 6).

22   For selections from the Townshend Revenue Act, the American Board 114–120 (see note 5).

23   A good examination of John Dickinson's life is to be found in the biography by Milton E. Flower, *John Dickinson, Conservative Revolutionary* (Charlottesville: University Press of Virginia, 1983).

24   Selections from Dickinson's *Letters from a Farmer* can be found in Greene, *Colonies to Nation*, 122–133 (see note 5). Quotations are on 130 and 128, respectively.

25   Quotations may be found respectively in Greene, *Colonies to Nation*, 129–130, 131, 125, 133 (see note 5).

26   For an excellent review of these events see Richard Knollenberg, *Growth of the American Revolution, 1766–1775* (New York: The Free Press, 1975), 61–81. More recently, Edward Countryman has written a highly readable narrative of these occurrences that stresses, in a fashion that would have pleased the Revolution's Tory critics, the violent inclinations of the American "rioters" and of the eighteenth century in general. See Countryman, *The American Revolution*,

74–104 (see note 1). On the question of standing armies in Whig political thought see Trenchard and Gordon's essays in Ronald Hamowy, ed., *Cato's Letters or Essays on Liberty, Civil and Religious, and Other Important Subjects 2* (Indianapolis: Liberty Fund, 1995), esp. 689–690. On Thomas Hutchinson's decision to remove the troops from Boston, see Bernard Bailyn, *The Ordeal of Thomas Hutchinson* (Cambridge, Massachusetts: Harvard University Press, 1974), 156–162. On the nonimportation agreements and their dissolution after the partial repeal of the Townshend duties, see Knollenberg, *Growth*, 54–60, 70–74.

27   On British concerns about repeal of the Townshend duties and the retention of the duty on tea see Knollenberg, *Growth*, 71, 91 (see note 26).

28   For the controversy over the payment of governors and justices see Ibid., 87–89; For the exchange between Hutchinson and Adams see Greene, *Colonies to Nation*, 178, 182–188 (see note 5).

29   Bailyn, *Ordeal of Thomas Hutchinson*, 1–34 (see note 26); see esp. 18–20 with regard to Hutchinson's writing style.

30   Ibid., 208.

31   A short biographical sketch of John Adams' life can be found in Edmund S. Morgan, *The Meaning of Independence* (New York: W. W. Norton and Co., 1978), 3–25. For a fuller treatment see C. Bradley Thompson, *John Adams and the Spirit of Liberty* (Lawrence, Kansas: University Press of Kansas, 1998); Peter Shaw, *The Character of John Adams* (Chapel Hill: University of North Carolina Press, 1976); and Anne Husted Burleigh, *John Adams* (New Rochelle, New York: Arlington House, 1969).

32   Greene, *Colonies to Nation*, 183–185 (see note 5).

33   Ibid., 185–188.

34   For selections from the Intolerable Acts (also called the Coercive Acts) see Greene, *Colonies to Nation*, 202–211 (see note 5). For a review essay of the acts, see David L. Ammerman, "The tea crisis and its consequences, through 1775," in Greene and Pole, *Blackwell Encyclopedia*, 201–202 (see note 2).

35   Greene, *Colonies to Nation*, 242–246 (see note 5).

36   Peterson, *Thomas Jefferson and the New Nation*, 70–71 (see note 10); Herbert Lawrence Ganter, "Jefferson's Pursuit of Happiness," *William and Mary Quarterly*, 1st series, 16 (Spring 1936): 565–566.

37   Peterson, *Thomas Jefferson and the New Nation*, 72–73 (see note 10); Adrienne Koch, *The Philosophy of Thomas Jefferson* (Chicago: Quadrangle Books, 1964), 133–148; David N. Mayer, *Constitutional Thought*, 28–37 (see note 10).

38   Hyneman and Lutz, *American Political Writing*, 76 (see note 10); Greene, *Colonies to Nation*, 64–65 (see note 5).

39   The importance of this earlier version goes to the nature of the Old Whig opposition and reveals that ideas usually associated with Locke regarding civil society

and the original contract did not constitute an anachronistic offshoot of Whig thought, but a fully integrated part of the tradition. The text read: "That King James the Second, having endeavored to subvert the constitution of this kingdom by breaking the original contract between king and people, and by the advice of Jesuits and other wicked persons, having violated the fundamental laws, and having withdrawn himself out of the kingdom, has abdicated the government; and that the throne is thereby vacant." Source for quotation in Lois G. Schwoerer, *The Declaration of Rights, 1689* (Baltimore: Johns Hopkins University Press, 1981), 24–25.

40   Ibid.; see also Blackstone, *Commentaries*, vol. 1, 226 (see note 15).

41   Merrill D. Peterson, ed., *The Portable Thomas Jefferson* (Kingsport, Tennessee: Penguin Books, 1975), 3–21; quotations on 9, 4, and 21, respectively.

42   Greene, *Colonies to Nation*, 220–227 (see note 5); Ganter, "Jefferson's Pursuit of Happiness," 431 (see note 36). On those passages of Wilson's essay that Jefferson was clearly familiar with, see Gilbert Chinard, ed., *The Commonplace Book of Thomas Jefferson* (Baltimore: Johns Hopkins University Press, 1926; Ann Arbor, Michigan: University Microfilms, 1975 [39–41]).

43   Greene, *Colonies to Nation*, 244 (see note 5).

44   Perry and Cooper, *Sources of Our Liberties*, 295–300 (see intro note 7).

45   Among the works to consult on the loyalists, see Egerton Ryerson, *The Loyalists of America and Their Times*, 2 vols. (New York: Haskell House, 1880; reprint 1970); Moses Coit Tyler, *The Literary History of the American Revolution,* vol. 1 (New York: Fredrick Ungar Publishing, 1957), 329–400; Jackson T. Main, *Rebel Versus Tory: The Crisis of the Revolution, 1773–1776* (Chicago: Rand McNally, 1963); Paul H. Smith, *Loyalists and Redcoats* (Chapel Hill: North Carolina Press, 1964); Catherine S. Crary, ed., *The Price of Loyalty: Tory Writings from the Revolutionary Era* (New York: McGraw Hill Book Company, 1973); Robert A. East and Jacob Judd, eds., *The Loyalist Americans, A Focus on Greater New York* (Tarrytown, New York: Sleepy Hollow Restorations, 1975); and Robert M. Calhoon, *The Loyalist Perception and Other Essays* (Columbia: University of South Carolina Press, 1989).

46   On Daniel Dulaney, see Tyler, *Literary History,* 102–110 (see note 45). On Joseph Galloway, see Calhoon, *Loyalist Perception,* 74–93 (see note 45).

47   Tyler, *Literary History,* 358, 359–368 (see note 45); Hyneman and Lutz, *Political Writing,* 209–216, 211 (see note 10). See also Calhoon, *Loyalist Perception,* 112–114 (see note 45).

48   Daniel Leonard, *Massachusettensis, Letters to the Inhabitants of the Province of Massachusetts–Bay* (Boston: J. Mathews, 1775; reprint Boston: Gregg Press, 1972 [9, 10]).

49   Hyneman and Lutz, *American Political Writing,* 211, 213 (see note 10).

50   Leonard, *Massachusettensis,* 64 (see note 48).

51   The nature of the loyalist opposition has produced a wealth of literature, some of which has appeared in the citations above. The view often taken is that the Revolution was a dispute within the Whig tradition, but that understanding overlooks a fundamental difference between loyalist and patriot in their conceptions of social order. The interpretation offered here is not that the loyalists were old-style Tories (to that extent the view expressed here is consistent with these other analyses), but that new Whigs and old Tories did share a basic belief in government as the primary source of social stability and order. For the new Whigs, all was justifiable by the idea of the supremacy of Parliament, which displaced the earlier Tory idea of the divine right of kings. These distinctions were recognized by contemporary observers. Daniel Leonard noted that "In America, the word Tory now implies *a friend to the supremacy of the British constitution all over the empire*; and the word Whig, *an asserter of colonial independence*, or (what is just the same) of legislations, distinct and divided from British legislation, in all the several provinces." David Ramsay similarly observed that Americans had "fancied themselves in the condition of the barons at Runnymede; but with this difference, that in addition to opposing the king, they had also to oppose the parliament. This difference was more nominal than real, for in the latter case the king and parliament stood precisely in the same relation to the people of America which subsisted in the former between the king and people of England." See Leonard, *Massachusettensis*, vi (see note 48); and David Ramsay, *American Revolution*, 199 (see note 48). Compare this "Whig" interpretation with Mary Beth Norton, "The Loyalist Critique," 127–144; 136 (see Intro. note 6).

52   Quotations as given in Tyler, *Literary History*, 341, 343–344 (see note 45).

53   Leonard, *Massachusettensis*, 8 (see note 48).

54   See the essays of Helvetius (1780) as presented in Randall M. Miller, *"A Warm and Zealous Spirit": John J. Zubly and the American Revolution, A Selection of His Writings* (Athens, Georgia: Mercer University Press, 1982), 288.

55   Charles Inglis, *Letters of Papinian in which the Conduct, Present State and Prospects of the American Congress are Examined* (New York: 1779), 119.

Chapter 2

1   Flower, *John Dickinson, Conservative Revolutionary* 129–130, 141–142 (see Ch. 1 note 23). A portion of the Olive Branch Petition can be found in Henry Steele Commager and Richard B. Morris, eds., *The Spirit of Seventy-Six* (New York: Da Capo Press, 1995), 279–280. On the Prohibitory Act and its consequences see Ramsay, *American Revolution*, 265–267 (see Ch. 1, note 10); and Warren, *Rise, Progress, and Termination*, 154–155 (see Intro. note 11).

2   On the influence of Paine see the review essay by Jack Fruchtman, Jr., "*Common Sense*," in Greene and Pole, *The Blackwell Encyclopedia*, 260–263 (see Ch. 1 note 2). First year sales were well over 100,000 in America alone.

3   Thomas Paine, *Political Writings*, ed. Bruce Kuklick (New York: Cambridge University Press, 1989), 28.

4   An early study of the influence of the states on the Declaration, especially the charges against the King, is to be found in Donald S. Lutz, *The Origins of American Constitutionalism* (Baton Rouge: Louisiana State University Press, 1988), 111–124. See also Maier, 63, 226–227 (see Intro. note 7); and Perry and Cooper, *Sources of Our Liberties*, 311 (see Ch. 1 note 18).

5   Lutz, *Origins of American Constitutionalism*, 114–115 (see note 4).

6   Perry and Cooper, *Sources of Our Liberties*, 328 (see ch. 1 note 18); See also Maier, *American Scripture*, 78, 82,163–164 (see Intro. note 7).

7   Lutz, *Origins of American Constitutionalism*, 114–115 (see note 4).

8   Julian P. Boyd, ed., *The Papers of Thomas Jefferson*, vol. 1, (Princeton, New Jersey: Princeton University Press, 1950), 377–379; Maier, *American Scripture*, 48–49 (see Intro. note 7).

9   Among the first to ask these questions were the critics of the Revolution. See especially, Thomas Hutchinson, *Strictures upon the Declaration of the Congress at Philadelphia in a Letter to a Noble Lord* (London, 1776) in appendix B (Please note: all page references to Hutchinson are to the original pagination given in [] in the text provided here); and John Lind, *An Answer to the Declaration of the American Congress* (London, 1776). On the effectiveness of the charges see the critical appraisal in Maier, *American Scripture*, 123 (see Intro. note 7). For the practice in common law see Blackstone, *Commentaries*, vol. 3, 295 (see Ch. 1. Note 15). Blackstone observes, "It is generally usual in actions upon the case to set forth several cases, by different *counts* in the same declaration; so that if the plaintiff fails in the proof of one, he may succeed in another."

10 Maier, *American Scripture*, 57 (see Intro. note 7); Perry and Cooper, *Sources of Our Liberties*, 311-313 (see Ch. 1 note 18). On the objective of the Declaration of Independence see also Cecelia M. Kenyon, "The Declaration of Independence," in *Fundamental Testaments of the American Revolution* (Washington: Library of Congress, 1973), 26; and Herbert Friedenwald, *The Declaration of Independence* (New York: The Macmillan Company, 1904; reprint New York: Da Capo Press, 1974 [168–171]).

11 Quotations as presented in Boyd, *Evolution of the Text*, 10 (see Intro. note 7).

12 Hazelton, *The Declaration of Independence,* 146–149 (see Intro. note 7); Friedenwald, *The Declaration of Independence*, 173–176 (see note 10); Dumbauld, *The Declaration of Independence and What It Means Today* (Norman, Oklahoma: University of Oklahoma Press, 1950), 21–23; Boyd, *Evolution of the Text*, 9–16, 39 (see Intro. note 7); Maier, *American Scripture*, 123–131 (see Intro. note 7).

13 Boyd, *Evolution of the Text*, 14–16, 19–21, 39 (see Intro. note 7).

14 Maier, *American Scripture*, 170–175 (see Intro. note 7). Jefferson to Henry Lee, Monticello, May 8, 1825, in Petersen, *Thomas Jefferson, Writings*, 1501 (see Intro. note 5).

15 The fullest account given by Thomas Jefferson can be found in his letter to James Madison of August 30, 1823, in James Morton Smith, ed., *The Republic of Letters: The Correspondence between Thomas Jefferson and James Madison, 1776–1826*, vol. 3 (New York: W. W. Norton and Co., 1995), 1875–1877. Here Jefferson extrapolates on his briefer account in his *Autobiography* (find in Peterson, *Thomas Jefferson Writings*; see Intro. note 5) wherein he writes that he alone is appointed by the whole group to compose the Declaration. For Maier's account see, Maier, *American Scripture*, 99–105 (see Intro. note 7). In regard to the Jefferson letter to Franklin, see the letter and commentary by Boyd in Boyd, *Papers of Thomas Jefferson*, 404–406 (see note 8). Regardless of the version of events, there is little to support a more activist view of the committee beyond what Jefferson recounts, and Adams' diary entry for June 23, 1779, seems to confirm Jefferson's version. Even Maier concedes that it is essentially his work. See Maier, *American Scripture* 100, 105 (see Intro. note 7). With regard to the number of changes, Boyd concludes that there were some sixteen changes made by Jefferson after what Boyd extrapolates to be his likely first version prior to its submission to the committee. The document then underwent some thirty-one changes, mostly by Jefferson, with four or five changes suggested by Franklin and Adams before its submission to Congress, where it was then subjected to some thirty-nine changes. See Boyd, *Evolution of the Text*, 22–34 (see Intro. note 7). See for comparison Maier, *American Scripture*, 144–149 (see Intro. note 7). The different counts appear to be based, not on any disagreement about what was changed, but on whether a change is counted as one alteration or more than one.

16 Maier, *American Scripture*, 105 (see Intro. note 7).

17 Hutchinson was a native of Massachusetts and among the leading loyalists. His essay is not necessarily the most informative, but because he was a native-born member of colonial society, it provides one of the best windows through which to perceive the American loyalist mind. John Lind wrote a response to the Declaration around the same time that is in many respects superior to Hutchinson's, but as a Londoner, it could be argued that he was less attuned to the culture of the empire's periphery. For a discussion of both works see Sydney George Fisher, "The Twenty-Eight Charges Against the King in the Declaration of Independence," *The Pennsylvania Magazine of History and Biography* 31 (July 1907): 257–303, 262.

18 Thomas Hutchinson, *Strictures upon the Declaration*, 4 (see note 9).

19 Ibid., 9.

20 Ibid., 9–10.

21 This approach is borrowed from the insightful analysis in Ross Lence, "Jefferson and the Declaration of Independence: The Power and Natural Rights of a Free People," *The Political Science Reviewer* 6 (Fall 1976): 1–31, 10.

22 Hutchinson, *Strictures upon the Declaration*, 10 (see note 9); Fisher, "Twenty-Eight Charges," 268 (see note 17); Friedenwald, *The Declaration of Independence*, 217–218 (see note 10).

23 The definitive study of the administration of the colonies and the use of the royal veto, instructions to governors, the disallowance, suspension, and the distinctions between each is to be found in Joseph Henry Smith, *Appeals to the Privy Council From the American Plantations* (New York: Octagon Books, 1965), see esp. 599–607 (I am indebted to my colleague G. M. Curtis for this reference). On the effect of these restrictions on American attitudes see John Adams, *Novanglus* no. 4, in *The Works of John Adams*, vol. 5, ed. Charles Francis Adams (Boston: Charles C. Little and James Brown, 1851), 49. For current interpretations of the currency question, the definitive work is Edwin J. Perkins, *American Public Finance and Financial Services*, 1700–1815 (Columbus: Ohio State University Press, 1994), 50–55.

24 Jefferson, *Summary View*, in Peterson, *The Portable Thomas Jefferson*, 14 (see Ch. 1 note 41).

25 Among the best efforts to analyze the grievances of the Declaration is the work by Dumbauld, *The Declaration of Independence* (see note 12). This chapter draws considerably from his findings, but seeks to embellish that work with the constitutional views of Hutchinson and others. See Dumbauld, 88–91; Fisher, "Twenty-Eight Charges," 264–265; Friedenwald, *The Declaration of Independence*, 215–217 (see note 10); Jefferson, *Summary View*, in Peterson, *The Portable Thomas Jefferson*, 14-15 (see Ch. 1 note 41); and Maier, *American Scripture*, 113 (see Intro. note 7).

26 Dumbauld, *The Declaration of Independence*, 88–89 (see note 12); and Maier, *American Scripture*, 113 (see Intro. note 7).

27 Hutchinson, *Strictures upon the Declaration*, 10 (see note 9). On colonial disregard of the law banning paper currency see Perkins, *American Public Finance*, 50 (see note 23). On American constitutional theory and the distinction drawn between the King's disallowance and Parliament's authority to legislate on the matter see Reid, *The Authority to Legislate*, 261–265 (see Ch. 1 note 15).

28 Dumbauld, *The Declaration of Independence*, 91 (see note 12).

29 The quotation of Parliament is as given in ibid., 92. See also Fisher, "Twenty-Eight Charges," 266–268 (see note 10); Reid, *The Authority to Legislate*, 261 (see Ch. 1 note 15).

30 Dumbauld, *The Declaration of Independence*, 92 (see note 12); Hutchinson, *Strictures upon the Declaration*, 11 (see note 9).

31 According to John Lind, this was not neglect, but the exercise of a useful tool of regulation. Rather than necessitating a forceful disallowance, the ministry had only to ignore legislation it did not like in order to keep it from going into effect. See Dumbauld, *The Declaration of Independence*, 93 (see note 12); Fisher, "Twenty-Eight Charges," 267 (see note 17).

32 Hutchinson, *Strictures upon the Declaration*, 13 (see note 9). See also Maier, *American Scripture*, 113–114 (see Intro. note 7).

33 For quote and discussion of the King's intent, see Hutchinson, *Strictures upon the Declaration*, 12 (see note 9). On the Massachusetts charter and the concession of the ministry to the Massachusetts legislature, see Dumbauld, *The Declaration of Independence*, 94–95 (see note 12). On Virginia see Jefferson's *Summary View*, in Peterson, *The Portable Thomas Jefferson*, 15–16 (see Ch. 1, note 41).

34 Hutchinson, *Strictures upon the Declaration*, 13 (see note 9); Dumbauld, *The Declaration of Independence*, 100–102 (see note 12).

35 Ibid.

36 Blackstone writes, before qualifying the King's power later in the same section, that "It is a branch of the royal prerogative, that no Parliament can be convened by it's own authority, or by the authority of any, except the king alone." Blackstone, *Commentaries*, vol. 1, 146 (see ch. 1 note 15).

37 J. C. D. Clark, *The Language of Liberty, 1660–1832* (Cambridge, U.K.: Cambridge University Press, 1994), 4–5. See also Blackstone, *Commentaries*, 155–156 (see ch. 1 note 15); and Reid, *The Authority of Law*, 54 (see Ch. 1 note 16).

38 As Reid notes, Americans understood the Glorious Revolution as a movement against arbitrary power, not simply a reshuffling of power from the king to Parliament. See Reid, *The Authority of Law*, 58 (see ch. 1 note 16).

39 Dumbauld, *The Declaration of Independence*, 102–103 (see note 12).

40 Jefferson, *Summary View*, in Peterson, *The Portable Thomas Jefferson*, 17 (see Ch. 1 note 41).

41 Ibid., 19; Dumbauld, *The Declaration of Independence*, 105–108 (see note 12).

42 Ibid., 107; Jefferson, *Summary View*, 18, 19. See also Fisher, 276–279 (see Ch. 1 note 41).

43 Ibid., 279-281; Dumbauld, *The Declaration of Independence*, 108–112 (see note 12).

44 Ibid. 113; Fisher, "Twenty-Eight Charges," 281 (see note 17); Hutchinson, *Strictures upon the Declaration*, 18 (see note 9).

45 Ibid., 18; Dumbauld, *The Declaration of Independence*, 112–115 (see note 12).

46 Quotations to be found in order respectively in Charles Francis Adams, *Works of John Adams*, 126, 124, 122, 126 (see note 23).

47 Dumbauld, *The Declaration of Independence*, 116–117 (see note 12); Fisher, "Twenty-Eight Charges," 281–283 (see note 17).

48 Dumbauld, *The Declaration of Independence*, 117–118 (see note 12). On the fear of standing armies in Whig thought see the fifth charge against King James

II in the English Bill of Rights in Perry and Cooper, *The Sources of Our Liber-ties*, 245 (see Intro. note 8); and Hamowy, *Cato's Letters*, 867–868, 890; quo-tation on 983 (see Ch. 1 note 26).

49   Dumbauld, *The Declaration of Independence*, 118–119 (see note 12); Hutchinson, *Strictures Upon the Declaration*, 19-20 (see note 9).

50   By far the best discussion of these developments is to be found in Reid, *The Authority of Law*, 54, 55–68 (see Ch. 1 note 16). Reid identifies three, rather than two, constitutional traditions, or theories. The first is the one associated here with the American Whig understanding and the small number of Rockingham Whigs in England. The second theory is that the constitution that restrained the Stuart monarchs restrained Parliament, but not in its rule over the colonies. The third is that Parliament was simply supreme over the entire empire. For Ameri-cans, the last two were the same, practically speaking; in fact, they resulted from the same Tory proclivity to view privileges in a purely customary light. The dis-agreement was only to what extent custom restrained Parliament at home. For Hutchinson's reference to Locke see his remarkable 1768 essay in Bernard Bailyn, ed., "A Dialogue between an American and a European Englishman by Thomas Hutchinson [1768]," *Perspectives in American History* 9 (1975): 369–410, 394–395. For Adams' interpretation of the Glorious Revolution see the excerpt from his 1773 response to Hutchinson in Reid, *The Authority to Legislate*, 71–72 (see Ch. 1 note 15).

51   Hutchinson, 20.

52   Ibid., 22–23.

53   Locke, *The Two Treatises of Government*, 400 (see Ch. 1 note 16). Reid's discussion of the Old Whigs is among the best, but he apparently feels so in-tensely the need to resist the popular shorthand of ascribing to Locke the theory of the Revolution, that he gives him little or no place in the pantheon of early Whigs. This despite the fact that he recognizes that natural law was invoked side by side with customary and constitutional arguments. He lists for certain Sidney, Selden and Coke, though revolutionaries like Adams, who figures quite promi-nently in all four of Reid's books, themselves commonly included Locke. See Charles Francis Adams, *Works of John Adams*, 15, 82, 83, 84 (see note 23); and Reid, *The Authority of Law*, 55–60 (see Ch. 1 note 16); and, *The Authority to Legislate*, 5 (see Ch. 1 note 15).

54   Hutchinson, *Strictures Upon the Declaration*, 28, 32 (see note 9).

55   Greene, *Colonies to Nation*, 266–267 (see Ch. 1 note 5).

Chapter 3

1   Carl J. Richard refers to the founders' "susceptibility to inconsistency." Richard, *The Founders and the Classics*, 6 (see Intro. note 4). I prefer, and think more accurate, Michael Zuckert's reference to the "unique amalgam" of American po-litical thought. See Zuckert, *Natural Rights Republic*, 6–7 (see Intro. note 4).

2 For an excellent, if brief, discussion of the origins of the state/society distinction, see David N. Mayer's *Constitutional Thought*, 69–74 (see Ch. 1 note 10). Though I would give more credit to John Locke in the development of this distinction than Mayer, he does a superb job relating the Whig notion of self-government to the thought of Thomas Jefferson.

3 George Burton Adams, *Outline Sketch*, 28–56 (see Intro. note 8). In connection with the American reading of medieval Saxon history see Trevor Colbourn, *The Lamp of Experience: Whig History and the Intellectual Origins of the American Revolution* (Indianapolis: Liberty Fund, 1998), 25–47. See also Mayer, *Constitutional Thought*, 30–31 (see Ch. 1 note 10).

4 On the law merchant see Bruce Benson, "The Spontaneous Evolution of Commercial Law," *Southern Economic Journal* 55 (January 1989): 644–661; Bruce Benson, *The Enterprise of Law* (San Francisco: Pacific Research Institute, 1990), 21–36; Harold J. Berman, *Law and Revolution, The Formation of the Western Legal Tradition* (Cambridge, Massachusetts: Harvard University Press, 1983), 341–344; Leon E. Trakman, *The Law Merchant: The Evolution of Commercial Law* (Littleton, Colorado: Fred B. Rothman and Co., 1983), 7–33; and Alan Harding, *The Law Courts of Medieval England* (New York: Barnes and Noble Inc., 1973), 41–43. A wealth of information on the law merchant is to be found in the three-volume collection of essays in legal history published at the turn of the century, *Select Essays in Anglo American Legal History*, Ernst Freund, William E. Mikell, and John H. Wigamore, eds. (Boston: Little, Brown, and Co., 1909). See especially the essay of Francis Marion Burdick, "Contributions of the Law Merchant to the Common Law," in vol. 3, 34–50. For a discussion of common law as an amalgam of different legal systems and jurisdictions see J. H. Baker, *An Introduction to English Legal History* (London: Butterworths, 1971), 9–64; and Arthur R. Hogue, *Origins of the Common Law* (Indianapolis: Liberty Fund, 1985), 5–6. On the incorporation of merchant law see Hogue, 248.

5 Adams, *Outline Sketch*, 57–79; Russell Kirk, *The Roots of American Order* (Washington, D.C.: Regnery Gateway, 1991), 195–199. On early radicalism in Parliament during the English Civil War, see the Introduction by Jack R. McMichael and Barbara Taft, eds., in *The Writings of William Walwyn* (Athens, Georgia: University of Georgia Press, 1989), 34–35. On the origins of the Whig and Tory parties, the classic explanation is to be found in David Hume, *The History of England*, vol. 6 (London: T. Cadell, 1778; reprint Indianapolis: Liberty Fund, 1983 [381]).

6 Blackstone, *Commentaries*, vol. 1, 67–68 (see Ch. 1 note 15).

7 For a discussion of the difference between American Whigs and English Whigs on the question of the royal prerogative, see Reid, *The Authority of Law*, 162–165 (see Ch. 1 note 16). A good example of the Tory view of obedience can be seen in the sermons of the loyalist minister Jonathan Boucher, who preached that "there can be no better way of asserting the people's lawful rights, than the disowning unlawful commands, by thus patiently suffering. When this doctrine was more generally embraced, our holy religion gained as much by submission, as

it is now in a fair way of losing for want of it." See Tyler, *Literary History*, 328 (see Ch. 1 note 26). The quintessentially Whig use of history can be seen by perusing the pages of Algernon Sidney's *Discourses Concerning Government* (London: J. Tolland, 1698; reprint Indianapolis: Liberty Fund, 1990) or of Trenchard and Gordon's *Cato's Letters* (see Ch. 1 note 26).

8   This was the real insight of those path-breaking scholars whose works are often included along with the more extreme claims of what came to be called "the republican synthesis." While they did indeed point to a new line of inquiry, they had no intention of writing off the rest of the Whig understanding of natural rights and liberal political economy. See the emphatic statement in favor of viewing the ideology of the American Revolution as a synthesis of many strands brought together originally in England's Glorious Revolution in Bernard Bailyn, *The Ideological Origins of the American Revolution* (Cambridge, Massachusetts: Harvard University Press, 1967), 54. See also the essays on the influence and contributions of Douglass Adair by three fellow contributors to the classical republican project—Trevor Colbourn, Caroline Robins, and Robert E. Shalhope—in the collection of essays by Douglass Adair, *Fame and the Founding Fathers*, ed. Trevor Colbourn (Indianapolis: Liberty Fund, 1998), xi–xliv.

9   For the Renaissance formulation of these ideas see J. G. A. Pocock, *The Machiavellian Moment*, 31–80 (see Intro. note 4) see esp. 78–79.

10   Sidney, *Discourses Concerning Government*, 140, 166, 248–249 (see note 6).

11   Ibid., 252, 255.

12   Hamowy, *Cato's Letters,* vol. 2, 803-804 (see Ch. 1 note 26). On the influence of Cato on America see Bailyn, *Ideological Origins*, 22–54 (see note 7). For one of the finest discussions of Trenchard and Gordon and their continuation of the Old Whig tradition in the early eighteenth century, with its blending of liberal political economy and republican political thought see Richard B. Vernier, "Political Economy and Political Ideology: The Public Debt in Eighteenth-Century Britain and America" (D. Phil. Diss., Oxford University, 1993), 71–77; see also his excellent discussion of "Old," or "True" Whigs, 28–53.

13   Hyneman and Lutz, *American Political Writing*, 341 (see Ch. 1 note 10).

14   Sidney, *Discourse Concerning Government*, 253 (see note 6).

15   See Trevor Colbourn's excellent discussion of the Whig understanding of history in *The Lamp of Experience*, (see note 3), citation of Bolingbroke on 5.

16   The source and strongest expression of the anti-Lockean and anti-commercial view is to be found in Pocock, *Machiavellian Moment*, 509 (see Intro. note 4). See also J. G. A. Pocock, "Virtue and Commerce in the Eighteenth Century," *Journal of Interdisciplinary History*, 3 (Summer 1972): 119–134. See also Stanley N. Katz, "Thomas Jefferson and the Right to Property in Revolutionary America," *The Journal of Law and Economics* 19 (October 1976): 467–488; 483. For a good review of the literature in this area, see Dworetz, *The Unvarnished Doctrine*, 3–38 (see Intro. note 4). In regard to commerce and in defense

of Pocock, Lance Banning noted that *Machiavellian Moment* never argued that commerce as simple exchange was opposed by the republican writers of the eighteenth century, but commerce as public finance and monopoly privileges. (On this point, see David M. Fitzsimons, "Tom Paine's New World Order," *Diplomatic History* 19, no. 4 [Fall 1995]: 572.) While Banning may be technically correct, Pocock's emphasis upon the tensions between virtue and commerce leaves little doubt that it is commerce in general, rather than political power, that he wishes to make the source of republican fears, whether or not the opposition writers themselves understood it as such. Ultimately, for Pocock, it is the elusive quality of money and its necessary relation to credit that undermines the stability of property as a source of republican independence and, therefore, real virtue. Thus, writing of the early American republic, Pocock states, "Dependent, subversive, and venal men in a commercial society are 'fit tools for the designs,' not only of classical demagogues like Burr, but also of architects of military-financial empire like Hamilton." See Lance Banning, "Jeffersonian Ideology Revisited: Liberal and Classical Ideas in the New American Republic," *William and Mary Quarterly*, 3d series, 43 (January 1986): 10; and Pocock, *Machiavellian Moment*, 462–505; 533 (see Intro. note 4).

17 Jefferson's understanding of the common law was shaped by his perception of its origins in the earlier, one might also say, mythical Saxon tradition, as well as by his experience of the common law as it had evolved in Virginia. He had difficulty, however, with the common law of England in his own time as it was being shaped by such luminaries as Blackstone and Lord Mansfield. Their works seemed for Jefferson to promote at every turn the subjection of the law to arbitrary power. Not only did they support the supremacy of Parliament; they also encouraged judges to set aside the decisions of juries, the rules of the common law, and the strict interpretation of statutes, in favor of the judge's personal perception of what was equitable. This fusion of equity with the traditional functions of a common law court illustrated for Jefferson the corrupt condition of the common law in England. On this see George M. Curtis' entry on Jefferson in W. Hamilton Bryson, ed., *The Virginia Law Reporters Before 1880* (Charlottesville: University Press of Virginia, 1977), 75–84. See also Maier, *American Scripture*, 260 (see Intro. note 7); and Merrill D. Peterson, *Thomas Jefferson and the New Nation* (New York: Oxford University Press, 1970), 155. On the legal libraries of the founding generation see, Trevor Colbourn, *The Lamp of Experience*, 15-24 (see note 3).

18 John Adams, "'U' to the Boston Gazette," *Boston Gazette*, September 5, 1763, in Robert J. Taylor, Mary-jo Kline, and Gregg L. Lint, eds., *The Papers of John Adams*, vol. 1 (Cambridge, Massachusetts: Harvard University Press, 1977), 86; Charles Francis Adams, *The Works of John Adams*, vol. 4, 124 (see Ch. 2 note 23).

19 Jefferson, *Summary View* and *Notes on the State of Virginia*, in Peterson, *The Portable Thomas Jefferson*, 18, 198, 20 (see Ch. 1 note 41).

20 Of course, for those deeply enmeshed in the philosophical arguments on this point, the interpretation of the meaning of "fulfillment" in natural law ethics is a very complicated matter. Is the ultimate good for human beings the life of intellectual

contemplation, or the life of practical reason? See, for example, John Cooper, *Reason and Human Good in Aristotle* (Cambridge, Massachusetts: Harvard University Press, 1975).

21   The outlines of this story have been given by Heinrich Rommen, and while I agree with his overall history, I see no reason to go along with his view that the Enlightenment conception of natural rights marked a decline or degeneration of the natural law tradition. See Heinrich A. Rommen, *The Natural Law* (Indianapolis: Liberty Fund, 1998), 67–108. On the influence of science on natural law and the founding, see I. Bernard Cohen, *Science and the Founding Fathers* (New York: W. W. Norton and Co., 1995), 61–134. See also Morton White's interpretation of the natural law understanding of late eighteenth-century Americans in *The Philosophy of the American Revolution* (New York: Oxford University Press, 1978). See also Dworetz, *The Unvarnished Doctrine*, 125–128 (see Intro. note 4).

22   Cohen, *Science*, 57 (see note 21); Carlo M. Cipolla, *Clocks and Culture, 1300–1700* (New York: W. W. Norton and Co., 1978), 33.

23   For a discussion of the origins of liberalism in political economy, and of Locke's ideas in particular, see Joyce Appleby, *Liberalism and Republicanism*, 58–89 (see Intro. note 4); Karen Iversen Vaughn, "The Economic Background to Locke's *Two Treatises of Government*," in Edward J. Harpham, ed., *John Locke's Two Treatises of Government* (Lawrence, Kansas: University Press of Kansas, 1992), 118–147. See also Karen Iverson Vaughn, *John Locke, Economist and Social Scientist* (Chicago: University of Chicago Press, 1980). On natural law, science, and political economy see Murray N. Rothbard, *Economic Thought Before Adam Smith* (Brookfield, Vermont: Edward Elgar Publishing Co., 1995), 272–273.

24   Gary Wills makes a clear association of political activity with the pursuit of happiness. See Wills, *Inventing America: Jefferson's Declaration of Independence* (New York: Vintage Books, 1979), 164. This is a common misperception as evidenced by Garrett Ward Sheldon's *The Political Philosophy of Thomas Jefferson* (Baltimore: Johns Hopkins University Press, 1991), 55, where he equates the social with the political. See also Richard K. Matthews, *Radical Politics*, 27 (see Intro. note 4); and his reference to the work of Robert Staughton Lynd, 28–29. Matthews is especially keen to invoke Jefferson's letter to Madison of September 6, 1789 where Jefferson contemplates a "revolution" every nineteen years, but Matthews fails to note that this was offered chiefly against the incursion of *public* debt (Peterson, *Thomas Jefferson Writings*, 959–964 [see Intro. note 5]). See also Dumas Malone, *Jefferson and the Rights of Man* (New York: Little, Brown and Co., 1951), 291. Matthews also cites the October 28, 1785 letter to Madison wherein Jefferson toys with the notion of property redistribution in France, but this was in reference to the unnatural distribution created by an *artificial* aristocracy—that is to say by political power (not by the workings of a commercial society of free exchange) or, as Jefferson styled it in his *Autobiography*, "the monstrous abuses of power under which this people were ground to powder." For citations of the letters and *Autobiography* see, Peterson, *Jefferson Writings*, 840–843 and 78 respectively (see Intro. note 5). In the New World, it was neces-

sary only to ensure that state governments would not automatically grant all property to the firstborn, or require such property to be entailed from one generation
to the next. Jefferson's contemplation of a graduated tax on land, as Lance Banning has noted, was in response to the grave inequalities arising from privileges
enshrined in law through which "great proprietors were placed 'above attention
to the increase of their revenues.'" See footnote 11 in chapter 2 of Lance Banning, *Jefferson and Madison, Three Conversations from the Founding* (Madison, Wisconsin: Madison House, 1995), 50. Some might insist that Jefferson's
was an unwarranted invasion of contracts based upon custom (and an abridge-
ment of natural law by some accounts), but it is important to keep the distinction
in view between customs enforced by the power of the state, prohibiting the free
disposal of one's property, and the right of an individual to leave his property to
anyone of his choosing. Jefferson never denied the propriety or justice of the
latter.

25 Vaughn, "Locke's *Two Treatises*," 120–121 (see note 23). See also, Peter Laslett,
    "The Great Recoinage, and the Origins of the Board of Trade," in John W. Yolton,
    ed., *John Locke, Problems and Perspectives* (Cambridge, U.K.: Cambridge Uni-
    versity Press, 1969), 144–145.

26 Hans Aarsleff, "The State of Nature and the Nature of Man in Locke," in Yolton,
    John Locke, 101–103, 105 (see note 25). The absolutism of both Filmer and
    Hobbes is recognized by Peter Laslett in his introduction to Locke, 67, 70 (see
    note 25).

27 This observation should come as little surprise when we consider that both au-
    thors were opposing the same groups that were fomenting the political upheavals
    of the seventeenth century in England. For quotations see Thomas Hobbes, *Le-
    viathan*, ed. C. B. Macpherson (New York: Penguin Books, 1986), 185; Sir Rob-
    ert Filmer, *Patriarcha and Other Writings*, ed. Johann P. Sommerville (New
    York: Cambridge University Press, 1991), 11.

28 On the question of interest rates see Vaughn, "Locke's *Two Treatises*," 121–123
    (see note 23). On the language of natural law and money in Locke's discussion of
    re-coinage, see Appleby, *Liberalism and Republicanism*, 58–89 (see Intro. note
    4). The best discussion of the economics of the historical controversy, however, is
    to be found in Rothbard, *Economic Thought*, 321–323. Quotation from Locke is
    as presented in Rothbard, 322 (see note 23).

29 Vaughn, *John Locke, Economist*, 80–100 (see note 23); Richard Ashcraft, "The
    Politics of Locke's Two Treatises," in Harpham, *Locke's Two Treatises*, 42–43
    (see note 23); Locke, *Two Treatises of Government*, 302 (see Ch. 1 note 16).
    Locke uses the term "societie" here to mean what he elsewhere clearly distin-
    guishes as "political society." The latter, when properly constituted, is meant to
    preserve the best of man's character in the state of nature; which is to say, his
    capacity for "Reason, the common Rule and Measure, God hath given to Man-
    kind." See, Locke, 274.

30 Ibid., 276–277.

31   Ibid., 280, 291, 336–337, 350. The term "parapolitical" was suggested to me by Professor John Alvis of the University of Dallas as being more descriptive and readily comprehendible by the standards of the present day. The interpretive framework, however, was first put forward, or perhaps more accurately, rediscovered, by Yehoshua Ariele in *Individualism and Nationalism in American Ideology* (Cambridge, Massachusetts: Harvard University Press, 1964), 91–157. The view of Locke in the present study differs from Arieli's due to the emphasis I have placed on the importance of economic thought to Locke's political ideas, but I am persuaded by Arieli's interpretation that "The image of a natural order of social life dominated the Jeffersonian Tradition" (Arieli, 97).

32   Locke, *Two Treatises of Government*, 275–276, 351, 352, 353 (see Ch. 1 note 16).

33   Allen Jayne, *Jefferson's Declaration of Independence: Origins, Philosophy, and Theology* (Lexington, Kentucky: University Press of Kentucky, 1998), 62–66. On the centrality of religion to Locke, see John Dunn, *The Political Thought of John Locke* (New York: Cambridge University Press, 1969), 97–101. A good review of the literature from the Locke-as-Christian perspective is to be found in Dworetz, *The Unvarnished Doctrine*, 97–134 (see Intro. note 4). See also Eldon Eisenach, "Religion and Locke's *Two Treatises of Government*," in Harpham, *Locke's Two Treatises*, 50–81 (see note 21).

34   Locke, *Two Treatises of Government*, 327, 338 (see Ch. 1 note 16). For quotation and commentary on the possible influence of Locke's *Essay Concerning the Human Understanding* see Herbert Lawrence Ganter, "Jefferson's Pursuit of Happiness and Some Forgotten Men," *William and Mary Quarterly*, 2d series, 16 (July 1936): 562, n.33; 563–564. See also Michael Zuckert, *Natural Rights Republic*, 83–85 (see Intro. note 4); Caroline Robbins, "The Pursuit of Happiness," in Stephen J. Tonsor, ed., *America's Continuing Revolution* (Washington, D.C.: American Enterprise Institute, 1975), 127; Boyd, *Papers of Thomas Jefferson*, 4–5 (see Ch. 2 note 8); and Jayne, *Jefferson's Declaration of Independence*, 110–111 (see note 33).

35   Quotations are to be found respectively in Algernon Sidney, *Discourses Concerning Government*, 524 (see note 7); Hamowy, *Cato's Letters*, vol. 2, 536; vol. 1, 432, 431; vol. 2, 537, 541 (see Ch. 1 note 26). See also the opening letter of dedication by Thomas Gordon to *Cato's Letters* which describes the essentially personal nature of happiness as belonging to "the private man," on pages 1–3.

36   Jayne, *Jefferson's Declaration of Independence* 34–40 (see note 33); Quotations to be found respectively in Jefferson to John Hollins, Washington, February 19, 1809, and Jefferson to Sir John Sinclair, Washington, June 30, 1803, in Peterson, *Thomas Jefferson Writings*, 1201, 1133 (see Intro. note 5); Hamowy, *Cato's Letters*, vol. 1, 181 (see Ch. 1 note 26).

37   Ibid., 433; Heyneman and Lutz, *American Political Writings*, 413, 443, 445 (see Ch. 1 note 10).

38   Jefferson, *Summary View*, in Peterson, *The Portable Thomas Jefferson*, 7 (see Ch. 1 note 41); idem, *Notes on the State of Virginia*, in ibid., 166, 198.

39   Jefferson to Joseph C. Cabell, February 2, 1816, in Peterson, ed., *Thomas Jefferson Writings*, 1380 (see Intro. note 5).

40   Samuel Sherwood, *A Sermon Containing Scriptural Instructions to Civil Rulers, and all Free-born Subjects*, August 31, 1774, in Ellis Sandoz, ed., *Political Sermons of the American Founding Era: 1730–1805* (Indianapolis: Liberty Fund, 1991), 382.

41   Quotations found respectively in Heyneman and Lutz, *American Political Writing*, 116, 188, 414–415, 72 (see Ch. 1 note 10).

42   Perry and Cooper, *Sources of Our Liberties*, 311 (see Intro. note 8).

43   Wills, *Inventing America*, see esp. 167–180 (see note 24). Quotations in Ronald Hamowy, "Jefferson and the Scottish Enlightenment: A Critique of Gary Wills' *Inventing America: Jefferson's Declaration of Independence*," *William and Mary Quarterly*, 3d series (October 1979): 503–523, 505. An example of the misreading of the implications of Hamowy's conclusions see Maier, *American Scripture*, 139 (see Intro. note 7).

44   See Intro. note 3 for a discussion of the problems raised by the use of "autonomous."

45   Wills, *Inventing America*, 215, 236 (see note 24). Locke, *Two Treatises of Government*, 318 (see Ch. 1 note 16).

46   For a discussion of Locke's understanding of the limits of reason, see Richard Ashcraft, "Faith and knowledge in Locke's philosophy," in Yolton, *John Locke*, 195–223; 216 (see note 25). See also Jayne, *Jefferson's Declaration of Independence*, 62–74 (see note 33). Thomas Hutcheson, *A System of Moral Philosophy* (Glasgow: R. and A. Foulis, 1755), 319.

47   Ibid., 322–323.

48   Wills explicitly equates what is social and public with government and what is private with the economy, failing to note that public activity can be both private and social in character—privately owned and controlled but conducted openly and in the public, with very public and very "social" ramifications and intentions. This is the real insight of thinkers like Hutcheson. But Wills mistakenly insists, "When Jefferson spoke of pursuing happiness, he had nothing vague or private in mind. He meant a public happiness which is measurable; which is indeed, the test and justification of any government." In fact, happiness had very little to do with government at all, except in so far as it did not interfere with the "pursuit of happiness," and performed those minimal duties required of a limited government. On Hutcheson's lack of influence on Jefferson at this time, however, see Hamowy, "Critique," 512–516 (see note 43).

49   For a discussion of the intellectual background of James Wilson and his work, see Stephen A. Conrad, "Polite Foundation: Citizenship and Common Sense in James

Wilson's Republican Theory," *1984 Supreme Court Review* (1985): 359–388. Quotations and an analysis of their influence on Jefferson to be found in Gilbert Chinard, *Commonplace Book*, 39–44 (see Ch. 1 note 42). See also Becker, *The Declaration of Independence*, 110–112 (see Intro. note 4).

50 Chinard, *Commonplace Book*, 39–42 (see Ch. 1 note 42).

51 Jayne, *Jefferson's Declaration of Independence*, 66–74 (see note 33). For further reading on the influence of the Scottish Enlightenment on Jefferson, see the recent work by Jean Yarbrough, *American Virtues: Thomas Jefferson on the Character of a Free People* (Lawrence, Kansas: University Press of Kansas, 1998), 27–54.

52 Hamowy, "Critique," 512 (see note 43). Jefferson to Skipwith, August 3, 1771, and Jefferson to Carr, August 10, 1787 in Peterson, *Thomas Jefferson Writings*, 743–745; 901–902 (see Intro. note 5). Jayne, *Jefferson's Declaration of Independence*, 74–81 (see note 33). See also Maier, *American Scripture*, 72–73 (see Intro. note 6).

53 Wills, *Inventing America*, 235–236 (see note 24).

54 The "hymn" or poem was in all editions of Kames' *Essays*, including the 1751 and 1758 editions which Jefferson would have read prior to writing the Declaration. Kames' reference to "pursues happiness" was probably one of many inspirations for Jefferson's use of the phrase, "pursuit of happiness." The most readily available version for the student of Kames' work is the reprinted third edition of 1779: Henry Home, Lord Kames, *Essays on the Principles of Morality and Natural Religion* (Edinburgh: John Bell and John Murray, 1779; reprint London: Routledge/Thoemmes Press, 1993), 376–377.

55 Quotations to be found respectively in appendix A, Declaration of Independence; Jefferson to Say, February 1, 1804, in Peterson, *Thomas Jefferson Writings*, 1144 (see Intro. note 5); and Jefferson to Joseph Milligan, August 16, 1813, as presented in Banning, *Jefferson and Madison*, 50 n. 11 (see note 24). On the letter to P. S. Dupont de Nemours, April 24, 1816, see Peterson, *Thomas Jefferson Writings*, 1386–1387 (see Intro. note 5). For more on Jefferson's idea of self-government and a natural social order see the excellent discussion in Mayer, *Constitutional Thought*, 69–74, 125 (see Ch. 1 note 10). Mayer derives his understanding from the work of Yehoshua Ariele (see note 31). On Jefferson's work to translate the material from de Tracy, see Koch, *Philosophy of Thomas Jefferson*, 54–64 (see Ch. 1 note 37); see esp. 61, n. 35. For a discussion of de Tracy's economics see Daniel Klein, "Deductive Economic Methodology in the French Enlightenment: Condillac and Destutt de Tracy," *History of Political Economy* 17 (January 1985): 51–71.

56 Jefferson to Duane, April 4, 1813, as cited in Appleby, *Liberalism and Republicanism*, 307 (see Intro. note 4); see also 313–315; and Koch, *Philosophy of Thomas Jefferson*, 56–57 (see note 55). On Jefferson's differences with de Tracy see Jefferson to Adams, October 14, 1816, in Lester J. Cappon, *The Adams-Jefferson Letters* (Chapel Hill: University of North Carolina Press, 1959), 490–

493. For a further discussion of Jefferson's interest in the work of de Tracy see
Mayer, *Constitutional Thought*, 136–141 (see Ch. 1 note 10). Yehoshua Areili
(see note 31) also makes use of Jefferson's interest in de Tracy, but his idea that
de Tracy was opposed to great fortunes because they are a threat to liberty misses
the point that de Tracy had the aristocracies of Europe with their feudal privileges
and political powers in mind and not the productive enterprises of commercial
wealth. In fact, he made a sharp distinction between the aristocratic consumers of
luxury living upon rents, and those active capitalists who pursued profits. In any
case, he never favored redistribution because of his fundamental commitment to
"the necessity of respect for property and justice in general." See Destutt de
Tracy, *A Treatise on Political Economy to which is prefixed a Supplement to
a Preceding Work on the Understanding, or Elements of Ideology; with an
Analytical Table and an Introduction on the Faculty of the Will* (Georgetown,
D.C.: Joseph Milligan, 1817), note on 159, 168–169, second note on 183.

57   Emerich de Vattel, *The Law of Nations* (Amsterdam: Van Harrevelt, 1775) as
cited in Boyd, *The Declaration*, 5 n. 10 (see Intro. note 7).

58   Paine, *Common Sense*, in Kuklick, *Political Writings*, 3 (see Ch. 2 note 3).

59   See discussion in the bibliographic essay.

60   There is an important debate over the meaning of self-evidence. Does it refer
essentially to an *assertion* of certain truths that must be affirmed to preserve a
just polity or is it a reference to those most basic truths that can be positively
discovered by reason? It is not clear to me that both positions are unalterably
opposed. One could, it seems to me, believe that certain truths are what an
enlightened public could, through reflection, agree upon as the most basic of
rights, and yet consider them also as the necessary foundation for establishing a
just political system. For both constructions see respectively, Zuckert, *Natural
Rights Republic*, 41–55 (see Intro. note 4); and White, *Philosophy of the American Revolution*, 61–96 (see note 21).

61   On the "Quarlsome and Contentious" and the proper place of government see
Locke, *Two Treatises of Government*, 290, 291, 326–327, 329, 352, 359 (see
Ch. 1 note 16). On "Safety and Happiness," see Heyneman and Lutz, *American
Political Writing*, 133, 415, 420 (see Ch. 1 note 10); and Perry and Cooper,
Sources of Our Liberties, 311 (see Intro. note 8). On the exercise of the right of
resistance by a people, see the discussion in Lence, "Jefferson," 1–31 (see Ch. 2
note 21). For quotations from the Declaration see appendix A.

62   Pauline Maier discusses the issue of audience briefly in *American Scripture*, 129–
132 (see Intro. note 7). The most informative analysis of the Declaration's prose,
however, is to be found in Jay Fliegelman's rhetorical analysis of the text. The
Declaration was intended to be "performed," or as Fliegelman points out, "The
locations of the marks on the rough draft of the Declaration as well as the locations of the 'quotation marks' on the proof copy of the Dunlap broadside represent not breath or punctuational pauses but precisely what Jefferson discusses:
rhythmic pauses of emphatical stress that divide the pieces into units comparable to musical bars or poetic lines." Jay Fliegelman, *Declaring Independence:*

Jefferson, Natural Language, and the Culture of Performance (Stanford, California: Stanford University Press, 1993), 10.

63   On this point, and for the definitive study of the social and cultural background to American ideological currents, see Jack P. Green's *Pursuits of Happiness: The Social Development of Early Modern British Colonies and the Formation of American Culture* (Chapel Hill: The University of North Carolina Press, 1988), 197–200.

Chapter 4

1   A good discussion of this tendency and its history is to be found in "Charles S. Hyneman on the Declaration of Independence and Personal Equality," which is the second appendix of Charles S. Hyneman, *The American Founding Experience*, ed. Charles E. Gilbert (Chicago: University of Illinois Press, 1994), 266–270. Another excellent account is that of Martin Daimond, "The Declaration and the Constitution: Liberty, Democracy and the Founders," in Martin Diamond, *As Far as Republican Principles Will Admit*, ed. William A. Schambra (Washington D.C.: The AEI Press, 1992), 224–240.

2   A number of authors who take such a view nevertheless approach their subject from various different interpretive perspectives such as classical republicanism, progressivism, and communitarianism. In the republican vein see Katz, "Right to Property" (October 1976): 467–488 (see Ch. 3 note 16). For a view that stresses the Scottish Enlightenment influence see Wills, *Inventing America*, 164, 244 (see Ch. 3 note 24). An interesting but more ambiguous view, from my perspective is Morton White's Lockean-Burlamaquian reading of the Declaration in *Philosophy of the American Revolution*, 97–141, 252–256 (see Ch. 3 note 21). From the perspective presented here, the tension that White sees within Jefferson's soul, torn between a desire to promote happiness through government and a desire to limit government to the protection of rights, is resolved by understanding society as distinct from the state. Government can then "promote" happiness by limiting violence in human affairs and by limiting itself, and the two are not in contradiction. Other government-centered views on the meaning of the pursuit of happiness can be found in Scott Douglas Gerber, *To Secure These Rights: The Declaration of Independence and Constitutional Interpretation* (New York: New York University Press, 1995), 193–195; and in the more extreme progressivist interpretation of Richard K. Matthews, *Radical Politics*, 122–126 (see Intro. note 4). Matthews' idea of happiness as the making of rules by a democratic government is the very antithesis of the liberal Whig notion that government and society are distinct forms of order. He comes close to equating Jefferson's vision with that of Rousseau's general will, which is a profound association—I would say confusion—of society with the state.

3   Robert H. Bork, *Slouching Towards Gomorrah* (New York: Regan Books, 1996), 57. Bork's perspective on the Declaration is unusually extreme among conservative thinkers in America. For the most part, American conservatives do not reject the Declaration, but argue about how it should be read. A nice example of such an

"in-house" disagreement is the exchange between Harry V. Jaffa and M. E. Bradford that is reprinted in George A. Panichas, ed., *Modern Age: The First Twenty-Five Years* (Indianapolis: Liberty Fund, 1988), 287–318.

4 This interpretation follows a long train of works that see a basic consistency in the Declaration and Constitution. Those who take such a position generally argue that the Declaration informs, to some degree, the moral and philosophical spirit of the later document. A very informative overview of this subject can be found in an essay that was brought to my attention by James Bond, Dean of the Seattle School of Law: Daniel L. Dreisbach, "In Search of A Christian Commonwealth: An Examination of Selected Nineteenth-Century Commentaries on References to God and the Christian Religion in the United States Constitution," *Baylor Law Review* 48 (1996): 928–1000; see esp. 967–1000. Dreisbach focuses on references to the divine in the Declaration and their applicability, if any, to the Constitution. Because this has formed a major part of the discussion of the relationship between the two documents, he has presented a nice survey of nineteenth-century sources, with some contemporary perspectives on the topic. It is especially useful for its references to current thoughts in the various law journals.

5 For a copy of the Articles of Confederation see Greene, *Colonies to Nation*, 428–436 (see Ch. 1 note 5). The classic study of the Articles is to be found in the two works by Merrill Jensen, *The Articles of Confederation* (see Intro. note 4), and, *The New Nation: A History of the United States During the Confederation 1781–1789* (New York: Alfred A. Knopf, 1962). On the semblance of the Articles to the colonial understanding of the old imperial constitution, see Greene, *Understanding the American Revolution*, 157–163 (see Intro. note 11).

6 Jensen, *The New Nation*, 422–428 (see Intro. note 6).

7 The definitive study of the financial and economic institutions of the period is to be found in Perkins, *American Public Finance*, quotation on 88; see also 95–105 (see Ch. 2 note 23).

8 Sidney, *Discourses Concerning Government*, 295 (see Ch. 3 note 10); Henry Home, Lord Kames, *Essays*, 47 (see Ch. 3 note 54); Adam Smith, *An Inquiry into the Nature and Causes of the Wealth of Nations* (London: W. Strahan and T. Cadell, in the Strand, 1776; reprint Indianapolis: Liberty Fund, 1981), 25–26.

9 Pelatiah Webster, *Political Essays on the Nature and Operation of Money, Public Finances and Other Subjects Published during the American War, and Continued up to the present Year 1791* (Philadelphia: 1791; reprint New York: Burt Franklin, 1969), 30.

10 Ibid., 130.

11 Ibid., respectively on 24, 9, 48, 203.

12 Ibid., 198–200.

13 Ibid., quotations at 211, 219, and 202, respectively.

14 Madison to Jefferson, Philadelphia, March 27 and 28, 1780; and August 12, 1786, Smith, *Republic of Letters*, vol. 1, 136, 428, 431 (see Ch. 2 note 15).

15 George Washington, "Circular to the States," June 14, 1783, in Colleen A. Sheehan and Gary L. McDowell, eds., *Friends of the Constitution: Writings of the "Other" Federalists, 1787–1788* (Indianapolis: Liberty Fund, 1998), 17.

16 James Madison, "Vices of the Political System of the United States," April 1787, in Marvin Meyers, ed., *The Mind of the Founder: Sources of the Political Thought of James Madison* (Hanover, New Hampshire: Brandeis University Press, 1981), 57–58, 64.

17 Ibid., 64.

18 Sidney, *Discourses Concerning Government*, 263 (see Ch. 3 note 10); see also 189, 217; and Hamowy, *Cato's Letters*, 421 (see Ch. 1 note 26).

19 Peterson, *Portable Thomas Jefferson*, 164 (see Ch. 1 note 41).

20 Webster, *Political Essays*, 425–426 (see note 9).

21 An excellent discussion of the role that the problems with paper money and finance played in the formation of the Constitutional Convention is to be found in Forrest McDonald, *Novus Ordo Seclorum: The Intellectual Origins of the Constitution* (Lawrence, Kansas: University Press of Kansas, 1985), 152–179. Whereas the account presented here refers to the centrality of contracts in Whig thought, McDonald refers to property, but these are really two sides of the same coin. Mankind's capacity to enter into contracts is premised, in Whig thought, on man's mastery of himself, which is the source from which the right of property is derived. See Locke, *Two Treatises of Government*, 298–299 (see Ch. 1 note 21).

22 Among the best introductory accounts of the history of the Constitutional Convention is to be found in Carl Van Doren, *The Great Rehearsal: The Story of the Making and Ratifying of the Constitution of the United States* (New York: Penguin Books, 1986).

23 McDonald, *Novus Ordo Seclorum*, 180–183, 185–186 (see note 21). See also Lance Banning, *The Sacred Fire of Liberty* (Ithaca: Cornell University Press, 1995), 111–137.

24 McDonald, *Novus Ordo Seclorum*, 226–227 (see note 21); quotation from the resolutions proposed by Edmond Randolph of Virginia at the Federal Convention on May 29, 1787, as given in James Madison, *Notes of the Debates in the Federal Convention of 1787* (New York: W. W. Norton and Co., 1987), 31.

25 Ibid., 84. Charles de Secondat, Baron de Montesquieu, *The Spirit of the Laws* (New York: Cambridge University Press, 1989), 38.

26 Madison, *Notes from the Debates*, 85 (see note 24).

27 Ibid., 86–87.

28   Ibid., 118–121.

29   Ibid., 153.

30   Ibid., 57, 77, 87, 103, 291, 650. Franklin is often given credit for originating the
      idea of equal representation in the Senate and proportional representation in the
      House. In actuality, it was Dickinson who first raised the idea, but it took the likes
      of Franklin to move it forward. See Van Doren, *The Great Rehersal*, 59 (see note
      22). See also McDonald, *Novus Ordo Seclorum*, 230–237 (see note 21).

31   Madison, *Notes of the Debates*, 215, 103, 224–225, 226, 616–617 (see note
      24). See also McDonald, *Noos Ordo Seclorum*, 236 (see note 21).

32   Madison, *Notes of the Debates*, 502, 503, 504 (see note 24).

33   Herbert J. Storing, ed., *The Anti-Federalist* (Chicago: University of Chicago
      Press, 1985), 13, 20.

34   Ibid., 35–36, 38–39.

35   Ibid., 40.

36   Ibid., 41, 48, 57.

37   Ibid., 167.

38   Alexander Hamilton, James Madison, and John Jay, *The Federalist Papers,* ed.
      Clinton Rossiter (New York: Mentor, 1961), 44.

39   Pauline Maier finds it surprising that there were not more references to the Dec-
      laration in these early debates of the late 1780s if the document was as funda-
      mental as later writers would claim it to be. But this seems to ignore the very
      context that Maier has herself made plain. The Declaration was an expression of
      the sentiments of its time, and was one of many statements of revolutionary
      principles. Rather than being ignored, it was *included* in the panoply of revolu-
      tionary symbols, and was, in fact, referred to when the nature of the confederacy
      was in doubt. As the common statement of independence, Federalists and Anti-
      federalists turned to the Declaration to decide the question of whether America
      was a union of separate states or of a single nation, and in Pennsylvania, as this
      work attempts to clarify, this was one of the most heated contests. See Maier,
      American Scripture, 168–170, 193 (see Intro. note 7).

40   Merrill Jensen, John P. Kaminski, and Gaspare J. Saladino, eds., *The Documen-
      tary History of the Ratification of the Constitution*, vol. 2 (Madison: State
      Historical Society of Wisconsin, 1976), 384–386.

41   Ibid., 393, 430, 472–473; see also "The Federalist's Political Creed," *Philadel-
      phia Independent Gazetteer*, May 10, 1788, in ibid., vol. 6, 5.

42   Rossiter, *The Federalist Papers*, 79, 83 (see note 38).

43   Ibid., 80, 83.

44   James Winthrop, "Agrippa, XIII," January 14, 1799, as cited in Wood, *Creation*, 538 (see Intro. note 4).

45   Madison to Jefferson, New York, October 24 and November 1, 1787 in Smith, *Republic of Letters*, 498–500, 502 (see Ch. 2 note 15). For comparison with his ealier notes see Ch. 2 note 16.

46   Jefferson to Madison, Paris, December 20, 1787, in ibid., 512.

47   Ibid., 512–513.

48   Ibid., 513–514; Jefferson to Alexander Donald, Paris, February 7, 1788, in Peterson, *Jefferson Writings*, 919 (see Intro. note 5).

49   The best documentary account of the making of the Bill of Rights is to be found in Helen E. Veit, Kenneth R. Bowling, and Charlene Bangs Bickford, eds., *Creating the Bill of Rights: The Documentary Record from the First Federal Congress* (Baltimore: Johns Hopkins University Press, 1991).

50   The distinction between a balanced constitution and a constitution of strictly separated powers has been frequently made in the context of the debates over the ideological character of the founding era. Forrest McDonald argues for a complete rejection of the doctrine of separation of powers as applying to the Constitution that goes, perhaps, a bit too far. Joyce Appleby, on the other hand, has argued that the "purpose of government was . . . not to raise power to check power but rather to ensure the conditions for liberating man's self-actualizing capacities." If those powers are seen to be rooted in ancient or medieval social estates, as the classical republican thesis holds, then that statement is accurate enough. Americans were not speaking in terms of balancing the social orders of established inherited ranks. They were, however, interested in *checking* power with power in the form of different offices, because that was the necessary precondition "for liberating man's self actualizing capacities." This reading would tend to fit better with Appleby's own conclusion that written constitutions "did not exist to establish a balance of power, as in the ancient constitution of England, but rather to define the power given to the people's representatives and to fix the limits beyond which they must not trespass." David N. Mayer makes a similar observation about the character of Jefferson's constitutional theory, adopting the approach of M. J. C. Vile to make a strong distinction between Jefferson's favoring of strict separation over balancing. But balancing was used liberally by all of the founders, and even Jefferson, throughout his life, whether in his *Notes on the State of Virginia* in 1784 or in his letter to Spencer Roane in 1819, had little difficulty employing the term. See Peterson, *Thomas Jefferson Writings*, 245, 1426 (see Intro. note 5). So long as it is clearly defined to refer to the separation and containment of powers ultimately derived from the people, the application of the word "balance" poses little difficulty for the Whig interpretation offered here, and, in fact, shows how the two constitutional positions, both the older one of a balanced constitution, and the newer one of strict separation, grew out of the same concern with the containment of power. See McDonald, *Novus Ordo Seclorum*, 258–259 (see note 21); Appleby, *Liberalism and Republicanism*, 299, 305 (see Intro. note 4); David N. Mayer, *Constitutional Thought*, 129–144

(see Ch. 1 note 10). See also Sidney, *Discourses Concerning Government*, 166–170 (see Ch. 3 note 10); M. J. C. Vile, *Constitutionalism and the Separation of Powers* (Indianapolis: Liberty Fund, 1998), 3, 5, 7, 27–28, 58–59.

51   Ibid., 172–176.

52   Storing, *The Anti-Federalist*, 41 (see note 33).

53   Thus Madison writes in essay fifty-one, "In the compound republic of America, the power surrendered by the people is first divided between two distinct governments, and then the portion allotted to each subdivided among distinct and separate departments. Hence a double security arises to the rights of the people. The different governments will control each other, at the same time that each will be controlled by itself." See Rossiter, *The Federalist Papers*, 323 (see note 38).

54   On Madison's strict construction of the Articles in regard to the Bank of North America, see Bray Hammond, *Banks and Politics in America* (Princeton, New Jersey: Princeton University Press, 1957), 50–51. On Madison's move to make incorporation an explicit part of the Constitution, see Madison, *Notes of the Debates*, 477, 638 (see note 24). On Madison's argument in Congress in 1791, see Gaillard Hunt, ed., *The Writings of James Madison*, vol. 6 (New York, G. P. Putnam's Sons, 1906), 26; and M. St. Claire Clarke and D. A. Hall, eds., *Legislative and Documentary History of the Bank of the United States* (Washington D.C.: Gales and Seaton, 1832; reprint New York: Augustus M. Kelley, 1967), 40–45. Madison even called attention to the fact that the Articles of Confederation had been insufficient to incorporate the earlier Bank of North America and that Congress had had to turn to the States to make good on the bank's legal standing. See Hunt, 29. For a discussion of Madison's strict constructionist views see Lance Banning, *The Sacred Fire of Liberty*, 8, 326–333 (see note 23).

55   For the opinions of both Jefferson and Hamilton see St. Claire Clarke and Hall, 91–94, 95–112; quotation of Jefferson on 93 (see note 54).

56   Ibid., 95; Gaillard Hunt, ed., 33.

57   St. Claire Clarke and Hall, 92 (see note 54); On Madison's disillusionment with Hamilton see Banning, *Sacred Fire*, 332–333 (see note 54). On the attitude of the Federalists to the Declaration see Maier, *American Scripture*, 170 (see Intro. note 6).

58   Ibid., 168–169, 170–175. This point was first made by Philip F. Detweiler in "The Changing Reputation of the Declaration of Independence: The First Fifty Years," *William and Mary Quarterly*, 3d series, 2 (1945): 557–574.

59   Ibid., 559.

60   Ibid., 565.

61   Ibid., 565–566, 569–570; Maier, *American Scripture*, 171 (see Intro. note 6).

62   Detweiler, "First Fifty Years," 569 (see note 58). For the citation of the *Aurora*, August 5, 1799, see the well researched historical novel by Richard N. Rosenfeld,

with a Foreword by Edmund S. Morgan, entitled, *American Aurora* (New York: St. Martin's Press, 1997), 675.

63 Thomas Paine, *The Rights of Mann*, Part 2, in *Political Writings*, 155 (see Ch. 2 note 3). This quotation was first brought to my attention in an essay by Murray N. Rothbard, "Frank S. Meyer: The Fusionist as Libertarian Manque," in George W. Carey, ed., *Freedom and Virtue* (Wilmington, Delaware: Intercollegiate Studies Institute, 1998), 154–155. Another very useful discussion of Paine's understanding is to be found in Tom G. Palmer's "The Literature of Liberty," in David Boaz, ed., *The Libertarian Reader* (New York: The Free Press, 1997), 428–429. A good discussion of the influence of Paine's brand of radicalism in the 1790s is to be found in Michael Durey, "Thomas Paine's Apostles: Radical Émigrés and the Triumph of Jeffersonian Republicanism," *The William and Mary Quarterly*, 3d series, 44 (October 1987): 661–688.

64 *Gazette of the United States*, November 23, 1798, as cited in John C. Miller, *Crisis in Freedom: The Alien and Sedition Acts* (Boston: Little, Brown and Co., 1952), 55; and *Annals of Congress*, X, 409, as cited in Ibid., 59–60.

65 On the Virginia and Kentucky Resolutions, see Mayer, *Constitutional Thought*, 201–208 (see Ch. 1 note 10), and Banning, *Sacred Fire*, 387–395 (see note 54).

66 On the political efficacy of the Virginia and Kentucky Resolutions see Miller, *Crisis in Freedom*, 177, 180, 181 (see note 64). On the questionable constitutionality of the embargo see Mayer, *Constitutional Thought*, 216–217 (see Ch. 1 note 10).

67 It is often argued that Jefferson's constitutional thought underwent a radical change during his years in France. From the perspective offered here, his adoption of a stricter separation of powers perspective over that of a balanced constitution was more of a refinement of his earlier commitments than a fundamental break in beliefs. See the discussion in note 50. Quotation is from Jefferson to Joseph C. Cabell, Monticello, February 2, 1816, in Peterson, *Thomas Jefferson Writings*, 1378, quotations on 1380–1381 (see Intro. note 5).

68 Ibid., 1380.

Conclusion

1 Lance Banning made such an observation in defense of the classical republican interpretation when he noted that Pocock never argued that commerce as exchange was opposed by the opposition writers of the eighteenth century, but it was commerce as public finance, and monopoly privileges that concerned them. Pocock's emphasis on the tensions between virtue and commerce, however, leaves little doubt that it is commerce in general that he wishes to make the source of English oppositionist fears, whether or not the opposition writers themselves understood it as such. Ultimately, for Pocock, it is the elusive quality of money and its necessary relation to credit that undermines the stability of property as a source of republican independence and, therefore, real virtue. Thus, writing of the early

republic, he lumps together commercial society and military-financial empire, observing that "Dependent, subversive, and venal men in a commercial society are 'fit tools for the designs,' not only of classical demagogues like Burr, but also of architects of military-financial empire like Hamilton." Gordon Wood is another who puts together very disparate social and political phenomena: "All the signs of England's economic and social development in the eighteenth century—the increasing capitalization of land and industry, the growing debt, the rising prices and taxes, the intensifying search for distinctions by more and more people— were counted as evidence of its 'present degeneracy, and its impending destruction.'" Nowhere does Wood clearly differentiate between the public debt (uppermost in the minds of republicans) from private or commercial debt. Nor does he discuss how republicans saw the rise of prices as attributable to government finance, as opposed to free and competitive commerce, or why corporations were seen as the suspect creatures of government, rather than the products of free competition. Banning, "Jeffersonian Ideology Revisited," 10 (see Ch. 3 note 16); J. G. A. Pocock, *Machiavellian Moment*, 462–505; 533 (see Intro. note 4); Wood, *Creation*, 36 (see Intro. note 4). See also on this point Fitzsimons, "New World Order," 572 (see Ch. 3 note 16).

2   Scott Douglas Gerber, *The Declaration and the Constitution* (New York: New York University Press, 1995), 1–56.

3   On Locke's skepticism as expressed in *Essays Concerning the Human Understanding* see Eldon Eisenach, "Religion and Locke's *Two Treatises of Government*," in Harpham, *Locke's Two Treatises*, 67 (see Ch. 3 note 23). The *Second Treatise* holds forth the importance of "manifest evidence" for justifying resistance to authority and reads, "For till the mischief be grown general, and the ill designs of the Rulers become visible, or their attempts sensible to the greater part, the People, who are more disposed to suffer, than right themselves by resistance, are not apt to stir. The examples of particular Injustice, or Oppression of here and there an unfortunate Man, moves them not. But if they universally have a perswasion, grounded upon manifest evidence, that designs are carrying on against their Liberties . . . who is to be blamed for it? . . . [H]e who does it is justly esteemed the common enemy." Locke's pragmatic skepticism can also be seen in his *A Letter Concerning Toleration*, wherein he advises princes to allow for a variety of expression of the Christian faith within their kingdoms, observing that "In the variety and contradiction of opinions in religion, wherein the princes of the world are as much divided as in their secular interests, the narrow way would be much straightened; one country alone would be in the right, and all the rest of the world put under an obligation of following their princes in the ways that lead to destruction." In a similar fashion, the federal structure of America, according to Madison's tenth essay of *The Federalist Papers*, would ensure that local evils "will be less apt to pervade the whole body of the Union than a particular member of it." Locke, *Two Treatises of Government*, 417–418 (see Ch. 1 note 16); Locke, *A Letter Concerning Toleration*, Buffalo, New York: Prometheus Books, 1990), 21. Rossiter, *The Federalist Papers*, 84 (see Ch. 4 note 38).

4   Gerber, *To Secure These Rights*, 193 (see Ch. 4 note 2); Jefferson to Judge
      Spencer Roane, Poplar Forest, September 6, 1819, in Peterson, ed., *Thomas
      Jefferson Writings*, 1426 (see Intro. note 5).

5   Quotations are from Jefferson to Joseph C. Cabell, Monticello, February 2, 1816,
      in ibid., 1380.

6   Alexis De Tocqueville, *Democracy in America*, ed. J. P. Mayer, trans. George
      Lawrence (New York: Harper and Row, 1988), 513.

7   The best survey of this complicated history, with extensive bibliographic refer-
      ences, is Jeffrey Rogers Hummel, *Emancipating Slaves, Enslaving Free Men*
      (Chicago: Open Court, 1996), 1–98.

8   Ibid., 16, 82–83, 137. For the quotation of Daniel Webster see Robert Remini,
      Daniel Webster: The Man and His Time (New York: W. W. Norton and Co.:
      1997), 128–129. For discussions of New Englanders who supported secession,
      many of whom were also members of the Constitutional Convention, see M. E.
      Bradford, *Founding Fathers: Brief Lives of the Framers of the United States
      Constitution* (Lawrence, Kansas: University Press of Kansas, 1994), 18, 38, 77.
      An excellent example of the sort of common legal reasoning behind the viability
      of secession is to be found in, St. George Tucker, *View of the Constitution of the
      United States: With Selected Writings*, ed. Clyde N. Wilson (Indianapolis: Lib-
      erty Fund, 1998), 85–86.

9   Hummel, *Emancipating Slaves*, 349–359 (see note 7); Robert H. Wiebe, *Self-
      Rule: A Cultural History of American Democracy* (Chicago: The University of
      Chicago Press, 1995), 162–180. For more on the consequences of the Civil War
      for the growth of the central state, see Richard Franklin Bensel, *Yankee Levia-
      than: The Origins of Central State Authority in America, 1859–1877* (New
      York: Cambridge University Press, 1991). By far the best book on the growth of
      government in the twentieth century is Robert Higgs' *Crisis and Leviathan: Critical
      Episodes in the Growth of American Government* (New York: Oxford Univer-
      sity Press, 1989).

10   See Carl N. Degler's "One Among Many: The Civil War in Comparative Perspec-
      tive," *29th Annual Robert Fortenbaugh Memorial Lecture* (Gettysburg, Penn-
      sylvania: Gettysburg College, 1990), 7–28. I am indebted to Jeffrey Rogers Hummel
      for his alerting me to this reference.

11   The scholars referred to are Cass R. Sunstein and Stephen Holmes, who cite the
      portion of the preamble that states, "to secure these Rights, Governments are
      established among Men." Avoiding the obvious meaning that rights inhere in the
      person and government is but an instrument for the individual's protection, they
      invoke the Declaration simply to present the "obvious truth" that "rights depend
      on government." Their argument is quintessentially Tory, denying the very basis
      of social order in individual self-government, contending that "Personal liberty, as
      Americans value and experience it, presupposes social cooperation managed by
      government officials. The private realm we rightly prize is sustained, indeed cre-
      ated, by public action." They conclude their work by denying the basic premise of
      the entire founding experience, to assert (in contradiction to the Declaration) that

there are no divine or natural rights, and all "rights are licenses for individuals to pursue their joint and separate purposes by taking advantage of collective assets, which include a share of those private assets accumulated under the community's protection." Community and government have been made one, and the Tory perception of a politically imposed social order is passed off as unexceptionable in the American tradition, without ever making explicit the authors' break with the past. See Stephen Holmes and Cass R. Sunstein, *The Cost of Rights: Why Liberty Depends on Taxes* (New York: W. W. Norton and Co., 1999), 15, 220–221.

Bibliographic Essay

1   Quotations are from Kamen, *People of Paradox*, 249 (see Intro. note 4); Michael Kamen, "The Discourse of Politics in 1787: The Constitution and Its Critics on Individualism, Community, and the State," in Herman Belz, Ronald Hoffman, Peter J. Albert, ed., *To Form a More Perfect Union: The Critical Ideas of the Constitution* (Charlottesville: University Press of Virginia, 1992), 168; Richard, *The Founders and the Classics*, 6 (see Intro. note 4).

2   See Wood, *Creation* (see Intro. note 4); J. G. A. Pocock, *Machiavellian Moment* (see Intro. note 4)); Lance Banning, *Jeffersonian Persuasion* (see Intro. note 4). On the republican synthesis see Shalhope, "Republicanism," 334–356 (see Intro. note 4).

Appendix A

1   The text of the Declaration presented here is based on the version of the Dunlap Broadside authorized by Congress and inserted into the rough Journal. The earliest printing by Dunlap began, "A DECLARATION by the REPRESENTATIVES of the UNITED STATES OF AMERICA in General Congress assembled." The title used here was that agreed to by Congress for the final engrossed copy authorized July 19, 1776 which is held by the Department of State. The complaints have been numbered in [ ] for ease of use. It is traditional to count twenty eight charges against the King, but by the construction of the text, it is more accurate to count nine of those grievances as illustrations of the thirteenth charge. Hence my count of the nineteen overall charges. For a discussion and comparison of the various printed copies of the Declaration, see Hazelton, *The Declaration of Independence*, 306–346 (see Intro. note 7); Boyd, *Evolution of the Text* (see Intro. note 7)); Ritz, *"Dunlap Broadside,"* 499–512 (see Intro. note 7); Maier, *American Scripture*, 97–153 (see Intro. note 7).

Appendix B

1   Original pagination is given in brackets [ ], designating the beginning of each page. The original pamphlet, from which this is taken, counted cover sheets and title page in its tally. Consequently, the text begins on page 3. Spelling and punctuation has been kept the same except for that of Massachusetts which has been

changed to conform to current spelling, and all letters have been changed to the modern style. Where Hutchinson's quotation of the Declaration departs from the actual document, the actual text is also given in brackets.

Index

('n' indicates a note)